DOCUMENTS
on the
MIDDLE EAST

Edited by
Ralph H. Magnus

AMERICAN ENTERPRISE INSTITUTE
FOR PUBLIC POLICY RESEARCH
1200 17th Street, N.W.
Washington, D.C. 20036
July 1969

AMERICAN ENTERPRISE INSTITUTE
for Public Policy Research

Middle East Research Project

Professor George Lenczowski
University of California, Berkeley
Director

This publication is presented by the American Enterprise Institute as the second in its series within the framework of the Middle East Research Project.

Library of Congress Catalog No. 75-93191

Price: $3.00

CONTENTS

Page

INTRODUCTION _____ 1

I. ORIGINS OF PROBLEMS AND POLICIES

  1. Convention Respecting the Free Navigation of the Suez Maritime Canal, Constantinople, October 29, 1888 _____ 8

  2. Great Britain Pledges to Support Arab Independence: The Hussein-McMahon Letters, 1915-1916 (Map) _____ 12

  3. The Balfour Declaration, November 2, 1917 _____ 27

  4. United States War Aims: President Wilson's XIV Points Speech to Congress (excerpts), January 8, 1918 _____ 27

  5. Recommendations of the King-Crane Commission on Syria and Palestine, August 28, 1919 _____ 28

  6. Oil Policy in the Middle Eastern Mandates: Letter from U.S. Ambassador Davis to British Foreign Secretary Lord Curzon, May 12, 1920 _____ 37

  7. Congress Endorses the Balfour Declaration: Public Resolution No. 73, 67th Congress, Second Session, September 21, 1922 _____ 40

  8. An "Open Door" Policy for Oil: Secretary Hughes to President Coolidge, November 8, 1923 _____ 40

  9. International Regulation of the Turkish Straits: The Montreux Convention, July 20, 1936 _____ 42

  10. German-Soviet Negotiations Regarding the Middle East: Documents from the German Foreign Office Archives, November, 1940 ____ 53

II. MUTUAL SECURITY TREATIES, AGREEMENTS AND POLICIES

  A. The Truman Doctrine

    11. Message from President Truman to Congress, March 12, 1947 _____ 63

    12. An Act to Provide for Assistance to Greece and Turkey (excerpts), May 22, 1947 _____ 67

  B. The North Atlantic Treaty

    13. The North Atlantic Treaty, April 4, 1949 _____ 70

    14. Note Verbale from the Secretary of State to the Turkish Ambassador in Washington on the Preliminary Association of Turkey with NATO, September 19, 1950 _____ 73

    15. Protocol to the Treaty on the Accession of Greece and Turkey, October 17, 1951 _____ 74

  C. Middle East Command Negotiations

    16. Proposals Presented to Egypt by the Governments of the United States, United Kingdom, France, and Turkey, October 13, 1951 ____ 75

iii

17. Rejection by Egypt of the Joint Proposals: Statement of Regret by the Secretary of State, October 17, 1951 _____ 77

D. The Baghdad Pact and CENTO

18. "Six Major Policy Issues": Speech by Secretary of State Dulles (excerpts), June 1, 1953 _____ 78

19. Pact of Mutual Cooperation Between the Kingdom of Iraq, the Republic of Turkey, the United Kingdom, the Dominion of Pakistan, and the Kingdom of Iran (Baghdad Pact), February 24, 1955 81

20. United States Support for the Pact: Department of State Press Statement, November 29, 1956 _____ 83

21. Iranian-United States Agreement for Cooperation in Promoting the Security and Defense of the Members of the Baghdad Pact Organization, March 5, 1959 _____ 83

22. Final Communique of the Fifteenth Meeting of the Ministerial Council of the Central Treaty Organization (CENTO), April 24, 1968 _____ 85

E. The Eisenhower Doctrine

23. Message from President Eisenhower to Congress, January 5, 1957 86

24. To Promote the Peace and Stability of the Middle East: Joint Resolution of Congress, March 9, 1957 _____ 93

25. Jordan Vital to the United States: Statement by the White House Press Secretary, April 24, 1957 _____ 95

26. Special Message from President Eisenhower to the Congress on the Sending of United States Forces to Lebanon, July 15, 1958 ____ 95

III. UNITED STATES RELATIONS WITH THE ARAB STATES

A. Problems of Giving and Receiving Aid

27. The United States Supports the Aswan High Dam Project: Statement by the Department of State, December 17, 1955 _____ 102

28. United States Withdraws from the Aswan High Dam Project: Announcement by the Department of State, July 19, 1956 _____ 103

29. President Kennedy Rejects the Use of Aid as a Weapon to Force Withdrawal of UAR Troops from Yemen: News Conference, November 14, 1963 _____ 104

30. "Whoever Does Not Like Our Conduct Can Go Drink Up the Sea": Speech by President Nasser (excerpts), December 23, 1964 104

31. President Johnson Requests Congressional Flexibility in Dealing With the UAR: News Conference, February 4, 1965 _____ 106

32. Congress Allows Food Aid to the UAR: Supplemental Appropriations for Fiscal Year 1965 to Finance P.L. 480 (partial text), February 11, 1965 _____ 107

33. Food Aid to the UAR is in the National Interest: Memorandum from the President to the Secretary of State, December 29, 1965___ 107

B. The Problem of Radical Arab Nationalism

34. United States Recognition of the United Arab Republic: Statement by the Department of State, February 25, 1958 _____ 108

35. United States Policy Respecting Arab Nationalism: Secretary of State Dulles' News Conference, July 31, 1958 _____ 108

36. Policy Toward the Iraqi Revolution: Selection from Ambassador Robert Murphy's Memoirs, August, 1958 _____ 108

37. United States Policies in the Middle East: Letter from President Kennedy to President Nasser, May 11, 1961 _____ 109

38. United States Recognition of the Yemen Arab Republic: State-ment by the Department of State, December 19, 1962 _____ 112

C. Saudi Arabian-United Arab Republic Dispute

39. United States Support for Saudi Arabia: Letter from President Kennedy to Crown Prince Faisal, October 25, 1962 _____ 112

40. United States Hopes for End to Yemeni Civil War, Supports Saudi Arabia: Department of State Press Officer's News Conference, August 4, 1965 _____ 113

41. President Johnson Praises the Agreement "Between Our Two Friends" (Saudi Arabia and the UAR) to End the Yemeni Civil War: News Conference, August 29, 1965 _____ 114

IV. UNITED STATES RELATIONS WITH THE NORTHERN TIER STATES

A. Iran

42. International Support for Iranian Independence: Declaration of the Three Powers Regarding Iran, December 1, 1943 _____ 119

43. United States Policy in Iran: Remarks by Ambassador George V. Allen, February 4, 1948 _____ 120

44. The Anglo-Iranian Oil Crisis: Impossibility of Increasing United States Economic Aid Pending a Settlement, Message from President Eisenhower to Prime Minister Mossagedh, June 29, 1953 _____ 122

45. The Anglo-Iranian Oil Crisis: United States Gratification Over the Settlement, Message from President Eisenhower to the Shah of Iran, August 5, 1954 _____ 123

46. 'Soviet-Iranian Relations Are Developing Auspiciously': Joint Communique Issued at End of Visit of the Shah of Iran to the Soviet Union, July 3, 1965 _____ 124

B. Turkey

47. The United States Position Regarding the Turkish Straits: Note From the American Ambassador to the Soviet Foreign Minister, October 9, 1946 _____ 126

48. United States and Turkish Views on NATO Obligations and the Cyprus Crisis: Correspondence Between President Johnson and Prime Minister Inonu, June 5 and 13, 1964 _____ 127

C. Emphasis on Economic Cooperation and Development

49. Regional Cooperation for Development: Joint Communique Issued by the Presidents of Pakistan and Turkey and the Shah of Iran, July 21, 1964 _____ 137

V. THE PALESTINE PROBLEM AND THE ARAB-ISRAELI DISPUTE

A. The Palestine Problem

50. United States Attitude Toward the Palestine Problem: Letter from President Roosevelt to the King of Saudi Arabia, April 5, 1945 ____ 144

51. The Partition of Palestine: Resolution of the United Nations General Assembly (excerpts), November 29, 1947 (Map) _____ 144

52. Creation of the Palestine Conciliation Commission: Resolution of the United Nations General Assembly, December 11, 1948 _____ 161

B. After Israel's Independence

53. Peace and Stability in the Middle East: Tripartite Declaration of the United States, the United Kingdom and France, May 25, 1950 163

54. Passage of Israeli Ships Through the Suez Canal: Resolution of the United Nations Security Council, September 1, 1951 _____ 164

55. United States Regret Over the Removal of the Israeli Foreign Ministry to Jerusalem: Statement by the Secretary of State, July 28, 1953 _____ 165

56. Retention of the American Embassy in Tel Aviv: Statement Issued by the Department of State, November 3, 1954 _____ 166

57. Reaffirmation of the Tripartite Declaration by the United States: Statement by the President, November 9, 1955 _____ 166

58. A Direct Appeal to the Israelis and Arabs: Speech by Assistant Secretary of State Byroade, April 9, 1954 _____ 167

C. The Suez War and Its Aftermath

59. Nationalization of the Suez Canal: Decree of the Egyptian Government, July 26, 1956 _____ 167

60. The United States Rejects the Use of Force: Speech by President Eisenhower (excerpts), October 31, 1956 _____ 169

61. The Establishment of the United Nations Emergency Force: Resolution of the United Nations General Assembly, November 5, 1956 172

62. Presence and Functions of the UNEF: Report of the Secretary General, November 20, 1956 _____ 172

63. Israel Refuses to Permit Stationing of the UNEF in Israel: Statement by Prime Minister Ben-Gurion to Knesset (excerpts), November 7, 1956 _____ 174

64. Presence and Functions of the UNEF: Secret Aide Memoire of Secretary General Hammarskjold, August 5, 1957 _____ 176

65. The United States Urges Israeli Withdrawal from Sinai: Aide Memoire from Secretary of State Dulles to Ambassador Eban, February 11, 1957 _____ 180

66. Israel Agrees to Withdraw from Sinai: Statement by Israeli Foreign Minister Meier in the United Nations General Assembly, March 1, 1957 _____ 182

D. The Second Truce: Continued Tensions

67. United States Opposition to the Introduction or Manufacture of Nuclear Weapons in the Middle East: President Kennedy's News Conference, April 3, 1963 _____ 185

68. United States Supports Security of Both Israel and Her Neighbors: President Kennedy's News Conference, November 14, 1963 _____ 186

VI. THE JUNE WAR AND ITS AFTERMATH

A. The Outbreak of War

69. The Palestinian Guerrillas Organize: Communique No. 1 from Headquarters of the Asifa Forces, January 6, 1965 _____ 192

70. Withdrawal of the UNEF from the United Arab Republic: Report by Secretary General U Thant to Security Council (excerpts), May 20, 1967 _____ 192

71. Closing of the Gulf of Aqaba: Speech to Armed Forces by President Nasser, May 22, 1967 _____ 195

72. United States Supports Independence and Integrity of All Nations in the Area: Statement by President Johnson, May 23, 1967 _____ 199

B. The Glassboro Summit Meeting

73. President Johnson's Report to the Nation, June 25, 1967 _____ 201

74. Premier Kosygin's News Conference Statement, June 25, 1967 ____ 202

C. The Status of Jerusalem

75. United Nations Rejects Israel's Changing the Status of Jerusalem: General Assembly Resolution, July 4, 1967 _____ 203

76. United States Explains Its Abstention on the Jerusalem Resolution: Statement by the United States Mission to the United Nations, July 4, 1967 _____ 203

D. Plans for Peace

77. Five Principles for Peace in the Middle East: Speech by President
Johnson (excerpts), June 19, 1967 _____ 204

78. The United Nations Peace Plan: Security Council Resolution Passed
Unanimously, November 22, 1967 _____ 205

79. United States Gratification at Passage of November 22 Resolution:
Statement by Ambassador Goldberg, November 22, 1967 _____ 206

80. "A Just and Dignified Peace . . . Is Possible": Speech by President
Johnson (excerpts), September 10, 1968 _____ 208

81. United States and Israel Support Spirit of November 22 Resolution
and President Johnson's Five Principles of Peace: Joint Statement
by President Johnson and Prime Minister Eshkol, January 8, 1968 210

82. An Arab Plan for Peace: Speech by King Hussein of Jordan (excerpt), April 10, 1969 _____ 211

E. Uncertain Cease Fire

83. The United States Condemns Violence on Both Sides: Statement
Released by the Department of State, March 21, 1968 _____ 212

84. Condemnation of Israeli Attacks on Jordan: United Nations Security Council Resolution Passed Unanimously, March 29, 1968 ____ 212

85. 'A Talk With President Nasser': Interview With *Newsweek* Editor,
February 10, 1969 _____ 213

86. 'Eshkol: A Reply to Nasser': Interview With *Newsweek* Editor,
February 17, 1969 _____ 218

F. New Initiatives of the United States

87. "A More Even-Handed Policy": Governor Scranton's News Conference Statement, December 13, 1968 _____ 223

88. 'We Are Not Going To Stand Back': President Nixon's News Conference, February 5, 1969 _____ 223

89. Progress Made Toward Middle East Talks: President Nixon's News
Conference, March 4, 1969 _____ 224

SOURCES _____ 227

AEI PUBLICATIONS _____ 231

Introduction

The purpose of this collection of documents is to illustrate the development of United States policies in the Middle East. The documents included are thus for the most part American, although a number of United Nations and foreign documents are also included. With two exceptions all of the selections are truly documentary—official instruments of governments or international organizations or statements of persons acting in their official capacities.

Any definition of the Middle East as a geographical concept must be arbitrary. The United States Department of State's own designation for the bureau dealing with this area of the world is "Near Eastern" rather than "Middle Eastern." However, we shall here take a restricted definition of the area involved by excepting North Africa, the Sudan, Greece, Afghanistan and, for most purposes, Pakistan, from our consideration. At times these "fringe" areas of the Middle East will come to affect the "heartland," that area bounded by Iran and Egypt on the east and west and between Turkey and the Indian Ocean on the north and south, but it is the central area which has been and remains the focus of the regional problems faced by United States policymakers. In a recent publication, *The United States and the Middle East* (1964), the State Department considered this area as constituting the Middle East.

This collection does not claim to be an exhaustive documentary history. Neither is it solely a collection of "basic" documents. In addition to the latter, it includes, firstly, those official explanations, speeches, letters, etc., illustrating the considerations which led to certain basic decisions; and, secondly, those other statements or documents which illustrate further development of policies.

The collection is arranged in six topical chapters, most of which are divided into sections. Chapters V and VI deal with the continuing conflict between the Arabs and the Israelis. The dividing point of the June war of 1967 is chronological rather than topical. The documents are numbered consecutively for the entire collection.

The editor hopes that this arrangement will aid the reader in understanding the development of the major issues, past and present, which the United States has faced in this area. This arrangement is to some extent arbitrary. One of the great problems of foreign policy formulation is that actions designed primarily for one purpose inevitably have influence in other areas. This means that a statement of United States support for the Baghdad Pact, here included under the heading of Mutual Security, also could have been placed either in the chapter dealing with United States relations with the Arab states or in the chapter dealing with the northern tier countries. Brief introductions to each chapter help to point out these relationships.

Most of the documents are reproduced in full. Where editing has been done this is indicated in the title or in the text. All sources are listed at the end of the collection. Notes on documents themselves have been kept to a minimum, the editorial comments being reserved for the introductions.

The editor would like to acknowledge the invaluable assistance and advice of Professor George Lenczowski of the University of California, Berkeley, in compiling this collection.

Ralph H. Magnus
May 20, 1969

I.

Origins
of Problems and Policies

In the period before the second world war, United States interest in the Middle East was limited and sporadic. Some outlines of the shape of future problems and policies emerged during this era, however, especially at the time of American involvement in the first world war.

The strategic importance of the Middle East as a meeting place of continents and oceans had long been an object of interest to European powers. The Suez Canal enhanced that interest immensely in the latter half of the nineteenth century. Protection of this "imperial life-line" became the major objective of British foreign policy in the Middle East. The first document in this collection is the Constantinople Convention of 1888, in which the European powers and Turkey established the principle of free navigation of the Suez Canal by all nations in peace and war. The question of free navigation of international waterways has remained a vital one down to the present day, and differing interpretations of this Convention remain a major cause of dispute between Israel and the United Arab Republic. As with many international agreements, it is possible to arrive at diametrically opposed interpretations on the right of Israeli ships to use the canal. Article I provides that the canal shall be open to all countries in peace and war. However, Article X acknowledges the right of Egypt to take steps to ensure its security.

With the entry of the Ottoman Empire on the side of the Central Powers in World War I, Britain found her traditional strategy in the Middle East in ruins. Earlier she had usually looked upon Ottoman Turkey as a friendly power to protect Britain's interests and communications in the Middle East. The major response of the British government to Turkey's entry into the war was to encourage the growing national and anti-Turkish spirit of the Arab subjects of the Ottoman Empire. This resulted in a series of letters exchanged between Sir Henry McMahon, the British High Commissioner in Egypt, and Sherif Hussein of Mecca, the Arab governor of the Moslem Holy Places under the Ottoman government. Britain promised to support the independence of the Arab areas of the Ottoman Empire if they would revolt against their masters. Certain areas along the Mediterranean coast were excluded from these pledges, although the precise borders of these excluded areas have never been established. In 1939 the British and Arab states met formally to consider these pledges and were still unable to resolve this dispute.

In excluding the coastal area the British were thinking primarily of the French claims to special influence and privileges in Lebanon and Syria, as well as the special character of Palestine as a center for three world religions. In 1916 the British, French, and Russian governments reached an agreement on the division of the Ottoman Empire after the war. This Sykes-Picot Agreement divided the Arab areas into British and French spheres of influence and an international area in Palestine. While some of this area had been excluded from the British promises to the Arabs, on the whole the Sykes-Picot Agreement constituted a secret repudiation of the British pledges to Sherif Hussein and formed the basis of the Arabs' later feeling that they had been tricked and robbed by the European imperialist powers.

Soon afterward, in 1917, the British government made a further pledge concerning the future of Palestine, at that time in the process of being taken from the Turks by the efforts of General Allenby's British Imperial army based in Egypt, and aided by the Arab forces of Sherif Hussein on Allenby's desert flank. The international Zionist movement had been aiming, for at least 20 years after the publication of Theodor Herzl's *The Jewish State,* at the establishment of a Jewish sovereignty in Palestine. In the late nineteenth and early twentieth centuries thousands of Jewish colonists, most of them from Russia, had immigrated to Ottoman-controlled Palestine. However, they were still in a distinct minority. During the war the Zionists attempted to get both sides to support their position. Eventually, in November, 1917, they received a qualified statement of support from the British cabinet in the form of a letter from the Foreign Secretary, Lord Balfour, to Lord Rothschild, the leader of the British Zionists. The hope of influencing the numerous and influential Jewish community in the United States as well as in Russia, was of prime importance in the motivation of the British cabinet. The declaration was qualified in two respects: it spoke of a "national home" *in* Palestine, rather than a sovereign state over the whole of Palestine; and it stated that the rights of the non-Jewish inhabitants of Palestine were not to be prejudiced. Although issued unilaterally by the British government, the Balfour Declaration had the concurrence of President Wilson.

With American participation as a belligerent in the war came the beginnings of a United States Middle Eastern policy. Although the United States never declared war on the Ottoman Empire, President Wilson's policies had a powerful influence on the final peace settlements in the Middle East. Since these settlements established the basic outlines of the Middle Eastern state system of today, an American share in responsibility for the origins of contemporary problems in the area must be acknowledged.

In January, 1918, President Wilson outlined in a famous speech to Congress his statement of American war aims. Some of his "Fourteen Points" dealt with specific areas and issues, such as Russia, Poland, and the Balkans. Others dealt with general principles, such as freedom of the seas and a permanent international organization of nations to preserve peace in the future. This collection includes Point XII, which deals specifically with the future of the Middle East, as well as other general points that had a powerful impact on the area. By asserting the rights of the non-Turkish areas of the Ottoman Empire to be free from both Ottoman and purely colonial rule Wilson made a powerful impact on Arab nationalist feelings. Point I was a repudiation of the secret deals, such as the Sykes-Picot Agreement. Point V stated that the interests of the local populations had to be considered equally with those of competing governments in their territorial claims.

The King-Crane Commission was an effort to implement this novel policy of consulting the wishes of the local population as to their future political development. The Commission was intended to be an international one, but the other powers at the Paris Peace Conference would not participate. With purely American personnel the Commission proceeded to the Middle East and consulted there with a wide variety of delegations holding various points of view. Their report advised against the creation of a Jewish state in Palestine and displayed the widespread popular image among the Arab people of the United States as a friendly and disinterested power which would aid their quest for self-determination. It was never formally accepted by the Peace Conference or the United States government. It is doubtful if the fatally ill President ever saw it. In the end, however, the idea of mandates under the League of Nations leading to eventual independence was the major contribution of President Wilson which came to be embodied in the peace settlements in the Middle East.

During the interwar period American direct involvement in the area declined. United States diplomacy did insist that the oil resources of the mandated territories should be open to American companies, as well as to those of the mandate holders. This allowed for American participation in the Iraq Petroleum Company concession. Other American oil companies were granted drilling concessions in the Arabian peninsula by the local rulers.

Many people in the United States were interested in the success of the "Jewish National Home" which had been embodied in the Palestine Mandate under British rule. Immigration expanded and it was felt that the British were dealing successfully with this issue. Congress, in a joint resolution, formally endorsed the Balfour Declaration, but in the text of this resolution—as in the original declaration—lay the seeds of future conflict. There was to be a "national home" for the Jewish people, but the rights of Christian and other non-Jewish Palestinians were not to be prejudiced.

Turkey had revived miraculously after the defeat of the Ottoman Empire. Under Kemal Ataturk she set a firm course toward national independence and modernization. By 1923 she was able to end the humiliating restrictions on her sovereignty imposed by the Treaty of Sevres. However, the Lausanne convention on the Turkish Straits of 1923 still demilitarized the vital waterway connecting the Black and Mediterranean Seas. With the growth of Axis power in Europe, Turkey, the USSR, and the Western powers became more favorable towards revising the regime of the Straits. The resulting Montreux Convention of 1936, while establishing international rules governing the Straits in peace and war, allowed Turkey to re-fortify them and to be the interpreter of the rules, rather than the international commission as provided in the Lausanne Convention.

By 1940, however, a new world war had already begun in Europe. The Soviet Union was first allied with Germany. In secret conversations the Russians and Germans discussed their respective territorial ambitions. The Soviet Union maintained the old ambitions of the Tsars for an outlet to the Mediterranean and the Persian Gulf. Turkey remained neutral until nearly the end of the war in Europe, but even before this war was over the USSR attempted to gain, on her own behalf and with the support of the United States and Britain, a new regime for the Turkish Straits, one which would allow the Soviet Union to set up bases in the area. These Soviet territorial ambitions, outlined to her Nazi ally and renewed in the demands on Turkey and Iran at the close of World War II, showed that the strategic importance of the Middle East would keep the area close to the center of world attention in the coming decades.

1. Convention Respecting the Free Navigation of the Suez Maritime Canal, Constantinople
October 29, 1888 [1]

Convention Between Great Britain, Austria-Hungary, France, Germany, Italy, the Netherlands, Russia, Spain, and Turkey, Respecting the Free Navigation of the Suez Maritime Canal

In the name of Almighty God,

Her Majesty the Queen of the United Kingdom of Great Britain and Ireland, Empress of India; His Majesty the German Emperor, King of Prussia; His Majesty the Emperor of Austria, King of Bohemia, etc., and Apostolic King of Hungary; His Majesty the King of Spain, and in His Name the Queen Regent of the Kingdom; the President of the French Republic; His Majesty the King of Italy; His Majesty the King of the Netherlands, Grand Duke of Luxemburg, etc.; His Majesty the Emperor of all the Russias; and His Majesty the Emperor of the Ottomans, being desirous of establishing, by a Conventional Act, a definitive system intended to guarantee, at all times and to all the Powers, the free use of the Suez Maritime Canal, and thus to complete the system under which the navigation of this canal has been placed by the Firman of His Imperial Majesty the Sultan, dated February 22, 1866 (2 Zilkadé, 1282), and sanctioning the Concessions of His Highness the Khedive, have appointed as their plenipotentiaries, to wit:

Her Majesty the Queen of the United Kingdom of Great Britain and Ireland, Empress of India, the Right Honorable Sir William Arthur White, Her Ambassador Extraordinary and Plenipotentiary;

His Majesty the German Emperor, King of Prussia, His Excellency Joseph de Radowitz, His Ambassador Extraordinary and Plenipotentiary;

His Majesty the Emperor of Austria, King of Bohemia, etc., and Apostolic King of Hungary, His Excellency Baron Henri de Calice, His Ambassador Extraordinary and Plenipotentiary;

His Majesty the King of Spain and in His Name the Queen Regent of the Kingdom, Mr. Miguel Florez y Garcia, His Chargé d'Affaires;

The President of the French Republic, His Excellency Gustav Louis Lannes, Count de Montebello, Ambassador Extraordinary and Plenipotentiary of France;

His Majesty the King of Italy, His Excellency Baron Albert Blanc, His Ambassador Extraordinary and Plenipotentiary;

His Majesty the King of the Netherlands, Grand Duke of Luxemburg, etc., Mr. Gustave Keun, His Chargé d'Affaires;

His Majesty the Emperor of all the Russias, His Excellency Alexandre de Nélidow, His Ambassador Extraordinary and Plenipotentiary;

His Majesty the Emperor of the Ottomans, Mehemmed Saïd Pasha, His Minister of Foreign Affairs;

---

[1] Translation by the Department of State from the French text in *British and Foreign State Papers, 1887-1888*, vol. 79, pp. 18-22.

Who, having communicated to each other their respective full powers, found in good and due form, have agreed upon the following articles:—

ART. I. The Suez Maritime Canal shall always be free and open, in time of war as in time of peace, to every vessel of commerce or of war, without distinction of flag.

The Canal shall never be subject to the exercise of the right of blockade.

ART. II. The High Contracting Parties, recognizing that the Fresh-Water Canal is indispensable to the Maritime Canal, take cognizance of the engagements of His Highness the Khedive towards the Universal Suez Canal Company as regards the Fresh-Water Canal; which engagements are stipulated in a Convention dated March 18, 1863, containing a preamble and four Articles.

They undertake not to interfere in any way with security of that Canal and its branches, the working of which shall not be the object of any attempt at obstruction.

ART. III. The High Contracting Parties likewise undertake to respect the equipment, establishments, buildings and work of the Maritime Canal and of the Fresh-Water Canal.

ART. IV. The Maritime Canal remaining open in time of war as a free passage, even to ships of war of the belligerents, under the terms of Article I of the present Treaty, the High Contracting Parties agree that no right of war, act of hostility or act having for its purpose to interfere with the free navigation of the Canal, shall be committed in the Canal and its ports of access, or within a radius of 3 nautical miles from those ports, even though the Ottoman Empire should be one of the belligerent Powers.

Warships of belligerents shall not take on fresh supplies or lay in stores in the Canal and its ports of access, except in so far as may be strictly necessary. The transit of the said vessels through the Canal shall be effected as quickly as possible, in accordance with the regulations in force, and without stopping except for the necessities of the service.

Their stay at Port Saïd and the roadstead of Suez shall not exceed 24 hours, except in case of putting in through stress of weather. In such case, they shall be bound to depart as soon as possible. A period of 24 hours shall always elapse between the sailing of a belligerent ship from a port of access and the departure of a ship belonging to the enemy Power.

ART. V. In time of war, belligerent powers shall not discharge or take on troops, munitions, or war materiel in the Canal and its ports of access. In case of an accidental hindrance in the Canal, however, troops broken up into groups not exceeding 1000 men, with a corresponding amount of equipment, may be embarked or disembarked at the ports of access.

ART. VI. Prizes shall in all respects be subject to the same rules and regulations as the warships of belligerents.

ART. VII. The Powers shall not keep any warship in the waters of the Canal (including Lake Timsah and the Bitter Lakes).

They may, however, have warships, the number of which shall not exceed two for each Power, stationed in the ports of access of Port Saïd and Suez.

This right shall not be exercised by belligerents.

ART. VIII. The Agents in Egypt of the Signatory Powers of the present Treaty shall be charged to see that it is carried out. In any circumstance threatening the security and free passage of the Canal, they shall meet at the summons of three of them and under the presidency of their Doyen, to make the necessary verifications. They shall inform the Khedivial Government of the danger perceived, in order that it may take proper steps to assure the protection and the free use of the Canal. In any case, they shall meet once a year to take note of the due execution of the Treaty.

These latter meetings shall be presided over by a Special Commissioner appointed for that purpose by the Imperial Ottoman Government. A Khedivial Commissioner may also take part in the meeting, and may preside over it in case of the absence of the Ottoman Commissioner.

They shall demand, in particular, the removal of any work or the dispersion of any assemblage on either bank of the Canal, the purpose or effect of which might be to interfere with the freedom and complete safety of navigation.

ART. IX. The Egyptian Government shall, within the limits of its powers based on the Firmans, and under the conditions provided for in the present Treaty, take the necessary measures for enforcing the execution of the said Treaty.

In case the Egyptian Government should not have sufficient means at its disposal, it shall appeal to the Imperial Ottoman Government, which shall take the necessary measures for responding to such appeal, give notice thereof to the other Signatory Powers of the Declaration of London of March 17, 1885, and, if necessary, consult with them on the matter.

The provisions of Articles IV, V, VI, and VII shall not stand in the way of the measures taken by virtue of the present Article.

ART. X. Likewise, the provisions of Articles IV, V, VII, and VIII shall not stand in the way of any measures which His Majesty the Sultan and His Highness the Khedive in the name of His Imperial Majesty, and within the limits of the Firmans granted, might find it necessary to take to assure by their own forces the defense of Egypt and the maintenance of public order.

In case His Imperial Majesty the Sultan or His Highness the Khedive should find it necessary to avail himself of the exceptions provided for in the present Article, the Signatory Powers of the Declaration of London would be notified thereof by the Imperial Ottoman Government.

It is also understood that the provisions of the four Articles in question shall in no case stand in the way of measures which the Imperial Ottoman Government considers it necessary to take to assure by its own forces the defense of its other possessions situated on the eastern coast of the Red Sea.

ART. XI. The measures taken in the cases provided for by Articles IX and X of the present Treaty shall not interfere with the free use of the Canal. In the same cases, the erection of permanent fortifications contrary to the provisions of Article VIII is prohibited.

ART. XII. The High Contracting Parties, by application of the principle of equality as regards free use of the Canal, a principle which forms one of the bases of the present Treaty, agree that none of them shall seek, with respect to the Canal, territorial or commercial advantages or privileges in any international arrangements that may be concluded. Furthermore, the rights of Turkey as the territorial Power are reserved.

ART. XIII. Aside from the obligations expressly provided for by the clauses of the present Treaty, the sovereign rights of His Imperial Majesty the Sultan and the rights and immunities of His Highness and Khedive based on the Firmans are in no way affected.

ART. XIV. The High Contracting Parties agree that the engagements resulting from the present Treaty shall not be limited by the duration of the Acts of Concession of the Universal Suez Canal Company.

ART. XV. The stipulations of the present Treaty shall not interfere with the sanitary measures in force in Egypt.

ART. XVI. The High Contracting Parties undertake to bring the present Treaty to the knowledge of those States which have not signed it, inviting them to accede thereto.

ART. XVII. The present Treaty shall be ratified, and the ratifications thereof shall be exchanged at Constantinople within one month or sooner if possible.

In witness whereof the respective Plenipotentiaries have signed the present Treaty, and have affixed thereto the seal of their arms.

Done at Constantinople, on the 29th day of the month of October, of the year 1888.

For Great Britain	(L.S.) W. A. WHITE
Germany	(L.S.) RADOWITZ
Austria-Hungary	(L.S.) CALICE
Spain	(L.S.) MIGUEL FLOREZ Y GARCIA
France	(L.S.) G. DE MONTEBELLO
Italy	(L.S.) A. BLANC
Netherlands	(L.S.) GUS. KEUN
Russia	(L.S.) NÉLIDOW
Turkey	(L.S.) M. SAÏD

2. Great Britain Pledges to Support Arab Independence: The Hussein-McMahon Letters, 1915-1916

No. 1.

Translation of a letter from the Sherif of Mecca to Sir Henry McMahon, His Majesty's High Commissioner at Cairo.

To his Honour: *July* 14, 1915.

WHEREAS the whole of the Arab nation without any exception have decided in these last years to live, and to accomplish their freedom, and grasp the reins of their administration both in theory and practice; and whereas they have found and felt that it is to the interest of the Government of Great Britain to support them and aid them to the attainment of their firm and lawful intentions (which are based upon the maintenance of the honour and dignity of their life) without any ulterior motives whatsoever unconnected with this object;

And whereas it is to their (the Arabs') interest also to prefer the assistance of the Government of Great Britain in consideration of their geographical position and economic interests, and also of the attitude of the above-mentioned Government, which is known to both nations and therefore need not be emphasized;

For these reasons the Arab nation see fit to limit themselves, as time is short, to asking the Governmnt of Great Britain, if it should think fit, for the approval, through her deputy or representative, of the following fundamental propositions, leaving out all things considered secondary in comparison with these, so that it may prepare all means necessary for attaining this noble purpose, until such time as it finds occasion for making the actual negotiations:—

Firstly.—England to acknowledge the independence of the Arab countries, bounded on the north by Mersina and Adana up to the 37° of latitude, on which degree fall Birijik, Urfa, Mardin, Midiat, Jezirat (Ibn 'Umar), Amadia, up to the border of Persia; on the east by the borders of Persia up to the Gulf of Basra; on the south by the Indian Ocean, with the exception of the position of Aden to remain as it is; on the west by the Red Sea, the Mediterranean Sea up to Mersina. England to approve of the proclamation of an Arab Khalifate of Islam.

Secondly.—The Arab Government of the Sherif to acknowledge that England shall have the preference in all economic enterprises in the Arab countries whenever conditions of enterprises are otherwise equal.

Thirdly.—For the security of this Arab independence and the certainty of such preference of economic enterprises, both high contracting parties to offer mutual assistance, to the best ability of their military and naval forces, to face any foreign Power which may attack either party. Peace not to be decided without agreement of both parties.

Fourthly.—If one of the parties enters upon an aggressive conflict, the other party to assume a neutral attitude, and in case of such party wishing the other to join forces, both to meet and discuss the conditions.

12

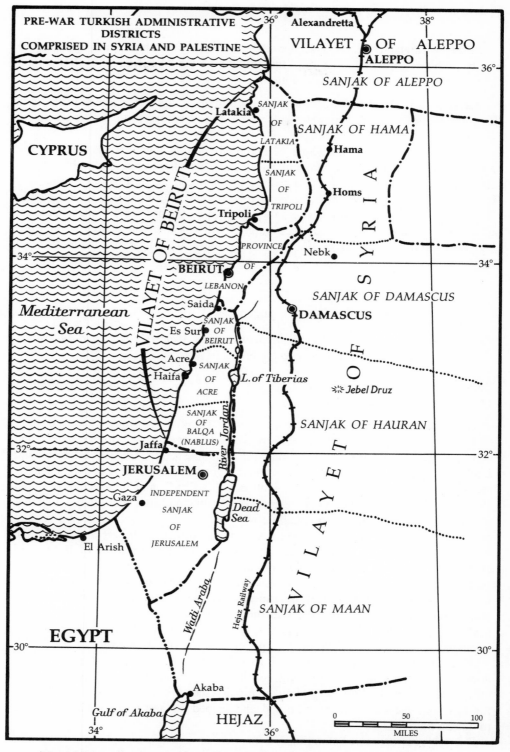

PRE-WAR TURKISH ADMINISTRATIVE
DISTRICTS
COMPRISED IN SYRIA AND PALESTINE

36°   Alexandretta   38°

VILAYET   OF   ALEPPO
ALEPPO

36°

SANJAK OF ALEPPO

SANJAK
OF
LATAKIA

Latakia

SANJAK OF HAMA

Hama

CYPRUS

SANJAK
OF
TRIPOLI

Homs

Tripoli

34°   PROVINCE   Nebk   34°

Mediterranean
Sea

BEIRUT   OF

LEBANON

Saida

SANJAK
OF
BEIRUT

Es Sur

Acre

Haifa

SANJAK
OF
ACRE

SANJAK
OF
BALQA
(NABLUS)

VILAYET OF BEIRUT

DAMASCUS

SANJAK OF DAMASCUS

L. of Tiberias

Jebel Druz

SANJAK OF HAURAN

River Jordan

32°   Jaffa   32°

JERUSALEM

Gaza

INDEPENDENT

SANJAK

OF

JERUSALEM

El Arish

OF   SYRIA

Dead
Sea

VILAYET

Wadi Araba

Hejaz Railway

SANJAK OF MAAN

EGYPT

30°   30°

Akaba

Gulf of Akaba   HEJAZ

34°   36°

0   50   100
MILES

Adapted from sketch included in McMahon-Hussein exchange of correspondence.

13

Fifthly.—England to acknowledge the abolition of foreign privileges in the Arab countries, and to assist the Government of the Sherif in an International Convention for confirming such abolition.

Sixthly.—Articles 3 and 4 of this treaty to remain in vigour for fifteen years, and, if either wishes it to be renewed, one year's notice before lapse of treaty to be given.

Consequently, and as the whole of the Arab nation have (praise be to God) agreed and united for the attainment, at all costs and finally, of this noble object, they beg the Government of Great Britain to answer them positively or negatively in a period of thirty days after receiving this intimation; and if this period should lapse before they receive an answer, they reserve to themselves complete freedom of action. Moreover, we (the Sherif's family) will consider ourselves free in word and deed from the bonds of our previous declaration which we made through Ali Effendi.

———

No. 2.

Translation of a letter from Sir H. McMahon, His Majesty's High Commissioner at Cairo, to the Sherif of Mecca.

To his Highness the Sherif Hussein.   *August* 30, 1915.
(After compliments and salutations.)

WE have the honour to thank you for your frank expressions of the sincerity of your feeling towards England. We rejoice, moreover, that your Highness and your people are of one opinion—that Arab interests are English interests and English Arab. To this intent we confirm to you the terms of Lord Kitchener's message, which reached you by the hand of Ali Effendi, and in which was stated clearly our desire for the independence of Arabia and its inhabitants, together with our approval of the Arab Khalifate when it should be proclaimed. We declare once more that His Majesty's Government would welcome the resumption of the Khalifate by an Arab of true race. With regard to the questions of limits and boundaries, it would appear to be premature to consume our time in discussing such details in the heat of war, and while, in many portions of them, the Turk is up to now in effective occupation; especially as we have learned, with surprise and regret, that some of the Arabs in those very parts, far from assisting us, are neglecting this their supreme opportunity and are lending their arms to the German and the Turk, to the new despoiler and the old oppressor.

Nevertheless, we are ready to send your Highness for the Holy Cities and the noble Arabs the charitable offerings of Egypt so soon as your Highness shall inform us how and where they should be delivered. We are, moreover, arranging for this your messenger to be admitted and helped on any journey he may make to ourselves.

Friendly reassurances. Salutations!

(Signed)   A. H. McMAHON.

14

Translation of a letter from the Sherif of Mecca to Sir H. McMahon, His Majesty's High Commissioner at Cairo.

September 9, 1915.

To his Excellency the Most Exalted, the Most Eminent—the British High Commissioner in Egypt; may God grant him Success.

WITH great cheerfulness and delight I received your letter dated the 19th Shawal, 1333 (the 30th August, 1915), and have given it great consideration and regard, in spite of the impression I received from it of ambiguity and its tone of coldness and hesitation with regard to our essential point.

It is necessary to make clear to your Excellency our sincerity towards the illustrious British Empire and our confession of preference for it in all cases and matters and under all forms and circumstances. The real interests of the followers of our religion necessitate this.

Nevertheless, your Excellency will pardon me and permit me to say clearly that the coolness and hesitation which you have displayed in the question of the limits and boundaries by saying that the discussion of these at present is of no use and is a loss of time, and that they are still in the hands of the Government which is ruling them, &c., might be taken to infer an estrangement or something of the sort.

As the limits and boundaries demanded are not those of one person whom we should satisfy and with whom we should discuss them after the war is over, but our peoples have seen that the life of their new proposal is bound at least by these limits and their word is united on this.

Therefore, they have found it necessary first to discuss this point with the Power in whom they now have their confidence and trust as a final appeal, viz., the illustrious British Empire.

Their reason for this union and confidence is mutual interest, the necessity of regulating territorial divisions and the feelings of their inhabitants, so that they may know how to base their future and life, so not to meet her (England?) or any of her Allies in opposition to their resolution which would produce a contrary issue, which God forbid.

For the object is, honourable Minister, the truth which is established on a basis which guarantees the essential sources of life in future.

Yet within these limits they have not included places inhabited by a foreign race. It is a vain show of words and titles.

May God have mercy on the Khalifate and comfort Moslems in it.

I am confident that your Excellency will not doubt that it is not I personally who am demanding of these limits which include only our race, but that they are all proposals of the people, who, in short, believe that they are necessary for economic life.

Is this not right, your Excellency the Minister?

In a word, your high Excellency, we are firm in our sincerity and declaring our preference for loyalty towards you, whether you are satisfied with us, as has been said, or angry.

With reference to your remark in your letter above mentioned that some of our people are still doing their utmost in promoting the interests of Turkey, your goodness (lit. "perfectness") would not permit you to make this an excuse for the tone of coldness and hesitation with regard to our demands, demands which I cannot admit that you, as a man of sound opinion, will deny to be necessary for our existence; nay, they are the essential essence of our life, material and moral.

Up to the present moment I am myself with all my might carrying out in my country all things in conformity with the Islamic law, all things which tend to benefit the rest of the Kingdom, and I shall continue to do so until it pleases God to order otherwise.

In order to reassure your Excellency I can declare that the whole country, together with those who you say are submitting themselves to Turco-German orders, are all waiting the result of these negotiations, which are dependent only on your refusal or acceptance of the question of the limits and on your declaration of safeguarding their religion first and then the rest of rights from any harm or danger.

Whatever the illustrious Government of Great Britain finds conformable to its policy on this subject, communicate it to us and specify to us the course we should follow.

In all cases it is only God's will which shall be executed, and it is God who is the real factor in everything.

With regard to our demand for grain for the natives, and the moneys ("surras") known to the Wakfs' Ministry and all other articles sent here with pilgrims' caravans, high Excellency, my intention in this matter is to confirm your proclamations to the whole world, and especially to the Moslem world, that your antagonism is confined only to the party which has usurped the rights of the Khalifate in which are included the rights of all Moslems.

Moreover the said grain is from the special Wakfs and has nothing to do with politics.

If you think it should be, let the grain of the two years be transported in a special steamer to Jedda in an official manner, in the name of all the natives as usual, and the captain of the steamer or the special "Mamur" detailed as usual every year to hand it over on his arrival at the port will send to the Governor of Jedda asking for the Mamur of the grain at Jedda or a responsible official to take over the grain and give the necessary receipt signed by the said Mamur, that is the Mamur of the grain himself. He should make it a condition that he would (? not) accept any receipt but that signed by this Mamur.

Let the captain of the steamer or the "Mamur" (detailed with the grain) be instructed that if he finds anything contrary to this arrangement he should warn them that he will return home with the cargo. Thereupon the Mamur and the special committee detailed with him, which is known as the committee of the grain for the natives, will take over the grain in the proper form.

Please accept my best regards and salutations.

If you choose to send a reply to this, please send it with the bearer.

29th Shawal, 1333.

Translation of a letter from Sir H. McMahon, His Majesty's High Commissioner at Cairo, to the Sherif of Mecca.

October 24, 1915.

I HAVE received your letter of the 29th Shawal, 1333, with much pleasure and your expressions of friendliness and sincerity have given me the greatest satisfaction.

I regret that you should have received from my last letter the impression that I regarded the question of the limits and boundaries with coldness and hesitation; such was not the case, but it appeared to me that the time had not yet come when that question could be discussed in a conclusive manner.

I have realised, however, from your last letter that you regard this question as one of vital and urgent importance. I have, therefore, lost no time in informing the Government of Great Britain of the contents of your letter, and it is with great pleasure that I communicate to you on their behalf the following statement, which I am confident you will receive with satisfaction:—

The two districts of Mersina and Alexandretta and portions of Syria lying to the west of the districts of Damascus, Homs, Hama and Aleppo cannot be said to be purely Arab, and should be excluded from the limits demanded.

With the above modification, and without prejudice to our existing treaties with Arab chiefs, we accept those limits.

As for those regions lying within those frontiers wherein Great Britain is free to act without detriment to the interests of her ally, France, I am empowered in the name of the Government of Great Britain to give the following assurances and make the following reply to your letter:—

(1) Subject to the above modifications, Great Britain is prepared to recognise and support the independence of the Arabs in all the regions within the limits demanded by the Sherif of Mecca.

(2) Great Britain will guarantee the Holy Places against all external aggression and will recognise their inviolability.

(3) When the situation admits, Great Britain will give to the Arabs her advice and will assist them to establish what may appear to be the most suitable forms of government in those various territories.

(4) On the other hand, it is understood that the Arabs have decided to seek the advice and guidance of Great Britain only, and that such European advisers and officials as may be required for the formation of a sound form of administration will be British.

(5) With regard to the *vilayets* of Bagdad and Basra, the Arabs will recognise that the established position and interests of Great Britain necessitate special administrative arrangements in order to secure these territories from foreign aggression, to promote the welfare of the local populations and to safeguard our mutual economic interests.

I am convinced that this declaration will assure you beyond all possible doubt of the sympathy of Great Britain towards the aspirations of her friends the Arabs and will result in a firm and lasting alliance, the immediate results of which will be the expulsion of the Turks from the Arab countries and the freeing of the Arab peoples from the Turkish yoke, which for so many years has pressed heavily upon them.

I have confined myself in this letter to the more vital and important questions, and if there are any other matters dealt with in your letters which I have omitted to mention, we may discuss them at some convenient date in the future.

It was with very great relief and satisfaction that I heard of the safe arrival of the Holy Carpet and the accompanying offerings which, thanks to the clearness of your directions and the excellence of your arrangements, were landed without trouble or mishap in spite of the dangers and difficulties occasioned by the present sad war. May God soon bring a lasting peace and freedom to all peoples!

I am sending this letter by the hand of your trusted and excellent messenger, Sheikh Mohammed Ibn Arif Ibn Uraifan, and he will inform you of the various matters of interest, but of less vital importance, which I have not mentioned in this letter.

(Compliments.)

(Signed)   A. HENRY McMAHON.

No. 5.

Translation of a letter from the Sherif of Mecca to Sir H. McMahon, His Majesty's High Commissioner at Cairo.

November 5, 1915.

(In the name of God, the Merciful, the Compassionate!)

To his Excellency the most exalted and eminent Minister who is endowed with the highest authority and soundness of opinion.

May God guide him to do His Will!

I RECEIVED with great pleasure your honoured letter, dated the 15th Zil Hijja (the 24th October, 1915), to which I beg to answer as follows:—

1. In order to facilitate an agreement and to render a service to Islam, and at the same time to avoid all that may cause Islam troubles and hardships—seeing moreover that we have great consideration for the distinguished qualities and dispositions of the Government of Great Britain—we renounce our insistence on the inclusion of the *vilayets* of Mersina and Adana in the Arab Kingdom. But the two *vilayets* of Aleppo and Beirut and their sea coasts are purely Arab *vilayets*, and there is no difference between a Moslem and a Christian Arab: they are both descendants of one forefather.

We Moslems will follow the footsteps of the Commander of the Faithful Omar ibn Khattab, and other Khalifs succeeding him, who ordained in the laws of the Moslem Faith that Moslems should treat the Christians as they treat themselves. He, Omar, declared with reference to Christians: "They will have the same

18

privileges and submit to the same duties as ourselves." They will thus enjoy their civic rights in as much as it accords with the general interests of the whole nation.

2. As the Iraqi *vilayets* are parts of the pure Arab Kingdom, and were in fact the seat of its Government in the time of Ali ibn Abu Talib, and in the time of all the Khalifs who succeeded him; and as in them began the civilisation of the Arabs, and as their towns were the first towns built in Islam where the Arab power became so great; therefore they are greatly valued by all Arabs far and near, and their traditions cannot be forgotten by them. Consequently, we cannot satisfy the Arab nations or make them submit to give us such a title to nobility. But in order to render an accord easy, and taking into consideration the assurances mentioned in the fifth article of your letter to keep and guard our mutual interests in that country as they are one and the same, for all these reasons we might agree to leave under the British administration for a short time those districts now occupied by the British troops without the rights of either party being prejudiced thereby (especially those of the Arab nation; which interests are to it economic and vital), and against a suitable sum paid as compensation to the Arab Kingdom for the period of occupation, in order to meet the expenses which every new kingdom is bound to support; at the same time respecting your agreements with the Sheikhs of those districts, and especially those which are essential.

3. In your desire to hasten the movement we see not only advantages, but grounds of apprehension. The first of these grounds is the fear of the blame of the Moslems of the opposite party (as has already happened in the past), who woud declare that we have revolted against Islam and ruined its forces. The second is that, standing in the face of Turkey which is supported by all the forces of Germany, we do not know what Great Britain and her Allies would do if one of the *Entente* Powers were weakened and obliged to make peace. We fear that the Arab nation will then be left alone in the face of Turkey together with her allies, but we would not at all mind if we were to face the Turks alone. Therefore it is necessary to take these points into consideration in order to avoid a peace being concluded in which the parties concerned may decide the fate of our people as if we had taken part in the war without making good our claims to official consideration.

4. The Arab nation has a strong belief that after this war is over the Turks under German influence will direct their efforts to provoke the Arabs and violate their rights, both material and moral, to wipe out their nobility and honour and reduce them to utter submission as they are determined to ruin them entirely. The reasons for the slowness shown in our action have already been stated.

5. When the Arabs know the Government of Great Britain is their ally who will not leave them to themselves at the conclusion of peace in the face of Turkey and Germany, and that she will support and will effectively defend them, then to enter the war at once will, no doubt, be in conformity with the general interest of the Arabs.

6. Our letter dated the 29th Shauâl, 1333 (the 9th September, 1915), saves us the trouble of repeating our opinions as to articles 3 and 4 of your honoured

last letter regarding administration, Government advisers and officials, especially as you have declared, exalted Minister, that you will not interfere with internal affairs.

7. The arrival of a clear and definite answer as soon as possible to the above proposals is expected. We have done our utmost in making concessions in order to come to an agreement satisfying both parties. We know that our lot in this war will be either a success, which will guarantee to the Arabs a life becoming their past history, or destruction in the attempt to attain their objects. Had it not been for the determination which I see in the Arabs for the attainment of their objects, I would have preferred to seclude myself on one of the heights of a mountain, but they, the Arabs, have insisted that I should guide the movement to this end.

May God keep you safe and victorious, as we devoutly hope and desire.

27th Zil Hijja, 1333.

———

No. 6.

Translation of a letter from Sir H. McMahon, His Majesty's High Commissioner at Cairo, to the Sherif of Mecca.

To Sherif Hussein: *December* 14, 1915.

(After customary greetings and acknowledgment of previous letter.)

I AM gratified to observe that you agree to the exclusion of the districts of Mersina and Adana from boundaries of the Arab territories.

I also note with great pleasure and satisfaction your assurances that the Arabs are determined to act in conformity with the precepts laid down by Omar Ibn Khattab and the early Khalifs, which secure the rights and privileges of all religions alike.

In stating that the Arabs are ready to recognise and respect all our treaties with Arab chiefs, it is, of course, understood that this will apply to all territories included in the Arab Kingdom, as the Government of Great Britain cannot repudiate engagements which already exist.

With regard to the *vilayets* of Aleppo and Beirut, the Government of Great Britain have fully understood and taken careful note of your observations, but, as the interests of our ally, France, are involved in them both, the question will require careful consideration and a further communication on the subject will be addressed to you in due course.

The Government of Great Britain, as I have already informed you, are ready to give all guarantees of assistance and support within their power to the Arab Kingdom, but their interests demand, as you yourself have recognised, a friendly and stable administration in the *vilayet* of Bagdad, and the adequate safeguarding of these interests calls for a much fuller and more detailed consideration than the present situation and the urgency of these negotiations permit.

We fully appreciate your desire for caution, and have no wish to urge you to hasty action, which might jeopardise the eventual success of your projects, but, in the meantime, it is most essential that you should spare no effort to attach all the

Arab peoples to our united cause and urge them to afford no assistance to our enemies.

It is on the success of these efforts and on the more active measures which the Arabs may hereafter take in support of our cause, when the time for action comes, that the permanence and strength of our agreement must depend.

Under these circumstances I am further directed by the Government of Great Britain to inform you that you may rest assured that Great Britain has no intention of concluding any peace in terms of which the freedom of the Arab peoples from German and Turkish domination does not form an essential condition.

As an earnest of our intentions, and in order to aid you in your efforts in our joint cause, I am sending you by your trustworthy messenger a sum of twenty thousand pounds.

(Customary ending.)

(Signed)   H. McMAHON.

———

No. 7.

Translation of a letter from the Sherif of Mecca to Sir H. McMahon, His Majesty's High Commissioner at Cairo.

January 1, 1916.

(In the name of God, the Merciful, the Compassionate!)

To his Excellency the eminent, energetic and magnanimous Minister.

WE received from the bearer your letter, dated the 9th Safar (the 14th December, 1915), with great respect and honour, and I have understood its contents, which caused me the greatest pleasure and satisfaction, as it removed that which had made me uneasy.

Your honour will have realised, after the arrival of Mohammed (Faroki) Sherif and his interview with you, that all our procedure up to the present was of no personal inclination or the like, which would have been wholly unintelligible, but that everything was the result of the decisions and desires of our peoples, and that we are but transmitters and executants of such decisions and desires in the position they (our people) have pressed upon us.

These truths are, in my opinion, very important and deserve your honour's special attention and consideration.

With regard to what had been stated in your honoured communication concerning El Iraq as to the matter of compensation for the period of occupation, we, in order to strengthen the confidence of Great Britain in our attitude and in our words and actions, really and veritably, and in order to give her evidence of our certainty and assurance in trusting her glorious Government, leave the determination of the amount to the perception of her wisdom and justice.

As regards the northern parts and their coasts, we have already stated in our previous letter what were the utmost possible modifications, and all this was only done so to fulfill those aspirations whose attainment is desired by the will of the Blessed and Supreme God. It is this same feeling and desire which impelled us to avoid what may possibly injure the alliance of Great Britain and France and the

21

agreement made between them during the present wars and calamities; yet we find it our duty that the eminent minister should be sure that, at the first opportunity after this war is finished, we shall ask you (what we avert our eyes from to-day) for what we now leave to France in Beirut and its coasts.

I do not find it necessary to draw your attention to the fact that our plan is of greater security to the interests and protection of the rights of Great Britain than it is to us, and will necessarily be so whatever may happen, so that Great Britain may finally see her friends in that contentment and advancement which she is endeavouring to establish for them now, especially as her Allies being neighbours to us will be the germ of difficulties and discussion with which there will be no peaceful conditions. In addition to which the citizens of Beirut will decidedly never accept such dismemberment, and they may oblige us to undertake new measures which may exercise Great Britain, certainly not less than her present troubles, because of our belief and certainty in the reciprocity and indeed the identity of our intersts, which is the only cause that caused us never to care to negotiate with any other Power but you. Consequently, it is impossible to allow any derogation that gives France, or any other Power, a span of land in those regions.

I declare this, and I have a strong belief, which the living will inherit from the dead, in the declarations which you give in the conclusion of your honoured letter. Therefore, the honourable and eminent Minister should believe and be sure, together with Great Britain, that we still remain firm to our resolution which Storrs learnt from us two years ago, for which we await the opportunity suitable to our situation, especially in view of that action the time of which has now come near and which destiny drives towards us with great haste and clearness, so that we and those who are of our opinion may have reasons for such action against any criticisms or responsibilities imposed upon us in future.

Your expression "we do not want to push you to any hasty action which might jeopardise the success of your aim" does not need any more explanation except what we may ask for, when necessary, such as arms, ammunition, &c.

I deem this sufficient, as I have occupied much of your Honour's time. I beg to offer you my great veneration and respect.

25th Safar, 1334.

———

No. 8.

Translation of a letter from Sir H. McMahon, His Majesty's High Commissioner at Cairo, to the Sherif of Mecca.

(After customary greetings.)   *January* 25, 1916.

WE have received with great pleasure and satisfaction your letter of the 25th Safar (the 1st January) at the hands of your trusty messenger, who has also transmitted to us your verbal messages.

We fully realise and entirely appreciate the motives which guide you in this important question, and we know well that you are acting entirely in the interests of the Arab peoples and with no thought beyond their welfare.

We take note of your remarks concerning the *vilayet* of Bagdad, and will take the question into careful consideration when the enemy has been defeated and the time for peaceful settlement arrives.

As regards the northern parts, we note with satisfaction your desire to avoid anything which might possibly injure the alliance of Great Britain and France. It is, as you know, our fixed determination that nothing shall be permitted to interfere in the slightest degree with our united prosecution of this war to a victorious conclusion. Moreover, when the victory has been won, the friendship of Great Britain and France will become yet more firm and enduring, cemented by the blood of Englishmen and Frenchmen who have died side by side fighting for the cause of right and liberty.

In this great cause Arabia is now associated, and God grant that the result of our mutual efforts and co-operation will bind us in a lasting friendship to the mutual welfare and happiness of us all.

We are greatly pleased to hear of the action you are taking to win all the Arabs over to our joint cause, and to dissuade them from giving any assistance to our enemies, and we leave it to your discretion to seize the most favourable moment for further and more decided measures.

You will doubtless inform us by the bearer of this letter of any manner in which we can assist you and your requests will always receive our immediate consideration.

You will have heard how El Sayed Ahmed el Sherif el Senussi has been beguiled by evil advice into hostile action, and it will be a great grief to you to know that he has been so far forgetful of the interests of the Arabs as to throw in his lot with our enemies. Misfortune has now overtaken him, and we trust that this will show him his error and lead him to peace for the sake of his poor misguided followers.

We are sending this letter by the hand of your good messenger, who will also bring to you all our news.

With salaams.

(Signed)   H. McMAHON.

———

No. 9.

Translation of a letter from the Sherif of Mecca to Sir H. McMahon, His Majesty's High Commissioner at Cairo.

February 18, 1916.

(In the name of the Merciful, the Compassionate!)

To the most noble His Excellency the High Commissioner. May God protect him. (After compliments and respects.)

WE received your Excellency's letter dated 25th Rabi El Awal, and its contents filled us with the utmost pleasure and satisfaction at the attainment of the required understanding and the intimacy desired. I ask God to make easy our purposes and prosper our endeavours. Your Excellency will understand the work that is being done, and the reasons for it from the following:—

Firstly.—We had informed your Excellency that we had sent one of our sons to Syria to command the operations deemed necessary there. We have received a detailed report from him stating that the tyrannies of the Government there have not left of the persons upon whom they could depend, whether of the different ranks of soldiers or of others, save only a few, and those of secondary importance; and that he is awaiting the arrival of the forces announced from different places, especially from the people of the country and the surrounding Arab regions as Aleppo and the south of Mosul, whose total is calculated at not less than 100,000 by their estimate; and he intends, if the majority of the forces mentioned are Arab, to begin the movement by them; and, if otherwise, that is, of the Turks or others, he will observe their advance to the Canal, and when they begin to fight, his movements upon them will be different to what they expect.

Secondly.—We purposed sending our eldest son to Medina with sufficient forces to strengthen his brother (who is) in Syria, and with every possibility of occupying the railway line, or carrying out such operations as circumstances may admit. This is the beginning of the principal movement, and we are satisfied in its beginning with what he had levied as guards to keep the interior of the country quiet; they are of the people of Hejaz only, for many reasons, which it would take too long to set forth; chiefly the difficulties in the way of providing their necessities with secrecy and speed (although this precaution was not necessary) and to make it easy to bring reinforcements when needed; this is the summary of what you wished to understand. In my opinion it is sufficient, and it is to be taken as a foundation and a standard as to our actions in the face of all changes and unforeseen events which the sequence of events may show. It remains for us to state what we need at present:—

Firstly.—The amount of £50,000 in gold for the monthly pay of the troops levied, and other things the necessity of which needs no explanation. We beg you to send it with all possible haste.

Secondly.—20,000 sacks of rice, 15,000 sacks of flour, 3,000 sacks of barley, 150 sacks of coffee, 150 sacks of sugar, 5,000 rifles of the modern pattern and the necessary ammunition, and 100 boxes of the two sample cartridges (enclosed) and of Martini-Henry cartridges and "Aza," that is those of the rifles of the factory of St. Etienne in France, for the use of those two kinds of rifles of our tribes; it would not be amiss to send 500 boxes of both kinds.

Thirdly.—We think it better that the place of deposit of all these things should be Port Sudan.

Fourthly.—As the above provisions and munitions are not needed until the beginning of the movement (of which we will inform you officially), they should remain at the above place, and when we need them we will inform the Governor there of the place to which they may be conveyed, and of the intermediaries who will carry orders for receiving them.

Fifthly.—The money required should be sent at once to the Governor of Port Sudan, and a confidential agent will be sent by us to receive it, either all at once, or in two instalments, according as he is able, and this (§) is the (secret) sign to be recognized for accepting the man.

Sixthly.—Our envoy who will receive the money will be sent to Port Sudan in three weeks' time, that is to say, he will be there on the 5th Jamad Awal (9th March) with a letter from us addressed to Al Khawaga Elias Effendi, saying that he (Elias) will pay him, in accordance with the letter, the rent of our properties, and the signature will be clear in our name, but we will instruct him to ask for the Governor of the place, whom you will apprise of this person's arrival. After perusal of the letter, the money should be given to him on condition that no discussion whatever is to be made with him of any question concerning us. We beg you most emphatically not to tell him anything, keeping this affair secret, and he should be treated apparently as if he were nothing out of the way.

Let it not be thought that our appointment of another man results from lack of confidence in the bearer; it is only to avoid waste of time, for we are appointing him to a task elsewhere. At the same time we beg you not to embark or send him in a steamer, or officially, the means already arranged being sufficient.

Seventhly.—Our representative, bearer of the present letter, has been definitely instructed to ensure the arrival of this, and I think that his mission this time is finished since the condition of things is known both in general and in detail, and there is no need for sending anyone else. In case of need for sending information, it will come from us; yet as our next representative will reach you after three weeks, you may prepare instructions for him to take back. Yet let him be treated simply in appearance.

Eighthly.—Let the British Government consider this military expenditure in accordance with the books which will be furnished it, explaining how the money has been spent.

To conclude, my best and numberless salutations beyond all increase.
14 *Rabi al Akhar,* 1334.

———

No. 10.

Translation of a letter from Sir H. McMahon, His Majesty's High Commissioner at Cairo, to the Sherif of Mecca.

(After customary greetings.)   *March* 10, 1916.

We have received your letter of the 14th Rabi el Akhar (the 18th February), duly delivered by your trusted messenger.

We are grateful to note the active measures which you propose to take. We consider them the most suitable in the existing circumstances, and they have the approval of His Majesty's Government. I am pleased to be able to inform you that His Majesty's Government have approved of meeting your requests, and that which you asked to be sent with all haste is being despatched with your messenger, who is also the bearer of this letter.

The remainder will be collected as quickly as possible and will be deposited at Port Sudan, where it will remain until we hear from you officialy of the beginning of the movement and of the places to which they may be conveyed and the intermediaries who will carry out the orders for receiving them.

The necessary instructions, as set forth in your letter, have been issued to the Governor at Port Sudan, and he will arrange everything in accordance with your wishes.

Your representative who brought your last letter has been duly facilitated in his journey to Jeizan, and every assistance has been given him in his mission, which we trust will be crowned with good results.

We have arranged that, on completion, he will be brought to Port Sudan, whence he will proceed by the safest means to join you and report the results of his work.

We take the opportunity, in sending this letter, to explain to you a matter which might otherwise not have been clear to you, and which might have given rise to misunderstanding. There are various Turkish posts and small garrisons along the coasts of Arabia who are hostile to us, and who are said to be planning injury to our naval interests in the Red Sea. We may, therefore, find it necessary to take hostile measures against these posts and garrisons, but we have issued strict instructions that every care must be taken by our ships to differentiate between the hostile Turkish garrisons and the innocent Arab inhabitants, towards whom we entertain such friendly feelings.

We give you notice of this matter in case distorted and false reports may reach you of the reasons for any action which we may be obliged to take.

We have heard rumours that our mutual enemies are endeavouring to construct boats for the purpose of laying mines in the Red Sea, and of otherwise injuring our interests there, and we beg of you that you will give us early information should you receive any confirmation of such reports.

We have heard that Ibn Rashid has been selling large quantities of camels to the Turks, which are being sent up to Damascus.

We hope that you will be able to use influence with him in order that he may cease from this practice and, if he still persists, that you will be able to arrange for the Arabs who lie between him and Syria to seize the camels as they pass, a procedure which will be to our mutual advantage.

I am glad to be able to inform you that those misguided Arabs under Sayed Ahmed el Senussi, who have fallen victims to the wiles of Turkish and German intriguers, are now beginning to see the error of their ways, and are coming in to us in large numbers, asking for forgiveness and friendship.

We have severely defeated the forces which these intriguers had collected against us, and the eyes of the Arabs are now becoming open to the deceit which has been praticed upon them.

The capture of Erzerum, and the defeats sustained by the Turks in the Caucasus, are having a great effect in our favour, and are greatly helping the cause for which we are both working.

We ask God to prosper your endeavors and to further the work which you have taken in hand.

In conclusion, we beg you to accept our warmest salutations and expressions of friendship.

6 Jamad Awwal, 1334.

(Signed)   A. H. McMAHON

3. The Balfour Declaration
November 2, 1917

I have much pleasure in conveying to you, on behalf of his Majesty's Government, the following declaration of sympathy with Jewish Zionist aspirations which has been submitted to and approved by the Cabinet:—

His Majesty's Government view with favour the establishment in Palestine of a national home for the Jewish people, and will use their best endeavours to facilitate the achievement of this object, it being clearly understood that nothing shall be done which may prejudice the civil and religious rights of existing non-Jewish communities in Palestine, or the rights and political status enjoyed by Jews in any other country.

I should be grateful if you would bring this declaration to the knowledge of the Zionist Federation.

4. United States War Aims: President Wilson's XIV Points
Speech to Congress (excerpts)
January 8, 1918

What we demand in this war, therefore, is nothing peculiar to ourselves. It is that the world be made fit and safe to live in; and particularly that it be made safe for every peace-loving nation which, like our own, wishes to live its own life, determine its own institutions, be assured of justice and fair dealing by the other peoples of the world as against force and selfish aggression. All the peoples of the world are in effect partners in this interest, and for our own part we see very clearly that unless justice be done to others it will not be done to us. The programme of the world's peace, therefore, is our programme; and that programme, the only possible programme, as we see it, is this:

I. Open covenants of peace, openly arrived at, after which there shall be no private international understandings of any kind but diplomacy shall proceed always frankly and in the public view. . . .

V. A free, open minded and absolutely impartial adjustment of all colonial claims based upon a strict observance of the principle that in determining all such questions of sovereignty the interests of the populations concerned must have equal weight with the equitable claims of the Government whose title is to be determined. . . .

XII. The Turkish portions of the present Ottoman Empire should be assured a secure sovereignty, but other nationalities which are now under Turkish rule should be assured an undoubted security of life and an absolutely unmolested opportunity of autonomous development, and the Dardanelles should be permanently opened as a free passage to ships and commerce of all nations under international guarantees. . . .

XIV. A general association of nations must be formed under specific covenants for the purpose of affording mutual guarantees of political independence and territorial integrity to great and small states alike.

5. Recommendations of the King-Crane Commission
On Syria and Palestine
August 28, 1919

At the meeting of the Big Four on 20 March 1919 (Doc. 22) President Wilson proposed that an Inter-Allied Commission visit Syria "to elucidate the state of opinion and the soil to be worked on by any mandatory" and to report their findings to the peace conference. Such "a Commission of men with no·previous contact with Syria," argued the President, would "convince the world that the Conference had tried to do all it could to find the most scientific basis possible for a settlement." The Supreme Council adopted Wilson's suggestion. But the French refused to appoint representatives, and, although the British had already named theirs, Whitehall also withdrew. As a result only the two American members, Henry C. King and Charles R. Crane, proceeded to the area with their staff. They arrived at Jaffa on 10 June and filed their report and recommendations with the American delegation at Paris less than forty days later. "Whether or not the methods were adequate or the time spent sufficient," one keen observer has noted, "the report remains the first instance of American concern, at the top level, with basic information about the area independently obtained" (E. A. Speiser, *The United States and the Near East*, p. 70). The King-Crane inquiry, however, proved to have no more than academic interest. Neither the European powers nor the United States gave it serious consideration. Reprinted here is only one segment of the long report.

The Commissioners make to the Peace Conference the following recommendations for the treatment of Syria:

1. We recommend, as most important of all, and in strict harmony with our instructions, that whatever foreign administration (whether of one or more powers) is brought into Syria, should come in, not at all as a colonizing Power in the old sense of that term, but as a Mandatory under the League of Nations, with the clear consciousness that "the well-being and development" of the Syrian people form for it a "sacred trust."

(1) To this end the mandate should have a limited term, the time of expiration to be determined by the League of Nations, in the light of all the facts as brought out from year to year, in the annual reports of the Mandatory to the League or in other ways.

(2) The Mandatory Administration should have, however, a period and power sufficient to ensure the success of the new State; and especially to make possible carrying through important educational and economic undertakings, essential to secure founding of the State.

(3) The Mandatory Administration should be characterized from the beginning by a strong and vital educational emphasis, in clear recognition of the imperative necessity of education for the citizens of a democratic state, and the development of a sound national spirit. This systematic cultivation of national spirit is particularly required in a country like Syria, which has only recently come to self-consciousness.

(4) The Mandatory should definitely seek, from the beginning of its trusteeship, to train the Syrian people to independent self-government as rapidly as conditions allow, by setting up all the institutions of a democratic state, and by sharing with them increasingly the work of administration, and so forming gradually an intelligent citizenship, interested unselfishly in the progress of the country, and forming at the same time a large group of disciplined civil servants.

(5) The period of "tutelage" should not be unduly prolonged, but independent self-government should be granted as soon as it can safely be done; remembering that the primary business of government is not the accomplishment of certain things, but the development of citizens.

(6) It is peculiarly the duty of the Mandatory in a country like Syria, and in this modern age, to see that complete religious liberty is ensured, both in the constitution and in the practice of the state, and that a jealous care is exercised for the rights of all minorities. Nothing is more vital than this for the enduring success of the new Arab State.

(7) In the economic development of Syria, a dangerous amount of indebtedness on the part of the new State should be avoided, as well as any entanglements financially with the affairs of the Mandatory Power. On the other hand the legitimate established privileges of foreigners such as rights to maintain schools, commercial concessions, etc., should be preserved, but subject to review and modification under the authority of the League of Nations in the interest of Syria. The Mandatory Power should not take advantage of its position to force a monopolistic control at any point to the detriment either of Syria or of other nations; but it should seek to bring the new State as rapidly as possible to economic independence as well as to political independence.

Whatever is done concerning the further recommendations of the Commission, the fulfillment of at least the conditions now named should be assured, if the Peace Conference and the League of Nations are true to the policy of mandatories already embodied in "The Covenant of the League of Nations." This should effectively guard the most essential interests of Syria, however the machinery of administration is finally organized. The Damascus Congress betrayed in many ways their intense fear that their country would become, though under some other name, simply a colonial possession of some other Power. That fear must be completely allayed.

2. We recommend, in the second place that the unity of Syria be preserved, in accordance with the earnest petition of the great majority of the people of Syria.

(1) The territory concerned is too limited, the population too small, and the economic, geographic, racial and language unity too manifest, to make the setting up of independent states within its boundaries desirable, if such division can possibly be avoided. The country is very largely Arab in language, culture, traditions, and customs.

(2) This recommendation is in line with important "general considerations" already urged, and with the principles of the League of Nations, as well as in answer to the desires of the majority of the population concerned.

(3) The precise boundaries of Syria should be determined by a special commission on boundaries, after the Syrian territory has been in general allotted.

The Commissioners believe, however, that the claim of the Damascus Conference to include Cilicia in Syria is not justified, either historically or by commercial or language relations. The line between the Arabic-speaking and the Turkish-speaking populations would quite certainly class Cilicia with Asia Minor, rather than with Syria. Syria, too, has no such need of further sea coast as the large interior sections of Asia Minor.

(4) In standing thus for the recognition of the unity of Syria, the natural desires of regions like the Lebanon, which have already had a measure of independence, should not be forgotten. It will make for real unity, undoubtedly, to give a large measure of local autonomy, and especially in the case of strongly unified groups. Even the "Damascus Program" which presses so earnestly the unity of Syria, itself urges a government "on broad decentralization principles."

Lebanon has achieved a considerable degree of prosperity and autonomy within the Turkish Empire. She certainly should not find her legitimate aspirations less possible within a Syrian national State. On the contrary, it may be confidently expected that both her economic and political relations with the rest of Syria would be better if she were a constituent member of the State, rather than entirely independent of it.

As a predominantly Christian country, too, Lebanon naturally fears Moslem domination in a unified Syria. But against such domination she would have a four-fold safeguard: her own large autonomy; the presence of a strong Mandatory for the considerable period in which the constitution and practice of the new State would be forming; the oversight of the League of Nations, with its insistence upon religious liberty and the rights of minorities; and the certainty that the Arab Government would feel the necessity of such a state, if it were to commend itself to the League of Nations. Moreover, there would be less danger of a reactionary Moslem attitude, if Christians were present in the state in considerable numbers, rather than largely segregated outside the state, as experience of the relations of different religious faiths in India suggests.

As a predominantly Christian country, it is also to be noted that Lebanon would be in a position to exert a stronger and more helpful influence if she were within the Syrian State, feeling its problems and needs, and sharing all its life, instead of outside it, absorbed simply in her own narrow concerns. For the sake of the larger interests, both of Lebanon and of Syria, then, the unity of Syria is to be urged. It is certain that many of the more thoughtful Lebanese themselves hold this view. A similar statement might be made for Palestine; though, as "the holy Land" for Jews and Christians and Moslems alike, its situation is unique, and might more readily justify unique treatment, if such treatment were justified anywhere. This will be discussed more particularly in connection with the recommendation concerning Zionism.

3. We recommend, in the third place, that Syria be placed under on[e] Mandatory Power, as the natural way to secure real and efficient unity.

(1) To divide the administration of the provinces of Syria among several mandatories, even if existing national unity were recognized; or to attempt a joint mandatory of the whole on the commission plan:—neither of these courses would be naturally suggested as the best way to secure and promote the unity of

the new State, or even the general unity of the whole people. It is conceivable that circumstances might drive the Peace Conference to some such form of divided mandate; but it is not a solution to be voluntarily chosen, from the point of view of the larger interests of the people, as considerations already urged indicate.

(2) It is not to be forgotten, either, that, however they are handled politically, the people of Syria are there, forced to get on together in some fashion. They are obliged to live with one another—the Arabs of the East and the people of the Coast, the Moslems and the Christians. Will they be helped or hindered, in establishing tolerable and finally cordial relations, by a single mandatory? No doubt the quick mechanical solution of the problem of difficult relations is to split the people up into little independent fragments. And sometimes, undoubtedly, as in the case of the Turks and Armenians, the relations are so intolerable as to make some division imperative and inevitable. But in general, to attempt complete separation only accentuates the differences and increases the antagonism. The whole lesson of the modern social consciousness points to the necessity of understanding "the other half," as it can be understood only by close and living relations. Granting reasonable local autonomy to reduce friction among groups, a single mandatory ought to form a constant and increasingly effective help to unity of feeling throughout the state, and ought to steadily improve group relations.

The people of Syria, in our hearings, have themselves often insisted that, so far as unpleasant relations have hitherto prevailed among various groups, it has been very largely due to the direct instigation of the Turkish Government. When justice is done impartially to all; when it becomes plain that the aim of the common government is the service of all classes alike, not their exploitation, decent human relations are pretty certain to prevail, and a permanent foundation for such relations to be secured—a foundation which could not be obtained by dividing men off from one another in antagonistic groups.

The Commissioners urge, therefore, for the largest future good of all groups and regions alike, the placing of the whole of Syria under a single mandate.

4. We recommend, in the fourth place, that Emir Feisal be made the head of the new united Syrian State.

(1) This is expressly and unanimously asked for by the representative Damascus Congress in the name of the Syrian people, and there seems to be no reason to doubt that the great majority of the population of Syria sincerely desire to have Emir Feisal as ruler.

(2) A constitutional monarchy along democratic lines, seems naturally adapted to the Arabs, with their long training under tribal conditions, and with their traditional respect for their chiefs. They seem to need, more than most people, a King as the personal symbol of the power of the State.

(3) Emir Feisal has come, too, naturally into his present place of power, and there is no one else who could well replace him. He had the great advantage of being the son of the Sherif of Mecca, and as such honored throughout the Moslem world. He was one of the prominent Arab leaders who assumed responsibility for the Arab uprising against the Turks, and so shared in the complete deliverance of the Arab-speaking portions of the Turkish Empire. He was consequently hailed by the "Damascus Congress" as having "merited their full confi-

dence and entire reliance." He was taken up and supported by the British as the most promising candidate for the headship of the new Arab State—an Arab of the Arabs, but with a position of wide appeal through his Sherifian connection, and through his broad sympathies with the best in the Occident. His relations with the Arabs to the east of Syria are friendly, and his kingdom would not be threatened from that side. He undoubtedly does not make so strong an appeal to the Christians of the West Coast, as to the Arabs of the East; but no man can be named who would have a stronger general appeal. He is tolerant and wise, skillful in dealing with men, winning in manner, a man of sincerity, insight, and power. Whether he has the full strength needed for his difficult task it is too early to say; but certainly no other Arab leader combines so many elements of power as he, and he will have invaluable help throughout the mandatory period.

The Peace Conference may take genuine satisfaction in the fact that an Arab of such qualities is available for the headship of this new state in the Near East.

5. We recommend, in the fifth place, serious modification of the extreme Zionist Program for Palestine of unlimited immigration of Jews, looking finally to making Palestine distinctly a Jewish State.

(1) The Commissioners began their study of Zionism with minds predisposed in its favor, but the actual facts in Palestine, coupled with the force of the general principles proclaimed by the Allies and accepted by the Syrians have driven them to the recommendation here made.

(2) The Commission was abundantly supplied with literature on the Zionist program by the Zionist Commission to Palestine; heard in conferences much concerning the Zionist colonies and their claims; and personally saw something of what had been accomplished. They found much to approve in the aspirations and plans of the Zionists, and had warm appreciation for the devotion of many of the colonists, and for their success, by modern methods, in overcoming great natural obstacles.

(3) The Commission recognized also that definite encouragement had been given to the Zionists by the Allies in Mr. Balfour's often quoted statement, in its approval by other representatives of the Allies. If, however, the strict terms of the Balfour Statement are adhered to—favoring "the establishment in Palestine of a national home for the Jewish people, it being clearly understood that nothing shall be done which may prejudice the civil and religious rights of existing non-Jewish communities in Palestine"—it can hardly be doubted that the extreme Zionist Program must be greatly modified. For a "national home for the Jewish people" is not equivalent to making Palestine into a Jewish State; nor can the erection of such a Jewish State be accomplished without the gravest trespass upon the "civil and religious rights of existing non-Jewish communities in Palestine." The fact came out repeatedly in the Commission's conference with Jewish representatives, that the Zionists looked forward to a practically complete dispossession of the present non-Jewish inhabitants of Palestine, by various forms of purchase.

In his address of July 4, 1918, President Wilson laid down the following principle as one of the four great "ends for which the associated peoples of the world were fighting": "The settlement of every question, whether of territory, of sovereignty, of economic arrangement, or of political relationship upon the basis of the free acceptance of that settlement by the people immediately concerned, and not upon the basis of the material interest or advantage of any other nation or people which may desire a different settlement for the sake of its own exterior influence or mastery." If that principle is to rule, and so the wishes of Palestine's population are to be decisive as to what is to be done with Palestine, then it is to be remembered that the non-Jewish population of Palestine—nearly nine-tenths of the whole—are emphatically against the entire Zionist program. The tables show that there was no one thing upon which the population of Palestine was more agreed than upon this. To subject a people so minded to unlimited Jewish immigration, and to steady financial and social pressure to surrender the land, would be a gross violation of the principle just quoted, and of the peoples' rights, though it kept within the forms of law.

It is to be noted also that the feeling against the Zionist program is not confined to Palestine, but shared very generally by the people throughout Syria, as our conferences clearly showed. More than 72 per cent—1350 in all—of all the petitions in the whole of Syria were directed against the Zionist program. Only two requests—those for a united Syria and for independence—had a larger support. This general feeling was only voiced by the "General Syrian Congress," in the seventh, eighth and tenth resolutions of their statement [paras. 7, 8, 10, Doc. 25]. . . .

The Peace Conference should not shut its eyes to the fact that the anti-Zionist feeling in Palestine and Syria is intense and not lightly to be flouted. No British officer, consulted by the Commissioners, believed that the Zionist program could be carried out except by force of arms. The officers generally thought a force of not less than fifty thousand soldiers would be required even to initiate the program. That of itself is evidence of a strong sense of the injustice of the Zionist program, on the part of the non-Jewish populations of Palestine and Syria. Decisions, requiring armies to carry out, are sometimes necessary, but they are surely not gratuitously to be taken in the interests of a serious injustice. For the initial claim, often submitted by Zionist representatives, that they have a "right" to Palestine, based on an occupation of two thousand years ago, can hardly be seriously considered.

There is a further consideration that cannot justly be ignored, if the world is to look forward to Palestine becoming a definitely Jewish state, however gradually that may take place. That consideration grows out of the fact that Palestine is "the Holy Land" for Jews, Christians, and Moslems alike. Millions of Christians and Moslems all over the world are quite as much concerned as the Jews with conditions in Palestine, especially with those conditions which touch upon religious feeling and rights. The relations in these matters in Palestine are most delicate and difficult. With the best possible intentions, it may be doubted whether the Jews could possibly seem to either Christians or Moslems proper guardians of the holy places, or custodians of the Holy Land as a whole. The reason is this: the places which are most sacred to Christians—those having to do with Jesus—and which are also sacred to Moslems, are not only not sacred to Jews, but abhorrent to them. It is simply impossible, under those circumstances, for Moslems and Christians to feel satisfied to have these places in Jewish hands, or under the custody of Jews. There are still other places about which Moslems must have the same feeling. In fact, from this point of view, the Moslems, just because the sacred places of all three religions are sacred to them, have made very naturally much more satisfactory custodians of the holy places than the Jews could be. It must be believed that the precise meaning, in this respect, of the complete Jewish occupation of Palestine has not been fully sensed by those who urge the extreme Zionist program. For it would intensify, with a certainty like fate, the anti-Jewish feeling both in Palestine and in all other portions of the world which look to Palestine as "the Holy Land."

In view of all these considerations, and with a deep sense of sympathy for the Jewish cause, the Commissioners feel bound to recommend that only a greatly reduced Zionist program be attempted by the Peace Conference, and even that, only very gradually initiated. This would have to mean that Jewish immigration should be definitely limited, and that the project for making Palestine distinctly a Jewish commonwealth should be given up.

There would then be no reason why Palestine could not be included in a united Syrian State, just as other portions of the country, the holy places being cared for by an International and Inter-religious Commission, somewhat as at present, under the oversight and approval of the Mandatory and of the League of Nations. The Jews, of course, would have representation upon this Commission.

6. The Recommendations now made lead naturally to the necessity of recommending what Power shall undertake the single Mandate for all Syria.

(1) The considerations already dealt with suggest the qualifications, ideally to be desired in this Mandatory Power: First of all it should be freely desired by the people. It should be willing to enter heartily into the spirit of the mandatory system, and its possible gift to the world, and so be willing to withdraw after a reasonable period, and not seek selfishly to exploit the country. It should have a passion for democracy, for the education of the common people and for the development of national spirit. It needs unlimited sympathy and patience in what is practically certain to be a rather thankless task; for no Power can go in, honestly to face actual conditions (like landownership, for example) and seek to correct these conditions, without making many enemies. It should have experience in dealing with less developed peoples, and abundant resources in men and money.

(2) Probably no Power combines all these qualifications, certainly not in equal degree. But there is hardly one of these qualifications that has not been more or less definitely indicated in our conferences with the Syrian people and they certainly suggest a new stage in the development of the self-sacrificing spirit in the relations of peoples to one another. The Power that undertakes the single mandate for all Syria, in the spirit of these qualifications, will have the possibility of greatly serving not only Syria but the world, and of exalting at the same time its own national life. For it would be working in direct line with the high aims of the Allies in the war, and give proof that those high aims had not been abandoned. And that would mean very much just now, in enabling the nations to keep their faith in one another and in their own highest ideals.

(3) The Resolutions of the Peace Conference of January 30, 1919, quoted in our Instructions, expressly state for regions to be "completely severed from the

Turkish Empire," that "the wishes of these communities must be a principal consideration in the selection of the Mandatory Power." Our survey left no room for doubt of the choice of the majority of the Syrian people. Although it was not known whether America would take a mandate at all; and although the Commission could not only give no assurances upon that point, but had rather to discourage expectation; nevertheless, upon the face of the returns, America was the first choice of 1152 of the petitions presented—more than 60 per cent—while no other Power had as much as 15 per cent for first choice.

And the conferences showed that the people knew the grounds upon which they registered their choice for America. They declared that their choice was due to knowledge of America's record: the unselfish aims with which she had come into the war; the faith in her felt by multitudes of Syrians who had been in America; the spirit revealed in American educational institutions in Syria, especially the College in Beirut, with its well known and constant encouragement of Syrian national sentiment; their belief that America had no territorial or colonial ambitions, and would willingly withdraw when the Syrian state was well established as her treatment both of Cuba and the Philippines seemed to them to illustrate; her genuinely democratic spirit; and her ample resources.

From the point of view of the desires of the "people concerned," the Mandate should clearly go to America.

(4) From the point of view of qualifications, too, already stated as needed in the Mandatory for Syria, America, as first choice of the people, probably need not fear careful testing, point by point, by the standard involved in our discussion of qualifications; though she has much less experience in such work than Great Britain, and is likely to show less patience; and though her definite connections with Syria have been less numerous and close than those of France. She would have at least the great qualification of fervent belief in the new mandatory system of the League of Nations, as indicating the proper relations which a strong nation should take toward a weaker one. And, though she would undertake the mandate with reluctance, she could probably be brought to see how logically the taking of such responsibility follows from the purposes with which she entered the war, and from her advocacy of the League of Nations.

(5) There is the further consideration, that America could probably come into the Syrian situation, in the beginning at least, with less friction than any other Power. The great majority of Syrian people, as has been seen, favor her coming, rather than that of any other power. Both the British and the French would find it easier to yield their respective claims to America than to each other. She would have no rival imperial interests to press. She would have abundant resources for the development of the sound prosperity of Syria; and this would inevitably benefit in a secondary way the nations which have had closest connection with Syria, and so help to keep relations among the Allies cordial. No other Power probably would be more welcome, as a neighbor, to the British, with their large interests in Egypt, Arabia, and Mesopotamia; or to the Arabs and Syrians in these regions; or to the French with their long-established and many-sided interests in Beirut and the Lebanon.

(6) The objections to simply recommending at once a single American Man-

date for all Syria are: first of all, that it is not certain that the American people would be willing to take the Mandate; that it is not certain that the British or French would be willing to withdraw, and would cordially welcome America's coming—a situation which might prove steadily harassing to an American administration; that the vague but large encouragement given to the Zionist aims might prove particularly embarrassing to America, on account of her large and influential Jewish population; and that, if America were to take any mandate at all, and were to take but one mandate, it is probable that an Asia Minor Mandate would be more natural and important. For there is a task there of such peculiar and world-wide significance as to appeal to the best in America, and demand the utmost from her, and as certainly to justify her in breaking with her established policy concerning mixing in the affairs of the Eastern Hemisphere. The Commissioners believe, moreover, that no other Power could come into Asia Minor, with hands so free to give impartial justice to all the peoples concerned.

To these objections as a whole, it is to be said, that they are all of such a kind that they may resolve themselves; and that they only form the sort of obstacles that must be expected, in so large and significant an undertaking. In any case they do not relieve the Commissioners from the duty of recommending the course which, in their honest judgment, is the best course, and the one for which the whole situation calls.

The Commissioners, therefore, recommend, as involved in the logic of the facts, that the United States of America be asked to undertake the single Mandate for all Syria.

If for any reason the mandate for Syria is not given to America, then the Commissioners recommend, in harmony with the express request of the majority of the Syrian people, that the mandate be given to Great Britain. The tables show that there were 1073 petitions in all Syria for Great Britain as Mandatory, if America did not take the mandate. This is very greatly in excess of any similar expression for the French. On the contrary—for whatever reason—more than 60 percent of all the petitions, presented to the Commission, directly and strongly protested against any French Mandate. Without going into a discussion of the reasons for this situation, the Commissioners are reluctantly compelled to believe that this situation itself makes it impossible to recommend a single French mandate for all Syria. The feeling of the Arabs of the East is particularly strong against the French. And there is grave reason to believe that the attempt to enforce a French Mandate would precipitate war between the Arabs and the French, and force upon Great Britain a dangerous alternative. The Commissioners may perhaps be allowed to say that this conclusion is contrary to their own earlier hope, that— because of France's long and intimate relations with Syria, because of her unprecedented sacrifices in the war, and because the British Empire seemed certain to receive far greater accessions of territory fom the war—it might seem possible to recommend that France be given the entire mandate for Syria. But the longer the Commission remained in Syria, the more clear it became that that course could not be taken.

The Commissioners recommend, therefore, that if America cannot take the mandate for all Syria, that it be given to Great Britain; because of the choice of the people concerned; because she is already on the ground and with much of the necessary work in hand; because of her trained administrators; because of her long and generally successful experience in dealing with less developed peoples; and because she has so many of the qualifications needed in a Mandatory Power, as we have already considered them.

We should hardly be doing justice, however, to our sense of responsibility to the Syrian people, if we did not frankly add at least some of the reasons and misgivings, variously expressed and implied in our conferences, which led to the preference for an American mandate over a British mandate. The people repeatedly showed honest fear that in British hands the mandatory power would become simply a colonizing power of the old kind; that Great Britain would find it difficult to give up the colonial theory, especially in case of a people thought inferior; that she would favor a civil service and pension budget too expensive for a poor people; that the interests of Syria would be subordinated to the supposed needs of the Empire; that there would be, after all, too much exploitation of the country for Britain's benefit; that she would never be ready to withdraw and give the country real independence; that she did not really believe in universal education, and would not provide adequately for it; and that she already had more territory in her possession—in spite of her fine colonial record—than was good either for herself or for the world. These misgivings of the Syrian people unquestionably largely explain their demand for "absolute independence," for a period of "assistance" of only twenty years, their protest against Article 22 of the Covenant of the League of Nations, etc. They all mean that whatever Power the Peace Conference shall send into Syria, should go in as a true mandatory under the League of Nations, and for a limited term. Anything else would be a betrayal of the Syrian people. It needs to be emphasized, too, that under a true mandatory for Syria, all the legitimate interests of all the nations in Syria would be safeguarded. In particular, there is no reason why any tie that France has had with Syria in the past should be severed or even weakened under the control of another mandatory power, or in an independent Syria.

There remains only to be added, that if France feels so intensely concerning her present claims in Syria, as to threaten all cordial relations among the Allies, it is of course possible to give her a mandate over the Lebanon (not enlarged), separated from the rest of Syria, as is desired by considerable groups in that region. For reasons already given, the Commissioners cannot recommend this course, but it is a possible arrangement.

6. Oil Policy in the Middle Eastern Mandates: Letter from U.S. Ambassador Davis to British Foreign Secretary Lord Curzon
May 12, 1920

Pursuant to the instructions of my Government, I have the honour to inform Your Lordship that the Government of the United States has been officially [*unofficially*] [1] informed that the Mandates for Mesopotamia and Palestine have

---

[1] The correction was authorized by a telegram from the Department, dated July 12, 1920, 4 p.m. (file no. 800.6363/148a).

been assigned to Great Britain; the Mandate for Mesopotamia being given subject to friendly arrangement with the Italian Government regarding economic rights.

The Government of the United States desires to point out that during the Peace negotiations at Paris leading up to the Treaty of Versailles, it consistently took the position that the future Peace of the world required that as a general principle any Alien territory which should be acquired pursuant to the Treaties of Peace with the Central Powers must be held and governed in such a way as to assure equal treatment in law and in fact to the commerce of all nations. It was on account of and subject to this understanding that the United States felt itself able and willing to agree that the acquisition of certain enemy territory by the victorious powers would be consistent with the best interests of the world. The representatives of the principal Allied Powers in the discussion of the Mandate principles expressed in no indefinite manner their recognition of the justice and far-sightedness of such a principle and agreed to its application to the Mandates over Turkish territory.

The Administration of Palestine and Mesopotamia during the interim period of military occupation has given rise to several communications between the United States Government and that of Great Britain relative to matters that had created the unfortunate impression in the minds of the American public that the Authorities of His Majesty's Government in the occupied region had given advantage to British oil interests which were not accorded to American Companies and further that Great Britain had been preparing quietly for exclusive control of the oil resources in this region. The impression referred to has, it is believed, been due in large part to reports of authoritative statements regarding the general Oil Policy of Great Britain and of actual work such as the construction of pipe lines, railways and refineries, the operations of certain oil wells, the acquisitions of dockyards, cotton investigations and permitted researches by certain individuals whose activities, though stated to be solely in behalf of the civil Administration, were attended by circumstances which created the impression that some benefit at least would accrue to British oil interests.

Certain of the occurrences above referred to have been explained by his Majesty's Government as due to military necessity, and certain others as due to laxity on the part of local authorities. It must be realized, however, that it has been difficult for the American people to reconcile all of these reports with the assurance of His Majesty's Government that "the provisional character of the military occupation does not warrant the taking of decisions by the occupying power in matters concerning the future economic development of the country," and that the invitation [*initiation*] of new undertakings and the exercise of rights under concessions would be prohibited. The United States Government has confidence in the good faith of His Majesty's Government in attempting to carry out the assurances given by His Majesty's Foreign Office, but desires to point out that the considerations above referred to indicate the difficulty in insuring the local execution of such undertakings and the necessity for careful measures to guarantee the practical fulfillment of the principles expressed and agreed to during the peace negotiations at Paris.

With this thought in mind, the Government of the United States ventures to

38

suggest the following propositions, which embody or illustrate the principles which the United States Government would be pleased to see applied in the occupied or mandated regions and which are submitted as furnishing a reasonable basis for discussions. In the event of such discussions it would be assumed that the legal situation as regards economic resources in the occupied or mandated regions would remain *in statu quo* pending an agreement:

(1) That the Mandatory Power strictly adhere and conform to the principles expressed and agreed to during the peace negotiations at Paris and to the principles embodied in Mandate "A" prepared in London for adoption by the League of Nations by the Commission on Mandatories.

(2) That there be guaranteed to the nationals or subjects of all nations treatment equal in law and in fact to that accorded nationals and subjects of the Mandatory Power with respect to taxation or other matters affecting residence, business, profession, concessions, freedom of transit for persons and goods, freedom of communication, trade, navigation, commerce, industrial property, and other economic rights or commercial activities.

(3) That no exclusive economic concession covering the whole of any Mandated region or sufficiently large to be virtually exclusive shall be granted and that no monopolistic concessions relating to any commodity or to any economic privilege subsidiary and essential to the production, development, or exploitation of such commodity shall be granted.

(4) That reasonable provision shall be made for publicity of applications for concessions and of Governmental Acts or Regulations relating to the economic resources of the Mandated territories; and that in general regulations or legislation regarding the granting of concessions relating to exploring or exploiting economic resources or regarding other privileges in connection with these shall not have the effect of placing American citizens or companies or those of other nations or companies controlled by American citizens or nationals of other countries at a disadvantage compared with the nationals or companies of the Mandate nation or companies controlled by nationals of the Mandate nation or others.

The fact that certain concessions were granted in the mandated regions by the Turkish Government is, of course, an important factor which must be given practical consideration. The United States Government believes that it is entitled to participate in any discussions relating to the status of such concessions not only because of existing vested rights of American citizens, but also because the equitable treatment of such concessions is essential to the initiation and application of the general principles in which the United States Government is interested.

No direct mention has been made herein of the question of establishment of monopolies directly or indirectly by or in behalf of the Mandatory Government. It is believed, however, that the establishment of monopolies by or in behalf of the Mandatory Government would not be consistent with the principles of trusteeship inherent in the Mandatory idea. His Majesty's Government has stated its conception of the necessity for the control of oil production in these territories in time of national emergency. The Government of the United States does not intend at present to suggest arrangements that shall extend to any consideration not included in an enlightened interpretation of what constitutes its legitimate commercial interests. The question of control in times of national emergencies of supplies which may be deemed essential by Great Britain is a subject which the United States Government deems a matter for separate discussion.

The Government of the United States realizes the heavy financial obligations which will arise in connection with the administration of the Mandatory. It believes, however, that any attempt toward reimbursement by the adoption of a policy of monopolization or of exclusive concessions and special favours to its own nationals, besides being a repudiation of the principles already agreed to would prove to be unwise even from the point of view of expediency both on economic and political grounds. It also believes that the interests of the world as well as that of the two respective countries can best be served by a friendly co-operation or a friendly and equal competition between the citizens of the two countries and citizens of ther nationalities.

The Government of the United States would be glad to receive an early expression of the views of His Majesty's Government, especially in order to reassure public opinion in the United States.

I have the honour further to acquaint Your Lordship that his Note is not designed by way of reply to the Allied Note from San Remo, which will be answered separately.

7. Congress Endorses the Balfour Declaration: Public Resolution No. 73, 67th Congress, Second Session
September 21, 1922

Resolved by the Senate and House of Representatives of the United States of America in Congress Assembled.

That the United States of America favors the establishment in Palestine of a national home for the Jewish people, it being clearly understood that nothing shall be done which may prejudice the civil and religious rights of Christian and all other non-Jewish communities in Palestine, and that the holy places and religious buildings and sites in Palestine shall be adequately protected.

8. An 'Open Door' Policy for Oil:
Secretary Hughes to President Coolidge
November 8, 1923

It has recently been brought to my attention that the Sinclair Oil Company has felt a certain dissatisfaction at what they consider their failure to receive proper support from this Department, particularly in connection with their effort to secure an oil concession in North Persia. In a letter I wrote to Mr. Harding under date of October 28, 1922, of which I attach a copy, I gave some of the details of the competition which had arisen in North Persia between the Sinclair and Standard Oil Companies, a matter which Mr. Archibald Roosevelt, of the former company, had laid before the President. In order that you may be fully advised I should be glad if you could find it posssible to glance through that letter.

This Department's attitude of impartiality as between the competing American companies, which I emphasized in that letter, has been scrupulously followed and I am now informing the Sinclair Oil Company that while I have no reason to believe that the Persian Government is in doubt on this point I am quite prepared to re-emphasize this position through our Legation at Teheran and also to indicate that it is the Government's policy to give appropriate diplomatic support to American interests abroad.

This general question raises a point which I feel to be of sufficient importance to bring to your attention; namely, the proper attitude of this Government toward American commercial enterprise abroad. From time to time there has been some dissatisfaction expressed in business circles because this Department's attitude toward American business interests in the foreign field differs somewhat from the attitude in similar matters of the British, French and other European governments. The latter are not loath to interfere politically in support of the business interests of their nationals to a degree which is not followed by this Department. Our position is that we are always ready to give appropriate support to our nationals in seeking opportunities for business enterprise abroad, but we do not undertake to make the government a party to the business negotiations or use political presssure for the benefit of private interests in order to obtain particular concessions, or intervene in favor of one Americcan interest as against another. We are persistent in our efforts to maintain the open door policy, or equality of commercial opportunity, but we do not attempt to assume obligations for the government, expressed or implied, which under our system we could not undertake to discharge.

American companies which might prefer a policy of more direct interference on their behalf by the government are inclined, in my opinion, to overlook the fact that American prestige and reputation for fairness has been enhanced, and consequently business opportunities of our nationals have been increased, by the correct policy which this government has followed. I find that in many parts of the world American business is welcomed largely because foreign countries realize that they can deal with American interests on a business basis without fearing political complications.

It is hardly necessary to point out that the other course desired by some businessmen, intent on their own immediate interests, would not only be contrary to our traditions and foreign policy, but if persistently followed would involve us in political intrigues and in difficulties which other governments with different exigencies and aims find it impossible to escape and from which we have happily been free.

While I do not feel that the question presented by the informal representations on the part of the Sinclair Company calls for any other action than I have indicated above, I desire briefly to summarize our attitude should the matter otherwise be brought to your attention.

9. International Regulation of the Turkish Straits: The Montreux Convention July 20, 1936

Article 1.

The High Contracting Parties recognise and affirm the principle of freedom of transit and navigation by sea in the Straits.

The exercise of this freedom shall henceforth be regulated by the provisions of the present Convention.

SECTION I.

MERCHANT VESSELS

Article 2.

In time of peace, merchant vessels shall enjoy complete freedom of transit and navigation in the Straits, by day and by night, under any flag and with any kind of cargo, without any formalities, except as provided in Article 3 below. No taxes or charges other than those authorised by Annex I to the present Convention shall be levied by the Turkish authorities on these vessels when passing in transit without calling at a port in the Straits.

In order to facilitate the collection of these taxes or charges merchant vessels passing through the Straits shall communicate to the officials at the stations referred to in Article 3 their name, nationality, tonnage, destination and last port of call (provenance).

Pilotage and towage remain optional.

Article 3.

All ships entering the Straits by the Ægean Sea or by the Black Sea shall stop at a sanitary station near the entrance to the Straits for the purposes of the sanitary control prescribed by Turkish law within the framework of international sanitary regulations. This control, in the case of ships possessing a clean bill of health or presenting a declaration of health testifying that they do not fall within the scope of the provisions of the second paragraph of the present Article, shall be carried out by day and by night with all possible speed, and the vessels in question shall not be required to make any other stop during their passage through the Straits.

Vessels which have on board cases of plague, cholera, yellow fever, exanthematic typhus or smallpox, or which have had such cases on board during the previous seven days, and vessels which have left an infected port within less than five times twenty-four hours shall stop at the sanitary stations indicated in the preceding paragraph in order to embark such sanitary guards as the Turkish authorities may direct. No tax or charge shall be levied in respect of these sanitary guards and they shall be disembarked at a sanitary station on departure from the Straits.

Article 4.

In time of war, Turkey not being belligerent, merchant vessels, under any flag or with any kind of cargo, shall enjoy freedom of transit and navigation in the Straits subject to the provisions of Articles 2 and 3.

Pilotage and towage remain optional.

Article 5.

In time of war, Turkey being belligerent, merchant vessels not belonging to a country at war with Turkey shall enjoy freedom of transit and navigation in the Straits on condition that they do not in any way assist the enemy.

Such vessels shall enter the Straits by day and their transit shall be effected by the route which shall in each case be indicated by the Turkish authorities.

Article 6.

Should Turkey consider herself to be threatened with imminent danger of war, the provisions of Article 2 shall nevertheless continue to be applied except that vessels must enter the Straits by day and that their transit must be effected by the route which shall, in each case, be indicated by the Turkish authorities.

Pilotage may, in this case, be made obligatory, but no charge shall be levied.

Article 7.

The term "merchant vessels" applies to all vessels which are not covered by Section II of the present Convention.

SECTION II.

Vessels of War

Article 8.

For the purposes of the present Convention, the definitions of vessels of war and of their specification together with those relating to the calculation of tonnage shall be as set forth in Annex II to the present Convention.

Article 9.

Naval auxiliary vessels specifically designed for the carriage of fuel, liquid or non-liquid, shall not be subject to the provisions of Article 13 regarding notification, nor shall they be counted for the purpose of calculating the tonnage which is subject to limitation under Articles 14 and 18, on condition that they shall pass through the Straits singly. They shall, however, continue to be on the same footing as vessels of war for the purpose of the remaining provisions governing transit.

The auxiliary vessels specified in the preceding paragraph shall only be entitled to benefit by the exceptional status therein contemplated if their armament does not include: for use against floating targets, more than two guns of a

43

maximum calibre of 105 millimetres; for use against aerial targets, more than two guns of a maximum calibre of 75 millimetres.

Article 10.

In time of peace, light surface vessels, minor war vessels and auxiliary vessels, whether belonging to Black Sea or non-Black Sea Powers, and whatever their flag, shall enjoy freedom of transit through the Straits without any taxes or charges whatever, provided that such transit is begun during daylight and subject to the conditions laid down in Article 13 and the Articles following thereafter.

Vessels of war other than those which fall within the categories specified in the preceding paragraph shall only enjoy a right of transit under the special conditions provided by Articles 11 and 12.

Article 11.

Black Sea Powers may send through the Straits capital ships of a tonnage greater than that laid down in the first paragraph of Article 14, on condition that these vessels pass through the Straits singly, escorted by not more than two destroyers.

Article 12.

Black Sea Powers shall have the right to send through the Straits, for the purpose of rejoining their base, submarines constructed or purchased outside the Black Sea, provided that adequate notice of the laying down or purchase of such submarines shall have been given to Turkey.

Submarines belonging to the said Powers shall also be entitled to pass through the Straits to be repaired in dockyards outside the Black Sea on condition that detailed information on the matter is given to Turkey.

In either case, the said submarines must travel by day and on the surface, and must pass through the Straits singly.

Article 13.

The transit of vessels of war through the Straits shall be preceded by a notification given to the Turkish Government through the diplomatic channel. The normal period of notice shall be eight days; but it is desirable that in the case of non-Black Sea Powers this period should be increased to fifteen days. The notification shall specify the destination, name, type and number of the vessels, as also the date of entry for the outward passage and, if necessary, for the return journey. Any change of date shall be subject to three days' notice.

Entry into the Straits for the outward passage shall take place within a period of five days from the date given in the original notification. After the expiry of this period, a new notification shall be given under the same conditions as for the original notification.

When effecting transit, the commander of the navel force shall, without being under any obligation to stop, communicate to a signal station at the entrance to the Dardanelles or the Bosphorus the exact composition of the force under his orders.

Article 14.

The maximum aggregate tonnage of all foreign naval forces which may be in course of transit through the Straits shall not exceed 15,000 tons, except in the cases provided for in Article 11 and in Annex III to the present Convention.

The forces specified in the preceding paragraph shall not, however, comprise more than nine vessels.

Vessels, whether belonging to Black Sea or non-Black Sea Powers, paying visits to a port in the Straits, in accordance with the provisions of Article 17, shall not be included in this tonnage.

Neither shall vessels of war which have suffered damage during their passage through the Straits be included in this tonnage; such vessels, while undergoing repair, shall be subject to any special provisions relating to security laid down by Turkey.

Article 15.

Vessels of war in transit through the Straits shall in no circumstances make use of any aircraft which they may be carrying.

Article 16.

Vessels of war in transit through the Straits shall not, except in the event of damage or peril of the sea, remain therein longer than is necessary for them to effect the passage.

Article 17.

Nothing in the provisions of the preceding Articles shall prevent a naval force of any tonnage or composition from paying a courtesy visit of limited duration to a port in the Straits, at the invitation of the Turkish Government. Any such force must leave the Straits by the same route as that by which it entered, unless it fulfills the conditions required for passage in transit through the Straits as laid down by Articles 10, 14 and 18.

Article 18.

(1) The aggregate tonnage which non-Black Sea Powers may have in that sea in time of peace shall be limited as follows:

(a) Except as provided in paragraph (b) below, the aggregate tonnage of the said Powers shall not exceed 30,000 tons;

(b) If at any time the tonnage of the strongest fleet in the Black Sea shall exceed by at least 10,000 tons the tonnage of the strongest fleet in that sea at the date of the signature of the present Convention, the aggregate tonnage of 30,000 tons mentioned in paragraph (a) shall be increased by the same amount, up to a maximum of 45,000 tons. For this purpose, each Black Sea Power shall, in conformity with Annex IV to the present Convention, inform the Turkish Government, on the 1st January and the 1st July of each year, of the total tonnage of its fleet in the Black Sea; and the Turkish Government shall transmit this information to the other High Contracting Parties and to the Secretary-General of the League of Nations;

(c) The tonnage which any one non-Black Sea Power may have in the Black Sea shall be limited to two-thirds of the aggregate tonnage provided for in paragraphs *(a)* and *(b)* above;

(d) In the event, however, of one or more non-Black Sea Powers desiring to send naval forces into the Black Sea, for a humanitarian purpose, the said forces, which shall in no case exceed 8,000 tons altogether, shall be allowed to enter the Black Sea without having to give the notification provided for in Article 13 of the present Convention, provided an authorization is obtained from the Turkish Government in the following circumstances: if the figure of the aggregate tonnage specified in paragraphs *(a)* and *(b)* above has not been reached and will not be exceeded by the despatch of the forces which it is desired to send, the Turkish Government shall grant the said authorization within the shortest possible time after receiving the request which has been addressed to it; if the said figure has already been reached or if the despatch of the forces which it is desired to send will cause it to be exceeded, the Turkish Government will immediately inform the other Black Sea Powers of the request for authorization, and if the said Powers make no objection within twenty-four hours of having received this information, the Turkish Government shall, within forty-eight hours at the latest, inform the interested Powers of the reply which it has decided to make to their request.

Any further entry into the Black Sea of naval forces of non-Black Sea Powers shall only be effected within the available limits of the aggregate tonnage provided for in paragraphs *(a)* and *(b)* above.

(2) Vessels of war belonging to non-Black Sea Powers shall not remain in the Black Sea more than twenty-one days, whatever be the object of their presence there.

Article 19.

In time of war, Turkey not being belligerent, warships shall enjoy complete freedom of transit and navigation through the Straits under the same conditions as those laid down in Articles 10 to 18.

Vessels of war belonging to belligerent Powers shall not, however, pass through the Straits except in cases arising out of the application of Article 25 of the present Convention, and in cases of assistance rendered to a State victim of aggression in virtue of a treaty of mutual assistance binding Turkey, concluded within the framework of the Covenant of the League of Nations, and registered and published in accordance with the provisions of Article 18 of the Covenant.

In the exceptional cases provided for in the preceding paragraph, the limitations laid down in Articles 10 to 18 of the present Convention shall not be applicable.

Notwithstanding the prohibition of passage laid down in paragraph 2 above, vessels of war belonging to belligerent Powers, whether they are Black Sea Powers or not, which have become separated from their bases, may return thereto.

Vessels of war belonging to belligerent Powers shall not make any capture, exercise the right of visit and search, or carry out any hostile act in the Straits.

Article 20.

In time of war, Turkey being belligerent, the provisions of Articles 10 to 18 shall not be applicable; the passage of warships shall be left entirely to the discretion of the Turkish Government.

Article 21.

Should Turkey consider herself to be threatened with imminent danger of war she shall have the right to apply the provisions of Article 20 of the present Convention.

Vessels which have passed through the Straits before Turkey has made use of the powers conferred upon her by the preceding paragraph, and which thus find themselves separated from their bases, may return thereto. It is, however, understood that Turkey may deny this right to vessels of war belonging to the State whose attitude has given rise to the application of the present Article.

Should the Turkish Government make use of the powers conferred by the first paragraph of the present Article, a notification to that effect shall be addressed to the High Contracting Parties and to the Secretary-General of the League of Nations.

If the Council of the League of Nations decide by a majority of two-thirds that the measures thus taken by Turkey are not justified, and if such should also be the opinion of the majority of the High Contracting Parties signatories to the present Convention, the Turkish Government undertakes to discontinue the measures in question as also any measures which may have been taken under Article 6 of the present Convention.

Article 22.

Vessels of war which have on board cases of plague, cholera, yellow fever, exanthematic typhus or smallpox or which have had such cases on board within the last seven days and vessels of war which have left an infected port within less than five times twenty-four hours must pass through the Straits in quarantine and apply by the means on board such prophylactic measures as are necessary in order to prevent any possibility of the Straits being infected.

SECTION III.

AIRCRAFT.

Article 23.

In order to assure the passage of civil aircraft between the Mediterranean and the Black Sea, the Turkish Government will indicate the air routes available for this purpose, outside the forbidden zones which may be established in the Straits. Civil aircraft may use these routes provided that they give the Turkish Government, as regards occasional flights, a notification of three days, and as regards flights on regular services, a general notification of the dates of passage.

The Turkish Government moreover undertake, notwithstanding any remilitarization of the Straits, to furnish the necessary facilities for the safe passage of civil aircraft authorized under the air regulations in force in Turkey to fly across

47

Turkish territory between Europe and Asia. The route which is to be followed in the Straits zone by aircraft which have obtained an authorization shall be indicated from time to time.

SECTION IV.

GENERAL PROVISIONS.

Article 24.

The functions of the International Commission set up under the Convention relating to the regime of the Straits of the 24th July, 1923, are hereby transferred to the Turkish Government.

The Turkish Government undertake to collect statistics and to furnish information concerning the application of Articles 11, 12, 14 and 18 of the present Convention.

They will supervise the execution of all the provisons of the present Convention relating to the passage of vessels of war through the Straits.

As soon as they have been notified of the intended passage through the Straits of a foreign naval force the Turkish Government shall inform the representatives at Angora of the High Contracting Parties of the composition of that force, its tonnage, the date fixed for its entry into the Straits, and, if necessary, the probable date of its return.

The Turkish Government shall address to the Secretary-General of the League of Nations and to the High Contracting Parties an annual report giving details regarding the movements of foreign vessels of war through the Straits and furnishing all information which may be of service to commerce and navigation, both by sea and by air, for which provision is made in the present Convention.

Article 25.

Nothing in the present Convention shall prejudice the rights and obligations of Turkey, or of any of the other High Contracting Parties members of the League of Nations, arising out of the Covenant of the League of Nations.

SECTION V.

FINAL PROVISIONS.

Article 26.

The present Convention shall be ratified as soon as possible.

The ratifications shall be deposited in the archives of the Government of the French Republic in Paris.

The Japanese Government shall be entitled to inform the Government of the French Republic through their diplomatic representative in Paris that the ratification has been given, and in that case they shall transmit the instrument of ratification as soon as possible.

A *procès-verbal* of the deposit of ratifications shall be drawn up as soon as six instruments of ratification, including that of Turkey, shall have been deposited. For this purpose the notification provided for in the preceding paragraph shall be taken as the equivalent of the deposit of an instrument of ratification.

The present Convention shall come into force on the date of the said *procès-verbal*.

The French Government will transmit to all the High Contracting Parties an authentic copy of the *procès-verbal* provided for in the preceding paragraph and of the *procès-verbaux* of the deposit of any subsequent ratifications.

Article 27.

The present Convention shall, as from the date of its entry into force, be open to accession by any Power signatory to the Treaty of Peace at Lausanne signed on the 24th July, 1923.

Each accession shall be notified, through the diplomatic channel, to the Government of the French Republic, and by the latter to all the High Contracting Parties.

Accessions shall come into force as from the date of notification to the French Government.

Article 28.

The present Convention shall remain in force for twenty years from the date of its entry into force.

The principle of freedom of transit and navigations affirmed in Article 1 of the present Convention shall however continue without limit of time.

If, two years prior to the expiry of the said period of twenty years, no High Contracting Party shall have given notice of denunciation to the French Government the present Convention shall continue in force until two years after such notice shall have been given. Any such notice shall be communicated by the French Government to the High Contracting Parties.

In the event of the present Convention being denounced in accordance with the provisions of the present Article, the High Contracting Parties agree to be represented at a conference for the purpose of concluding a new Convention.

Article 29.

At the expiry of each period of five years from the date of the entry into force of the present Convention each of the High Contracting Parties shall be entitled to initiate a proposal for amending one or more of the provisions of the present Convention.

To be valid, any request for revision formulated by one of the High Contracting Parties must be supported, in the case of modifications to Articles 14 or 18, by one other High Contracting Party, and, in the case of modifications to any other Article, by two other High Contracting Parties.

Any request for revision thus supported must be notified to all the High Contracting Parties three months prior to the expiry of the current period of five years. This notification shall contain details of the proposed amendments and the reasons which have given rise to them.

Should it be found impossible to reach an agreement on these proposals through the diplomatic channel, the High Contracting Parties agree to be represented at a conference to be summoned for this purpose.

Such a conference may only take decisions by a unanimous vote, except as regards cases of revision involving Articles 14 and 18, for which a majority of three-quarters of the High Contracting Parties shall be sufficient.

The said majority shall include three-quarters of the High Contracting Parties which are Black Sea Powers, including Turkey.

In witness whereof, the above-mentioned Plenipotentiaries have signed the present Convention.

Done at Montreux the 20th July, 1936, in eleven copies, of which the first copy, to which the seals of the Plenipotentiaries have been affixed, will be deposited in the archives of the Government of the French Republic and of which the remaining copies have been transmitted to the signatory Powers.

The undersigned, Plenipotentiaries of Japan, declare, in the name of their Government, that the provisions of the present Convention do not in any sense modify the position of Japan as a State not a member of the League of Nations, whether in relation to the Covenant of the League of Nations or in regard to treaties of mutual assistance concluded within the framework of the said Covenant, and that in particular Japan reserves full liberty of interpretation as regards the provisions of Articles 19 and 25 so far as they concern that Covenant and those treaties.

NOTE: ANNEX I REGARDING TAXES AND CHARGES IS DELETED.

ANNEX II.[1]

A. STANDARD DISPLACEMENT.

(1) The standard displacement of a surface vessel is the displacement of the vessel, complete, fully manned, engined, and equipped ready for sea, including all armament and ammunition, equipment, outfit, provisions and fresh water for crew, miscellaneous stores and implements of every description that are intended to be carried in war, but without fuel or reserve feed water on board.

(2) The standard displacement of a submarine is the surface displacement of the vessel complete (exclusive of the water in non-watertight structure), fully manned, engined and equipped ready for sea, including all armament and ammunition, equipment, outfit, provisions for crew, miscellaneous stores and implements of every description that are intended to be carried in war, but without fuel, lubricating oil, fresh water or ballast water of any kind on board.

(3) The word "ton" except in the expression "metric tons" denotes the ton of 2,240 lb. (1,016 kilos).

B. CATEGORIES.

(1) *Capital Ships* are surface vessels of war belonging to one of the two following sub-categories:

(a) Surface vessels of war, other than aircraft-carriers, auxiliary vessels, or capital ships of sub-category (b), the standard displacement of which exceeds 10,000 tons (10,160 metric tons) or which carry a gun with a calibre exceeding 8 in. (203 mm.);

---

[1] The wording of the present Annex is taken from the London Naval Treaty of March 25th, 1936.

(b) Surface vessels of war, other than aircraft-carriers, the standard displacement of which does not exceed 8,000 tons (8,128 metric tons) and which carry a gun with a calibre exceeding 8 in. (203 mm.).

(2) *Aircraft-Carriers* are surface vessels of war, whatever their displacement, designed or adapted primarily for the purpose of carrying and operating aircraft at sea. The fitting of a landing-on or flying-off deck on any vessel of war, provided such vessel has not been designed or adapted primarily for the purpose of carrying and operating aircraft at sea, shall not cause any vessel so fitted to be classified in the category of aircraft-carriers.

The category of aircraft-carriers is divided into two sub-categories as follows:

(a) Vessels fitted with a flight deck, from which aircraft can take off, or on which aircraft can land from the air;

(b) Vessels not fitted with a flight deck as described in *(a)* above.

(3) *Light Surface Vessels* are surface vessels of war other than aircraft-carriers, minor war vessels or auxiliary vessels, the standard displacement of which exceeds 100 tons (102 metric tons) and does not exceed 10,000 tons (10,160 metric tons), and which do not carry a gun with a calibre exceeding 8 in. (203 mm.).

The category of light surface vessels is divided into three sub-categories as follows:

(a) Vessels which carry a gun with a calibre exceeding 6.1 in. (155 mm.);

(b) Vessels which do not carry a gun with a calibre exceeding 6.1 in. (155 mm.) and the standard displacement of which exceeds 3,000 tons (3,048 metric tons);

(c) Vessels which do not carry a gun with a calibre exceeding 6.1 in. (155 mm.) and the standard displacement of which does not exceed 3,000 tons (3,048 metric tons).

(4) *Submarines* are all vessels designed to operate below the surface of the sea.

(5) *Minor War Vessels* are surface vessels of war, other than auxiliary vessels, the standard displacement of which exceeds 100 tons (102 metric tons) and does not exceed 2,000 tons (2,032 metric tons), provided they have none of the following characteristics:

(a) Mount a gun with a calibre exceeding 6.1 in. (155 mm.);

(b) Are designed or fitted to launch torpedoes;

(c) Are designed for a speed greater than twenty knots.

(6) *Auxiliary Vessels* are naval surface vessels the standards displacement of which exceeds 100 tons (102 metric tons), which are normally employed on fleet duties or as troop transports, or in some other way than as fighting ships, and which are not specifically built as fighting ships, provided they have none of the following characteristics:

(a) Mount a gun with a calibre exceeding 6.1 in. (155 mm.);

(b) Mount more than eight guns with a calibre exceeding 3 in. (76 mm.);

(c) Are designed or fitted to launch torpedoes;

(d) Are designed for protection by armour plate;

(e) Are designed for a speed greater than twenty-eight knots;

(f) Are designed or adapted primarily for operating aircraft at sea;

(g) Mount more than two aircraft-launching apparatus.

C. OVER-AGE.

Vessels of the following categories and sub-categories shall be deemed to be "over-age" when the undermentioned number of years have elapsed since completion:

(a) Capital ships _____ 26 years;

(b) Aircraft-carriers _____ 20 years;

(c) Light surface vessels, sub-categories *(a)* and *(b)*:

    (i) If laid down before 1st January, 1920 _____ 16 years;

    (ii) If laid down after 31st December, 1919 _____ 20 years;

(d) Light surface vessels, sub-category *(c)* _____ 16 years;

(e) Submarines _____ 13 years;

NOTE: ANNEX III REGARDING CERTAIN JAPANESE TRAINING SHIPS IS DELETED.

ANNEX IV.

1. The categories and sub-categories of vessels to be included in the calculation of the total tonnage of the Black Sea Powers provided for in Article 18 of the present Convention are the following:

Capital Ships:
    Sub-category *(a)*;
    Sub-category *(b)*.

Aircraft-Carriers:
    Sub-category *(a)*;
    Sub-category *(b)*.

Light Surface Vessels:
    Sub-category *(a)*;
    Sub-category *(b)*;
    Sub-category *(c)*.

Submarines:
    As defined in Annex II to the present Convention.

The displacement which is to be taken into consideration in the calculation of the total tonnage is the standard displacement as defined in Annex II. Only those vessels shall be taken into consideration which are not over-age according to the definition contained in the said Annex.

2. The notification provided for in Article 18, paragraph *(b)*, shall also include the total tonnage of vessels belonging to the categories and sub-categories mentioned in paragraph 1 of the present Annex.

PROTOCOL.

At the moment of signing the Convention bearing this day's date, the undersigned Plenipotentiaries declare for their respective Governments that they accept the following provisions:

(1) Turkey may immediately remilitarize the zone of the Straits as defined in the Preamble to the said Convention.

(2) As from the 15th August, 1936, the Turkish Government shall provisionally apply the régime specified in the said Convention.

(3) The present Protocol shall enter into force as from this day's date.

Done at Montreux, the 20th July, 1936.

10. German-Soviet Negotiations Regarding the Middle East: Documents from the German Foreign Office Archives November, 1940

The State Secretary in the German Foreign Office (Weizsäcker)
To All German Diplomatic Missions and the Offices in Paris and Brussels

[Circular telegram]

Multex 425   BERLIN, November 15, 1940.

The conversations between the German and the Soviet-Russian Governments on the occasion of the presence of Molotov in Berlin were conducted on the basis of the treaties concluded last year and resulted in complete agreement regarding the firm determination of both countries to continue in the future the policy inaugurated by these treaties. Beyond that, they served the purpose of coordinating the policy of the Soviet Union with the policy of the Tripartite Pact. As already expressed in the final communiqué regarding the visit of Molotov, this exchange of views took place in an atmosphere of mutual confidence and resulted in agreement by both sides on all important questions of interest to Germany and the Soviet Union. This result clearly proves that all conjectures regarding alleged German-Russian conflicts are in the realm of fantasy and that all speculations of the foe as to a disturbance in the German-Russian relationship of trust and friendship are based on self-deception.

This is particularly stressed by the friendly visit of Molotov in Berlin. [This sentence added in Ribbentrop's handwriting.]

Same text to all missions.

Please acknowledge receipt.

WEIZSACKER

53

Draft [1]

AGREEMENT BETWEEN THE STATES OF THE THREE POWER PACT, GERMANY, ITALY, AND JAPAN, ON THE ONE SIDE, AND THE SOVIET UNION ON THE OTHER SIDE

The Governments of the states of the Three Power Pact, Germany, Italy and Japan, on the one side,

and

the Government of the U.S.S.R. on the other side,
motivated by the desire to establish in their natural spheres of influence in Europe, Asia, and Africa a new order serving the welfare of all peoples concerned and to create a firm and enduring foundation for their common labors toward this goal, have agreed upon the following:

ARTICLE I

In the Three Power Pact of Berlin, of September 27, 1940, Germany, Italy, and Japan agreed to oppose the extension of the war into a world conflict with all possible means and to collaborate toward an early restoration of world peace. They expressed their willingness to extend their collaboration to nations in other parts of the world which are inclined to direct their efforts along the same course as theirs. The Soviet Union declares that it concurs in these aims of the Three Power Pact and is on its part determined to cooperate politically in this course with the Three Powers.

ARTICLE II

Germany, Italy, Japan, and the Soviet Union undertake to respect each other's natural spheres of influence. In so far as these spheres of interest come into contact with each other, they will constantly consult each other in an amicable way with regard to the problems arising therefrom.

Germany, Italy, and Japan declare on their part that they recognize the present extent of the possessions of the Soviet Union and will respect it.

ARTICLE III

Germany, Italy, Japan, and the Soviet Union undertake to join no combination of powers and to support no combination of powers which is directed against one of the Four Powers.

The Four Powers will assist each other in economic matters in every way and will supplement and extend the agreements existing among themselves.

ARTICLE IV

This agreement shall take effect upon signature and shall continue for a period of ten years. The Governments of the Four Powers shall consult each other in due time, before the expiration of that period, regarding the extension of the agreement.

Done in four originals, in the German, Italian, Japanese, and Russian languages.

Moscow,   1940.

---

[1] This draft was found in the secret files of the German Embassy in Moscow. It bears no date; apparently it formed the basis for Schulenburg's conversation with Molotov reported on November 26, 1940.

Draft

SECRET PROTOCOL NO. 1

Upon the signing today of the Agreement concluded among them, the Representatives of Germany, Italy, Japan and the Soviet Union declare as follows:

1) Germany declares that, apart from the territorial revisions in Europe to be carried out at the conclusion of peace, her territorial aspirations center in the territories of Central Africa.

2) Italy declares that, apart from the territorial revisions in Europe to be carried out at the conclusion of peace, her territorial aspirations center in the territories of Northern and Northeastern Africa.

3) Japan declares that her territorial aspirations center in the area of Eastern Asia to the south of the Island Empire of Japan.

4) The Soviet Union, declares that its territorial aspirations center south of the national territory of the Soviet Union in the direction of the Indian Ocean.

The Four Powers declare that, reserving the settlement of specific questions, they will mutually respect these territorial aspirations and will not oppose their achievement.

Moscow, on

Draft

SECRET PROTOCOL NO. 2 TO BE CONCLUDED AMONG GERMANY, ITALY, AND THE SOVIET UNION

On the occasion of the signing today of the Agreement among Germany, Italy, Japan, and the Soviet Union, the Representatives of Germany, Italy and the Soviet Union declare as follows:

1) Germany, Italy, and the Soviet Union agree in the view that it is in their common interest to detach Turkey from her existing international commitments and progressively to win her over to political collaboration with themselves. They declare that they will pursue this aim in close consultation, in accordance with a common line of action which is still to be determined.

2) Germany, Italy, and the Soviet Union declare their agreement to conclude, at a given time, a joint agreement with Turkey, wherein the Three Powers would recognize the extent of Turkey's possessions.

3) Germany, Italy, and the Soviet Union will work in common toward the replacement of the Montreux Straits Convention now in force by another convention. By this convention the Soviet Union would be granted the right of unrestricted passage of its navy through the Straits at any time, whereas all other Powers except the other Black Sea countries, but including Germany and Italy, would in principle renounce the right of passage through the Straits for their naval vessels. The passage of commercial vessels through the Straits would, of course, have to remain free in principle.

Moscow,   1940.

The German Ambassador in the Soviet Union (Schulenburg) to the
German Foreign Office

Telegram

VERY URGENT   Moscow, November 26, 1940—5:34 a.m.
STRICTLY SECRET   Received November 26, 1940—8:50 a.m.
No. 2362 of November 25

For the Reich Minister in person.

Molotov asked me to call on him this evening and in the presence of Dekanosov stated the following:

The Soviet Government has studied the contents of the statements of the Reich Foreign Minister in the concluding conversation on November 13 and takes the following stand:

"The Soviet Government is prepared to accept the draft of the Four Power Pact which the Reich Foreign Minister outlined in the conversation of November 13, regarding political collaboration and reciprocal economic [support[2]] subject to the following conditions:

"1) Provided that the German troops are immediately withdrawn from Finland, which, under the compact of 1939, belongs to the Soviet Union's sphere of influence. At the same time the Soviet Union undertakes to ensure peaceful relations with Finland and to protect German economic interests in Finland (export of lumber and nickel).

"2) Provided that within the next few months the security of the Soviet Union in the straits is assured by the conclusion of a mutual assistance pact between the Soviet Union and Bulgaria, which geographically is situated inside the security zone of the Black Sea boundaries of the Soviet Union, and by the establishment of a base for land and naval forces of the U.S.S.R. within range of the Bosporus and the Dardanelles by means of a long-term lease.

"3) Provided that the area south of Batum and Baku in the general direction of the Persian Gulf is recognized as the center of the aspirations of the Soviet Union.

"4) Provided that Japan [renounces][3] her rights to concessions for coal and oil in Northern Sakhalin.

"In accordance with the foregoing, the draft of the protocol concerning the delimitation of the spheres of influence as outlined by the Reich Foreign Minister would have to be amended so as to stipulate the focal point of the aspirations of the Soviet Union south of Batum and Baku in the general direction of the Persian Gulf.

"Likewise, the draft of the protocol or agreement between Germany, Italy, and the Soviet Union with respect to Turkey should be amended so as to guarantee a base for light naval and land forces of the U.S.S.R. on [am] the Bosporus

---

[2] *"Unterstützung"* in Moscow Embassy draft; garbled in text as received in Berlin.
[3] *"Verzichtet"* in Moscow draft; omitted in text as received in Berlin.

and the Dardanelles by means of a long-term lease, including—in case Turkey declares herself willing to join the Four Power Pact—a guarantee of the independence and of the territory of Turkey by the three countries named.

"This protocol should provide that in case Turkey refuses to join the Four Powers, Germany, Italy, and the Soviet Union agree to work out and to carry through the required military and diplomatic measures, and a separate agreement to this effect should be concluded.

"Furthermore there should be agreement upon:

"*a*) a third secret protocol between Germany and the Soviet Union concerning Finland (see Point 1 above).

"*b*) a fourth secret protocol between Japan and the Soviet Union concerning the renunciation by Japan of the oil and coal concession in Northern Sakhalin (in return for an adequate compensation).

"*c*) a fifth secret protocol between Germany, the Soviet Union, and Italy, recognizing that Bulgaria is geographically located inside the security zone of the Black Sea boundaries of the Soviet Union and that it is therefore a political necessity that a mutual assistance pact be concluded between the Soviet Union and Bulgaria, which in no way shall affect the internal regime of Bulgaria, her sovereignty or independence."

In conclusion Molotov stated that the Soviet proposal provided for five protocols instead of the two envisaged by the Reich Foreign Minister. He would appreciate a statement of the German view.

SCHULENBURG

II.

Mutual Security Treaties, Agreements, and Policies

Maintaining the security of the Middle East against Soviet expansionism and influence, both direct and indirect, has been the single most important aim of United States policy in the area since the end of the second world war. Great Britain decided in 1947 that she could no longer maintain her historic role as the protector of Greece and Turkey from foreign aggression, although she remained dominant in the Arab states of the Middle East for another decade. The United States response to Soviet threats against Turkey and Kremlin support for Communist rebels in Greece was the Truman Doctrine. This had both a specific intent and a larger purpose. Specifically, it put the United States in the traditional British role of preventing Russian expansion to the south. The larger purpose of the Truman Doctrine was to arouse the American people and Congress, and to serve notice to the Soviet Union that the United States would no longer be content with diplomatic protests in cases of Soviet aggression and expansion. This call to protect free peoples of the world against totalitarian regimes was a revival of the idealism of Wilson's Fourteen Points and of Franklin D. Roosevelt's Atlantic Charter.

America's security arrangements in the Middle East developed a striking dichotomy. They were almost uniformly successful in the area of their original application—the non-Arab states bordering on or close to the Soviet bloc. These included Greece, Turkey, Iran, and Pakistan. However, they encountered considerable difficulties among the Arab states. These difficulties may be assigned to three reasons:

1. The Arabs felt little or no threat from the Soviet Union;

2. The Arabs were embittered by the creation of Israel, blaming this on the West in general and the United States in particular;

3. The Arabs were just emerging from a period of foreign domination by the West, and felt that security treaties were mere subtrefuges to perpetuate imperialism.

The northern tier moved towards closer relations with the United States. In the direct aid of the Truman Doctrine, in the membership of Greece and Turkey in the North Atlantic Treaty Organization, in the Baghdad Pact (which later became the Central Treaty Organization), and in bilateral agreements of Turkey, Iran, and Pakistan with the United States there developed a series of close and formal mutual security arrangements.

In contrast, the Middle East Command negotiations of 1951, the inclusion of Arab Iraq in the Baghdad Pact, the efforts to extend the Pact to other Arab states, and, finally, the Eisenhower Doctrine proved to be of limited effectiveness at best. In some cases these policies may have had a destabilizing effect in the Arab world.

The Middle East Command proposals were rejected out of hand by the royalist Egyptian government, which simultaneously denounced its defense treaty of 1936 with Britain and the Anglo-Egyptian condominium over the Sudan. The fighting that developed between British troops and Egyptians in the Suez Canal Zone led to political conflicts in Egypt, and to the rioting in Cairo on "Black Friday," January 26, 1952. This breakdown of public order was in turn a major factor in the decision of the "Committee of Free Officers" to stage the coup d'etat of July 23, 1952, which set Egypt on the course of revolution.

The Baghdad Pact provided another issue which aided the radicalization of Arab politics. The Hashimite monarchy in Iraq and its leading statesman Nuri as-Said Pasha welcomed the idea of links with the West and with her non-Arab neighbors. But this feeling was not shared by other Arab leaders, or by many Iraqi opposition elements. The United States did not join the pact formally, although Secretary of State Dulles' speech of June 1, 1953, had been a major influence on its creation. The reasons for the United States not becoming a signatory, although participating in the major working committees of the pact organization, illustrate the problems raised by a formal association of an Arab state with the West. Article 5 effectively excluded Israel from becoming a member of the pact, since any new member would have to be fully recognized by Iraq. The pact also included Great Britain, and this was viewed by the Arabs as a trick of the British and Hashemites to continue Britain's special position and bases in Iraq. The United States was thus in the position of supporting the pact because of her interest in mutual security, but being reluctant to join it formally because it excluded Israel while arming some Arab states and antagonizing Nasser, the most vocal critic of the pact.

The Iraqi Revolution of 1958 soon removed Iraq from the pact. It also eliminated the major Arab supporter of the West—Nuri as-Said. As the Central Treaty Organization (CENTO) the former Baghdad Pact became more realistic. More genuinely fearful of Soviet attack or subversion and with the example of Iraqi before them, the non-Arab members of CENTO pressed for additional United States support. This resulted in the signing of identical bilateral security agreements with Turkey, Iran, and Pakistan. The subsequent relationships of these countries to the United States will be more fully covered in Chapter IV; however, the 1968 communique of the CENTO Ministerial Council (an otherwise undistinguished document) is interesting for two reasons. It refers more prominently to economic cooperation and development than to military security. It is also the first time that a meeting of the Council had not been attended by the United States Secretary of State. The formal structure of security pacts remained intact in the northern tier, but later developments in both the United States and in the Middle East lessened their importance to both parties.

The Eisenhower Doctrine was an attempt to regain the initiative for the West after the fiasco of the Anglo-French attack on Egypt in the Suez war. The Doctrine's main purpose was to block indirect Communist aggression but it was found necessary in 1957-58 to extend it to include protection of certain friendly Arab states against intervention by other Arab states. The Doctrine proved to be of no value in preserving the Iraqi monarchy, but American intervention in

Lebanon was probably instrumental in preserving Lebanese independence. At the same time it demonstrated that equating radical Arab nationalism with Communist subversion was false. President Eisenhower's special envoy, Ambassador Robert Murphy, later wrote that the Lebanese civil war largely concerned domestic issues, and that outside influences came from Syria and Egypt. The compromise agreement worked out for Lebanon, with American aid, replaced the pro-western government of President Chamoun with a neutralist president having a former rebel leader as his prime minister.

Eventually, United States relations with the Arab states entered into an era of lessened tension when compared with the period between 1955 and 1958. It became accepted that although radical Arab nationalism could still present problems for the United States and its allies, it was nevertheless a distinct entity in itself to be differentiated from international communism. Significant temporary or even long-range alliances between the two movements have been established and cultivated whenever their interests seemed to coincide, nevertheless even the radical Arab nationalist regimes would at times come into conflict with Soviet wishes and policies if they deemed it to be in their own national interest.

A. THE TRUMAN DOCTRINE

11. Message from President Truman to Congress, March 12, 1947

Mr. President, Mr. Speaker, Members of the Congress of the United States:

The gravity of the situation which confronts the world today necessitates my appearance before a joint session of the Congress.

The foreign policy and the national security of this country are involved.

One aspect of the present situation, which I wish to present to you at this time for your consideration and decision, concerns Greece and Turkey.

The United States has received from the Greek Government an urgent appeal for financial and economic assistance. Preliminary reports from the American Economic Mission now in Greece and reports from the American Ambassador in Greece corroborate the statement of the Greek Government that assistance is imperative if Greece is to survive as a free nation.

I do not believe that the American people and the Congress wish to turn a deaf ear to the appeal of the Greek Government.

Greece is not a rich country. Lack of sufficient natural resources has always forced the Greek people to work hard to make both ends meet. Since 1940 this industrious and peace-loving country has suffered invasion, four years of cruel enemy occupation, and bitter internal strife.

When forces of liberation entered Greece they found that the retreating Germans had destroyed virtually all the railways, roads, port facilities, communications, and merchant marine. More than a thousand villages had been burned. Eighty-five percent of the children were tubercular. Livestock, poultry, and draft animals had almost disappeared. Inflation had wiped out practically all savings.

As a result of these tragic conditions, a militant minority, exploiting human want and misery, was able to create political choas which, until now, has made economic recovery impossible.

Greece is today without funds to finance the importation of those goods which are essential to bare subsistence. Under these circumstances the people of Greece cannot make progress in solving their problems of reconstruction. Greece is in desperate need of financial and economic assistance to enable it to resume purchases of food, clothing, fuel, and seeds. These are indispensable for the subsistence of its people and are obtainable only from abroad. Greece must have help to import the goods necessary to restore internal order and security so essential for economic and political recovery.

The Greek Government has also asked for the assistance of experienced American administrators, economists, and technicians to insure that the financial and other aid given to Greece shall be used effectively in creating a stable and self-sustaining economy and in improving its public administration.

The very existence of the Greek state is today threatened by the terrorist activities of several thousand armed men, led by Communists, who defy the Government's authority at a number of points, particularly along the northern boundaries. A commission appointed by the United Nations Security Council is at present investigating disturbed conditions in northern Greece and alleged border violations along the frontier between Greece on the one hand and Albania, Bulgaria, and Yugoslavia on the other.

Meanwhile, the Greek Government is unable to cope with the situation. The Greek Army is small and poorly equipped. It needs supplies and equipment if it is to restore authority to the Government throughout Greek territory.

Greece must have assistance if it is to become a self-supporting and self-respecting democracy.

The United States must supply that assistance. We have already extended to Greece certain types of relief and economic aid, but these are inadequate.

There is no other country to which democratic Greece can turn.

No other nation is willing and able to provide the necessary support for a democratic Greek Government.

The British Government, which has been helping Greece, can give no further financial or economic aid after March 31. Great Britain finds itself under the necessity of reducing or liquidating its commitments in several parts of the world, including Greece.

We have considered how the United Nations might assist in this crisis. But the situation is an urgent one requiring immediate action, and the United Nations and its related organizations are not in a position to extend help of the kind that is required.

It is important to note that the Greek Government has asked for our aid in utilizing effectively the financial and other assistance we may give to Greece, and in improving its public administration. It is of the utmost importance that we supervise the use of any funds made available to Greece, in such a manner that each dollar spent will count toward making Greece self-supporting, and will help to build an economy in which a healthy democracy can flourish.

No government is perfect. One of the chief virtues of a democracy, however, is that its defects are always visible and under democratic processes can be pointed out and corrected. The Government of Greece is not perfect. Nevertheless it represents 85 percent of the members of the Greek Parliament who were chosen in an election last year. Foreign observers, including 692 Americans, considered this election to be a fair expression of the views of the Greek people.

The Greek Government has been operating in an atmosphere of chaos and extremism. It has made mistakes. The extension of aid by this country does not mean that the United States condones everything that the Greek Government has done or will do. We have condemned in the past, and we condemn now, extremist measures of the right or the left. We have in the past advised tolerance, and we advise tolerance now.

Greece's neighbor, Turkey, also deserves our attention.

The future of Turkey as an independent and economically sound state is clearly no less important to the freedom-loving peoples of the world than the future of Greece. The circumstances in which Turkey finds itself today are considerably different from those of Greece. Turkey has been spared the disasters that have beset Greece. And during the war the United States and Great Britain furnished Turkey with material aid.

Nevertheless, Turkey now needs our support.

Since the war Turkey has sought additional financial assistance from Great Britain and the United States for the purpose of effecting that modernization necessary for the maintenance of its national integrity.

That integrity is essential to the preservation of order in the Middle East.

The British Government has informed us that, owing to its own difficulties, it can no longer extend financial or economic aid to Turkey.

As in the case of Greece, if Turkey is to have the assistance it needs, the United States must supply it. We are the only country able to provide that help.

I am fully aware of the broad implications involved if the United States extends assistance to Greece and Turkey, and I shall discuss these implications with you at this time.

One of the primary objectives of the foreign policy of the United States is the creation of conditions in which we and other nations will be able to work out a way of life free from coercion. This was a fundamental issue in the war with Germany and Japan. Our victory was won over countries which sought to impose their will, and their way of life, upon other nations.

To insure the peaceful development of nations, free from coercion, the United States has taken a leading part in establishing the United Nations. The United Nations is designed to make possible lasting freedom and independence for all its members. We shall not realize our objectives, however, unless we are willing to help free peoples to maintain their free institutions and their national integrity against aggressive movements that seek to impose upon them totalitarian regimes. This is no more than a frank recognition that totalitarian regimes imposed upon free peoples, by direct or indirect aggression, undermine the foundations of international peace and hence the security of the United States.

The peoples of a number of countries of the world have recently had totalitarian

65

regimes forced upon them against their will. The Government of the United States has made frequent protests against coercion and intimidation, in violation of the Yalta agreement, in Poland, Rumania, and Bulgaria. I must also state that in a number of other countries there have been similar developments.

At the present moment in world history nearly every nation must choose between alternative ways of life. The choice is too often not a free one.

One way of life is based upon the will of the majority, and is distinguished by free institutions, representative government, free elections, guarantees of individual liberty, freedom of speech and religion, and freedom from political oppression.

The second way of life is based upon the will of a minority forcibly imposed upon the majority. It relies upon terror and oppression, a controlled press and radio, fixed elections, and the suppression of personal freedoms.

I believe that it must be the policy of the United States to support free peoples who are resisting attempted subjugation by armed minorities or by outside pressures.

I believe that we must assist free peoples to work out their own destinies in their own way.

I believe that our help should be primarily through economic and financial aid which is essential to economic stability and orderly political processes.

The world is not static, and the *status quo* is not sacred. But we cannot allow changes in the *status quo* in violation of the Charter of the United Nations by such methods as coercion, or by such subterfuges as political infiltration. In helping free and independent nations to maintain their freedom, the United States will be giving effect to the principles of the Charter of the United Nations.

It is necessary only to glance at a map to realize that the survival and integrity of the Greek nation are of grave importance in a much wider situation. If Greece should fall under the control of an armed minority, the effect upon its neighbor, Turkey, would be immediate and serious. Confusion and disorder might well spread throughout the entire Middle East.

Moreover, the disappearance of Greece as an independent state would have a profound effect upon those countries in Europe whose peoples are struggling against great difficulties to maintain their freedoms and their independence while they repair the damages of war.

It would be an unspeakable tragedy if these countries, which have struggled so long against overwhelming odds, should lose that victory for which they sacrificed so much. Collapse of free institutions and loss of independence would be disastrous not only for them but for the world. Discouragement and possibly failure would quickly be the lot of neighboring peoples striving to maintain their freedom and independence.

Should we fail to aid Greece and Turkey in this fateful hour, the effect will be far-reaching to the West as well as to the East.

We must take immediate and resolute action.

I therefore ask the Congress to provide authority for assistance to Greece and Turkey in the amount of $400,000,000 for the period ending June 30, 1948. In requesting these funds, I have taken into consideration the maximum amount of relief assistance which would be furnished to Greece out of the $350,000,000 which I recently requested that the Congress authorize for the prevention of starvation and suffering in countries devastated by the war.

In addition to funds, I ask the Congress to authorize the detail of American civilian and military personnel to Greece and Turkey, at the request of those countries, to assist in the tasks of reconstruction, and for the purpose of supervising the use of such financial and material assistance as may be furnished. I recommend that authority also be provided for the instruction and training of selected Greek and Turkish personnel.

Finally, I ask that the Congress provide authority which will permit the speediest and most effective use, in terms of needed commodities, supplies, and equipment, of such funds as may be authorized.

If further funds, or further authority, should be needed for purposes indicated in this message, I shall not hesitate to bring the situation before the Congress. On this subject the Executive and Legislative branches of the Government must work together.

This is a serious course upon which we embark.

I would not recommend it except that the alternative is much more serious.

The United States contributed $341,000,000,000 toward winning World War II. This is an investment in world freedom and world peace.

The assistance that I am recommending for Greece and Turkey amounts to little more than one-tenth of one percent of this investment. It is only common sense that we should safeguard this investment and make sure that it was not in vain.

The seeds of totalitarian regimes are nurtured by misery and want. They spread and grow in the evil and soil of poverty and strife. They reach their full growth when the hope of a people for a better life has died.

We must keep that hope alive.

The free peoples of the world look to us for support in maintaining their freedoms.

If we falter in our leadership, we may endanger the peace of the world— and we shall surely endanger the welfare of our own Nation.

Great responsibilities have been placed upon us by the swift movement of events.

I am confident that the Congress will face these responsibilities squarely.

12. An Act to Provide for Assistance to Greece and Turkey (excerpts), May 22, 1947 [1]

Whereas the Governments of Greece and Turkey have sought from the Government of the United States immediate financial and other assistance which is necessary for the maintenance of their national integrity and their survival as free nations; and

Whereas the national integrity and survival of these nations are of importance to the security of the United States and of all freedom-loving peoples and depend upon the receipt at this time of assistance; and

---

[1] Public Law 75, 80th Cong., 1st sess.

Whereas the Security Council of the United Nations has recognized the seriousness of the unsettled conditions prevailing on the border between Greece on the one hand and Albania, Bulgaria, and Yugoslavia on the other, and, if the present emergency is met, may subsequently assume full responsibility for this phase of the problem as a result of the investigation which its commission is currently conducting; and

Whereas the Food and Agriculture Organization mission for Greece recognized the necessity that Greece receive financial and economic assistance and recommended that Greece request such assistance from the appropriate agencies of the United Nations and from the Governments of the United States and the United Kingdom; and

Whereas the United Nations is not now in a position to furnish to Greece and Turkey the financial and economic assistance which is immediately required; and

Whereas the furnishing of such assistance to Greece and Turkey by the United States will contribute to the freedom and independence of all members of the United Nations in conformity with the principles and purposes of the Charter: Now, therefore,

Be it enacted by the Senate and House of Representatives of the United States of America in Congress assembled, That, notwithstanding the provisions of any other law, the President may from time to time when he deems it in the interest of the United States furnish assistance to Greece and Turkey, upon request of their governments, and upon terms and conditions determined by him—

(1) by rendering financial aid in the form of loans, credits, grants, or otherwise, to those countries;

(2) by detailing to assist those countries any persons in the employ of the Government of the United States; and the provisions of the Act of May 25, 1938 (52 Stat. 442), as amended, applicable to personnel detailed pursuant to such Act, as amended, shall be applicable to personnel detailed pursuant to this paragraph: *Provided, however,* That no civilian personnel shall be assigned to Greece or Turkey to administer the purposes of this Act until such personnel have been investigated by the Federal Bureau of Investigation;

(3) by detailing a limited number of members of the military services of the United States to assist those countries, in an advisory capacity only; and the provisions of the Act of May 19, 1926 (44 Stat. 565), as amended, applicable to personnel detailed pursuant to such Act, as amended, shall be applicable to personnel detailed pursuant to this paragraph;

(4) by providing for (A) the transfer to, and the procurement for by manufacture or otherwise and the transfer to, those countries of any articles, services, and information, and (B) the instruction and training of personnel of those countries; and

(5) by incurring and defraying necessary expenses, including administra-

tive expenses and expenses for compensation of personnel, in connection with the carrying out of the provisions of this Act..

* * *

SEC. 3. As a condition precedent to the receipt of any assistance pursuant to this Act, the government requesting such assistance shall agree (a) to permit free access of United States Government officials for the purpose of observing whether such assistance is utilized effectively and in accordance with the undertakings of the recipient government; (b) to permit representatives of the press and radio of the United States to observe freely and to report fully regarding the utilization of such assistance; (c) not to transfer, without the consent of the President of the United States, title to or possession of any article or information transferred pursuant to this Act nor to permit, without such consent, the use of any such article or the use or disclosure of any such information by or to anyone not an officer, employee, or agent of the recipient government; (d) to make such provisions as may be required by the. President of the United States for the security of any article, service, or information received pursuant to this Act; (e) not to use any part of the proceeds of any loan, credit, grant, or other form of aid rendered pursuant to this Act for the making of any payment on account of the principal or interest on any loan made to such government by any other foreign government; and (f) to give full and continuous publicity within such country as to the purpose, source, character, scope, amounts, and progress of the United States economic assistance carried on therein pursuant to this Act.

SEC. 4. (a) Notwithstanding the provisions of any other law, the Reconstruction Finance Corporation is authorized and directed, until such time as an appropriation shall be made pursuant. to subsection (b) of this section, to make advances, not to exceed in the aggregate $100,000,000, to carry out the provisions of this Act, in such manner and in such amounts as the President shall determine.

(b) There is hereby authorized to be appropriated to the President not to exceed $400,000,000 to carry out the provisions of this Act. From appropriations made under this authority there shall be repaid to the Reconstruction Finance Corporation the advances made by it under subsection (a) of this section.

SEC. 5. The President may from time to time prescribe such rules and regulations as may be necessary and proper to carry out any of the provisions of this Act; and he may exercise any power or authority conferred upon him pursuant to this Act through such department, agency, independent establishment, or officer of the Government as he shall direct.

The President is directed to withdraw any or all aid authorized herein under any of the following circumstances:

(1) If requested by the Government of Greece or Turkey, respectively, representing a majority of the people of either such nation;

(2) If the Security Council finds (with respect to which finding the United States waives the exercise of any veto) or the General Assembly finds that action taken or assistance furnished by the United Nations makes the continuance of such assistance unnecessary or undesirable;

(3) If the President finds that any purposes of the Act have been sub-

stantially accomplished by the action of any other intergovernmental organizations or finds that the purposes of the Act are incapable of satisfactory accomplishment; and

(4) If the President finds that any of the assurances given pursuant to section 3 are not being carried out.

SEC. 6. Assistance to any country under this Act may, unless sooner terminated by the President, be terminated by concurrent resolution by the two Houses of the Congress.

SEC. 7. The President shall submit to the Congress quarterly reports of expenditures and activities, which shall include uses of funds by the recipient governments, under authority of this Act.

SEC. 8. The chief of any mission to any country receiving assistance under this Act shall be appointed by the President, by and with the advice and consent of the Senate, and shall perform such functions relating to the administration of this Act as the President shall prescribe.

Approved May 22, 1947.

B. THE NORTH ATLANTIC TREATY

13. The North Atlantic Treaty, April 4, 1949

Text of the North Atlantic Treaty, 63 Stat. 2241, Treaties and Other International Act Series 1964; Signed at Washington, April 4, 1949; Ratification Advised by the Senate July 21, 1949; Ratified by the President July 25, 1949; Proclaimed by the President and Entered Into Force August 24, 1949; as Modified by Article II of the Protocol to the North Atlantic Treaty on the Accession of Greece and Turkey, Treaties and Other International Act Series 2390; Signed at London, October 17, 1951; Ratification Advised by the Senate February 7, 1952; Ratified by the President February 11, 1952; Entered Into Force February 15, 1952

The Parties to this Treaty [1] reaffirm their faith in the purposes and principles of the Charter of the United Nations and their desire to live in peace with all peoples and all governments.

They are determined to safeguard the freedom, common heritage and civilization of their peoples, founded on the principles of democracy, individual liberty and the rule of law.

They seek to promote stability and well-being in the North Atlantic area.

They are resolved to unite their efforts for collective defense and for the preservation of peace and security.

They therefore agree to this North Atlantic Treaty:

---

[1] Belgium, Canada, Denmark, France, Germany, Greece, Iceland, Italy, Luxembourg, Netherlands, Norway, Portugal, Turkey, United Kingdom and the United States. Germany became a party to the North Atlantic Treaty by virtue of the Protocol to the North Atlantic Treaty on the Accession of the Federal Republic of Germany; Signed at Paris, October 23, 1954; Ratification advised by the Senate April 1, 1955; Ratified by the President April 7, 1955; Entered into Force May 5, 1955.

ARTICLE 1

The Parties undertake, as set forth in the Charter of the United Nations, to settle any international disputes in which they may be involved by peaceful means in such a manner that international peace and security, and justice, are not endangered, and to refrain in their international relations from the threat or use of force in any manner inconsistent with the purposes of the United Nations.

ARTICLE 2

The Parties will contribute toward the further development of peaceful and friendly international relations by strengthening their free institutions, by bringing about a better understanding of the principles upon which these institutions are founded, and by promoting conditions of stability and well being. They will seek to eliminate conflict in their international economic policies and will encourage economic collaboration between any or all of them.

ARTICLE 3

In order more effectively to achieve the objectives of this Treaty, the Parties, separately and jointly, by means of continuous and effective self-help and mutual aid, will maintain and develop their individual and collective capacity to resist armed attack.

ARTICLE 4

The Parties will consult together whenever, in the opinion of any of them, the territorial integrity, political independence or security of any of the Parties is threatened.

ARTICLE 5

The Parties agree that an armed attack against one or more of them in Europe or North America shall be considered an attack against them all; and consequently they agree that, if such an armed attack occurs, each of them, in exercise of the right of individual or collective self-defense recognized by Article 51 of the Charter of the United Nations, will assist the Party or Parties so attacked by taking forthwith, individually and in concert with the other Parties, such action as it deems necessary, including the use of armed force, to restore and maintain the security of the North Atlantic area.

Any such armed attack and all measures taken as a result thereof shall immediately be reported to the Security Council. Such measures shall be terminated when the Security Council has taken the measures necessary to restore and maintain international peace and security.

ARTICLE 6 [2]

For the purpose of Article 5, an armed attack on one or more of the Parties is deemed to include an armed attack—

---

[2] As modified by the Protocol on the Assession of Greece and Turkey. The Article originally read as follows:

"ARTICLE 6

"For the purpose of Article 5 an armed attack on one or more of the Parties is deemed to include an armed attack on the territory of any of the Parties in Europe or North America, on the Algerian Departments of France, on the occupation forces of any Party in Europe, on the islands under the jurisdiction of any Party in the North Atlantic area north of the Tropic of Cancer or on the vessels or aircraft in this area of any of the Parties."

(i) on the territory of any of the Parties in Europe or North America, on the Algerian Departments of France, on the territory of Turkey or the islands under the jurisdiction of any of the Parties in the North Atlantic area north of the Tropic of Cancer;

(ii) on the forces, vessels or aircraft of any of the Parties, when in or over these territories or any other area in Europe in which occupation forces of any of the Parties were stationed on the date when the Treaty entered into force or the Mediterranean Sea or the North Atlantic area north of the Tropic of Cancer.

ARTICLE 7

The Treaty does not affect, and shall not be interpreted as affecting in any way the rights and obligations under the Charter of the Parties which are members of the United Nations, or the primary responsibility of the Security Council for the maintenance of international peace and security.

ARTICLE 8

Each Party declares that none of the international engagements now in force between it and any other of the Parties or any third state is in conflict with the provisions of this Treaty, and undertakes not to enter into any international engagements in conflict with this Treaty.

ARTICLE 9

The Parties hereby establish a council, on which each of them shall be represented, to consider matters concerning the implementation of this Treaty. The council shall be so organized as to be able to meet promptly at any time. The council shall set up such subsidiary bodies as may be necessary; in particular it shall establish immediately a defense committee which shall recommend measures for the implementation of Articles 3 and 5.

ARTICLE 10

The Parties may, by unanimous agreement, invite any other European state in a position to further the principles of this Treaty and to contribute to the security of the North Atlantic area to accede to this Treaty. Any state so invited may become a party to the Treaty by depositing its instrument of accession with the Government of the United States of America. The Government of the United States of America will inform each of the Parties of the deposit of each such instrument of accession.

ARTICLE 11

This Treaty shall be ratified and its provisions carried out by the Parties in accordance with their respective constitutional processes. The instruments of ratification shall be deposited as soon as possible with the Government of the United States of America, which will notify all the other signatories of each deposit. The Treaty shall enter into force between the states which have ratified it as soon as the ratification of the majority of the signatories, including the ratifications of Belgium, Canada, France, Luxembourg, the Netherlands, the United Kingdom and the United States, have been deposited and shall come into effect with respect to other states on the date of deposit of their ratifications.

ARTICLE 12

After the Treaty has been in force for ten years, or at any time thereafter, the Parties shall, if any of them so requests, consult together for the purpose of reviewing the Treaty, having regard for the factors then affecting peace and security in the North Atlantic area, including the development of universal as well as regional arrangements under the Charter of the United Nations for the maintenance of international peace and security.

ARTICLE 13

After the Treaty has been in force for twenty years, any Party may cease to be a party one year after its notice of denunciation has been given to the Government of the United States of America, which will inform the Governments of the other Parties of the deposit of each notice of denunciation.

ARTICLE 14

This Treaty, of which the English and French texts are equally authentic, shall be deposited in the Archives of the Government of the United States of America. Duly certified copies thereof will be transmitted by that Government to the Governments of the other signatories.

14. Note Verbale from the Secretary of State to the Turkish Ambassador in Washington on the Preliminary Association of Turkey with NATO, September 19, 1950

In connection with the examination of security problems confronting the Fifth Session of the North Atlantic Council, it was recognized that, in the case of the Mediterranean area, it would be desirable, if the Trukish Government so wished, to make arrangements which would permit Turkey to be associated with such appropriate phases of the military planning work of the North Atlantic Treaty Organization as are concerned with the defense of the Mediterranean.

The Council is keenly aware of the active support which Turkey, as a member of the United Nations, has accorded the principles of the United Nations and of the important role which Turkey is playing in the maintenance of the stability of the eastern Mediterranean area.

It is the view of the Council that association of the Turkish Government with the appropriate phase of the planning work of the North Atlantic Treaty Organization with regard to the defense of the Mediterranean would contribute significantly to the defense of that area.

15. Protocol to the Treaty on the Accession of Greece and Turkey, October 17, 1951

The Parties to the North Atlantic Treaty, signed at Washington on 4th April, 1949,

Being satisfied that the security of the North Atlantic area will be enhanced by the accession of the Kingdom of Greece and the Republic of Turkey to that Treaty,

Agree as follows:—

ARTICLE I

Upon the entry into force of this Protocol, the Government of the United States of America shall, on behalf of all the Parties, communicate to the Government of the Kingdom of Greece and the Government of the Republic of Turkey an invitation to accede to the North Atlantic Treaty, as it may be modified by Article II of the present Protocol. Thereafter the Kingdom of Greece and the Republic of Turkey shall each become a Party on the date when it deposits its instrument of accession with the Government of the United States of America in accordance with Article 10 of the Treaty

ARTICLE II

If the Republic of Turkey becomes a Party to the North Atlantic Treaty, Article 6 of the Treaty shall, as from the date of the deposit by the Government of the Republic of Turkey of its instrument of accession with the Government of the United States of America, be modified to read as follows:—

"For the purpose of Article 5, an armed attack on one or more of the Parties is deemed to include an armed attack—

(i) on the territory of any of the Parties in Europe or North America, on the Algerian Departments of France, on the territory of Turkey or on the islands under the jurisdiction of any of the Parties in the North Atlantic area north of the Tropic of Cancer;

(ii) on the forces, vessels or aircraft of any of the Parties, when in or over these territories or any other area in Europe in which occupation forces of any of the Parties were stationed on the date when the Treaty entered into force or the Mediterranean Sea or the North Atlantic area north of the Tropic of Cancer."

ARTICLE III

The present Protocol shall enter into force when each of the Parties to the North Atlantic Treaty has notified the Government of the United States of America of its acceptance thereof. The Government of the United States of America shall inform all the Parties to the North Atlantic Treaty of the date of the receipt of each such notification and of the date of the entry into force of the present Protocol.

ARTICLE IV

The present Protocol, of which the English and French texts are equally authentic, shall be deposited in the Archives of the Government of the United

States of America. Duly certified copies thereof shall be transmitted by that Government to the Governments of all the Parties to the North Atlantic Treaty.

In witness whereof, the undersigned plenipotentiaries have signed the present Protocol.

Open for signature at London the 17th day of October, 1951.

C. MIDDLE EAST COMMAND NEGOTIATIONS

16. Proposals Presented to Egypt by the Governments of the United States, the United Kingdom, France, and Turkey, October 13, 1951

DOCUMENT A

POINT I

Egypt belongs to the free world and in consequence her defense and that of the Middle East in general is equally vital to other democratic nations.

POINT II

The defense of Egypt and of other countries in the Middle East against aggression from without can only be secured by the cooperation of all interested powers.

POINT III

The defense of Egypt can only be assured through the effective defense of the Middle East area and the coordination of this defense with that of adjacent areas.

POINT IV

It therefore seems desirable to establish an Allied Middle East Command in which the countries able and willing to contribute to the defense of the area should participate. France, Turkey, the United Kingdom and the United States are prepared to participate with other interested countries in establishing such a Command. Invitations to participate in the Command have been addressed to Australia, New Zealand, the Union of South Africa, who have indicated their interest in the defense of the area and who have agreed in principle.

POINT V

Egypt is invited to participate as a founder member of the Middle East Command on a basis of equality and partnership with other founder members.

POINT VI

If Egypt is prepared to cooperate fully in the Allied Command Organization in accordance with the provisions of the attached annex, His Majesty's Government for their part would be willing to agree to supersession of the 1936 Treaty [1] and would also be willing to agree to withdraw from Egypt such British forces

---

[1] Treaty of Aug. 26, 1936; *British and Foreign State Papers,* vol. 140, pp. 179 ff.

as are not allocated to the Allied Middle East Command by agreement between the Egyptian Government and the Governments of other countries also participating as founder members.

POINT VII

As regards armed forces to be placed at the disposal of the Allied Middle East Command and the provision to that Command of the necessary strategic defense facilities, such as military and air bases, communications, ports, etc., Egypt will be expected to make her contribution on the same footing as other participating powers.

POINT VIII

In keeping with the spirit of these arrangements Egypt would be invited to accept a position of high authority and responsibility with the Allied Middle East Command and to designate Egyptian officers for integration in the Allied Middle East Command Headquarters staff.

POINT IX

Facilities to train and equip her forces will be given to Egypt by those participating members of the Allied Command in a position to do so.

POINT X

The detailed organization of the Allied Middle East Defense Organization and its exact relationship with the N.A.T.O. have yet to be worked out in consultation between all the powers concerned. For this purpose it is proposed that all founding members of the Allied Middle East Command should send military representatives to a meeting to be held in the near future with the object of preparing detailed proposals for submission to the governments concerned.

DOCUMENT B

TECHNICAL ANNEX

[1]

In common with other participating powers who are making similar contributions to the defense of the area.

(a) Egypt will agree to furnish to proposed Allied Middle East Command Organization such strategic defense and other facilities on her soil as are indispensable for the organization in peacetime of the defense of the Middle East

(b) that she will undertake to grant forces of the Allied Middle East Command all necessary facilities and assistance in the event of war, imminent menace of war, or apprehended international emergency including the use of Egyptian ports, airfields and means of communication.

[2]

We should also hope that Egypt would agree to the Allied Supreme Commander's Headquarters being located in her territory.

In keeping with the spirit of these arrangements, it would be understood

(a) that the present British base in Egypt would be formally handed over to the Egyptians on the understanding that it would simultaneously become an Allied base within the Allied Middle East Command with full Egyptian participation in the running of this base in peace and war

(b) that the strength of the Allied force of participating nations to be stationed in Egypt in peacetime would be determined between the participating nations including Egypt from time to time as progress is made in building up the force of the Allied Middle East Command.

It also would be understood that an air defense organization including both the Egyptian and Allied forces would be set up under the command of an officer with joint responsibility to the Egyptian Government and to the Allied Middle East Command for the protection of Egypt and Allied bases.

17. Rejection by Egypt of the Joint Proposals: Statement of Regret by the Secretary of State, October 17, 1951

It is with genuine regret that the U.S. Government received notification on October 15 of the rejection by the Egyptian Government of the proposals presented to it on October 13 by the United States, France, Turkey, and the United Kingdom. This Government has noted with surprise that the Egyptian Government rejected proposals of such importance without having given them the careful and considered deliberation which they merited. These proposals were formulated by the nations interested in the welfare and security of the Middle East after the most intensive and thorough consideration of the special problems of the area. The invitation to join with the other sovereign nations of the free world in a joint and cooperative effort to make the world safe from aggression was wholly consistent with the independence and sovereignty of Egypt.

Vigilance in protecting the liberties we enjoy is the responsibility of every nation of the free world. The spirit of responsibility to others requires that no nation carelessly precipitate events which can have no constructive end but which by their nature create those elements of confusion and weakness which tempt aggression. It is the hope of the U.S. Government that Egypt will carefully reconsider the course of action on which it has embarked and will recognize that its own interest will be served by joining the other nations of the free world in assuring the defense of the Middle East against the common danger.

The U.S. Government must reaffirm its belief that the action of the Egyptian Government with respect to the Anglo-Egyptian Treaty of 1936 and the agreements of 1899 regarding the Sudan is not in accord with proper respect for international obligations. For its part, the U.S. Government considers the action of the Egyptian Government to be without validity.

It is the sincere hope of the United States that great restraint will be shown in the present situation and that the obligation of all nations towards the preservation of world law and order will be respected.

D. THE BAGHDAD PACT AND CENTO

18. "Six Major Policy Issues":
Speech by Secretary of State Dulles (excerpts), June 1, 1953

About 3 weeks ago, the Director for Mutual Security, Mr. Harold Stassen, and I and our associates set out, at President Eisenhower's request, on a trip to 12 countries which lie in between the Mediterranean in Europe and China in Asia. I shall give you our country-by-country impressions and then our general conclusions.

First, let me say that everywhere we were well received. This was encouraging, for several of the countries feel that the United States policies have, in recent years, been harmful and even antagonistic to them. The Communists have vigorously exploited this feeling. They staged some hostile demonstrations. But these were inconsequential. The governments received us with warm hospitality, and as we drove through the streets, the people usually greeted us with friendly smiles and applause. The political leaders talked intimately with us, and we gained new friendships and new understanding which will stand us in good stead for the future. Also in each capital I spoke to all of the United States Foreign Service personnel. They are a fine body of men and women of whom we can be proud.

It is high time that the United States Government paid more attention to the Near East and South Asia, which, until our trip, no United States Secretary of State has ever visited. Our postwar attention has been primarily given to Western Europe. That area was and is very important, but not all-important.

It came as a surprising shock when the 450 million Chinese people, whom we had counted as friends, fell under Communist domination. There could be equally dangerous developments in the Near East and South Asia. The situation calls for urgent concern.

The area we visited contains about one-fourth of the world's population. It represents about one-half of the people of the world who are still free of Communist domination.

The Near East possesses great strategic importance as the bridge between Europe, Asia, and Africa. The present masters of the Kremlin, following the lead of past military conquerors, covet this position. In 1940 Soviet leaders specified, in secret negotiations with the Nazis, that Soviet "territorial aspirations center . . . in the direction of the Indian Ocean and . . . the Persian Gulf."

This area contains important resources vital to our welfare—oil, manganese, chrome, mica, and other minerals. About 60 percent of the proven oil reserves of the world are in the Near East.

Most important of all, the Near East is the source of three great religions—the Jewish, the Christian, and the Moslem—which have for centuries exerted an immense influence throughout the world. Surely we cannot ignore the fate of the peoples who have first perceived and then passed on to us the great spiritual truths from which our own society derives its inner strength.

* * *

Let me turn now to conclusions.

1. *Colonialism.* Most of the peoples of the Near East and South Asia are deeply concerned about political independence for themselves and others. They are suspicious of the colonial powers. The United States too is suspect because, it is reasoned, our NATO alliance with France and Britain requires us to try to preserve or restore the old colonial interests of our allies.

I am convinced that United States policy has become unnecessarily ambiguous in this matter. The leaders of the countries I visited fully recognize that it would be a disaster if there were any break between the United States and Great Britain and France. They don't want this to happen. However, without breaking from the framework of Western unity, we can pursue our traditional dedication to political liberty. In reality, the Western powers can gain, rather than lose, from an orderly development of self-government.

I emphasize, however, the word "orderly." Let none forget that the Kremlin uses extreme nationalism to bait the trap by which it seeks to capture the dependent peoples.

2. *Living Standards.* The peoples of the Near East and Asia demand better standards of living, and the day is past when their aspirations can be ignored. The task is one primarily for the government and the peoples themselves In some cases they can use their available resources, such as oil revenues, to better advantage. There are, however, ways in which the United States can usefully help, not with masses of money but by contributing advanced technical knowledge about transport, communication, fertilization, and use of water for irrigation. Mr. Stassen and I feel that money wisely spent for this area under the mutual security program will give the American people a good return in terms of better understanding and cooperation.

3. *Arab Good Will.* The United States should seek to allay the deep resentment against it that has resulted from the creation of Israel. In the past we had good relations with the Arab peoples. American educational institutions had built up a feeling of good will, and also American businessmen had won a good reputation in this area. There was mutual confidence to mutual advantage.

Today the Arab peoples are afraid that the United States will back the new State of Israel in aggressive expansion. They are more fearful of Zionism than of communism, and they fear lest the United States become the backer of expansionist Zionism.

On the other hand, the Israelis fear that ultimately the Arabs may try to push them into the sea.

In an effort to calm these contradictory fears the United States joined with Britain and France in a Declaration of May 25, 1950 which stated that "the three

Governments, should they find that any of these states (of the Near East) was preparing to violate frontiers or armistice lines, would, consistently with their obligations as members of the United Nations, immediately take action, both within and outside the United Nations, to prevent such violation." That Declaration when made did not reassure the Arabs. It must be made clear that the present U.S. administration stands fully behind that Declaration. We cannot afford to be distrusted by millions who could be sturdy friends of freedom. They must not further swell the ranks of Communist dictators.

The leaders in Israel themselves agreed with us that United States policies should be impartial so as to win not only the respect and regard of the Israeli but also of the Arab peoples. We shall seek such policies.

4. *Peace Between Israel and the Arab Nations.* There is need for peace in the Near East. Today there is an uneasy military armistice between Israel and the Arab States, while economic warfare is being conducted by the Arab States, in retaliation for alleged Israeli encroachments. The area is enfeebled by fear and by wasteful measures which are inspired by fear and hate.

Israel should become part of the Near East community and cease to look upon itself, or be looked upon by others, as alien to this community. This is possible. To achieve it will require concessions on the part of both sides. But the gains to both will far outweigh the concessions required to win those gains.

The parties concerned have the primary responsibility of bringing peace to the area. But the United States will not hesitate by every appropriate means to use its influence to promote a step-by-step reduction of tension in the area and the conclusion of ultimate peace.

5. *Middle East Defense Organization.* A Middle East Defense Organization is a future rather than an immediate policy. Many of the Arab League countries are so engrossed with their quarrels with Israel or with Great Britain or France that they pay little heed to the menace of Soviet communism. However, there is more concern where the Soviet Union is near. In general, the northern tier of nations shows awareness of the danger.

There is a vague desire to have a collective security system. But no such system can be imposed from without. It should be designed and grow from within out of a sense of common destiny and common danger.

While awaiting the formal creation of a security association, the United States can usefully help strengthen the interrelated defense of those countries which want strength, not as against each other or the West, but to resist the common threat to all free peoples.

6. *Friendly Understanding.* In conclusion, let me recall that the primary purpose of our trip was to show friendliness and to develop understanding. These peoples we visited are proud peoples who have a great tradition and, I believe, a great future. We in the United States are better off if we respect and honor them, and learn the thoughts and aspirations which move them. It profits nothing merely to be critical of others.

President Eisenhower's administration plans to make friendship—not fault-finding—the basis of its foreign policy. President Eisenhower brought with him from Europe an unprecedented measure of understanding and personal friendships.

Before he was inaugurated, he went to Korea. Twice since inauguration, Mr. Stassen and I have been to Europe. Now we have been to the Near East and South Asia. Later this month, the President's brother, Dr. Milton Eisenhower, and Assistant Secretary of State Cabot will go to South America.

Thus your Government is establishing the worldwide relationships and gathering the information which will enable us better to serve you, the American people.

19. Pact of Mutual Cooperation Between the Kingdom of Iraq, the Republic of Turkey, the United Kingdom, the Dominion of Pakistan, and the Kingdom of Iran (Baghdad Pact) February 24, 1955

Whereas the friendly and brotherly relations existing between Iraq and Turkey are in constant progress, and in order to complement the contents of the Treaty of Friendship and Good Neighbourhood concluded between His Majesty the King of Iraq and his Excellency the President of the Turkish Republic signed in Ankara on March 29, 1946, which recognized the fact that peace and security between the two countries is an integral part of the peace and security of all the nations of the world and in particular the nations of the Middle East, and that it is the basis for their foreign policies;

Whereas article 11 of the Treaty of Joint Defence and Economic co-operation between the Arab League States provides that no provision of that treaty shall in any way affect, or is designed to affect, any of the rights and obligations accruing to the Contracting Parties from the United Nations Charter;

And having realised the great responsibilities borne by them in their capacity as members of the United Nations concerned with the maintenance of peace and security in the Middle East region which necessitate taking the required measures in accordance with article 51 of the United Nations Charter;

They have been fully convinced of the necessity of concluding a pact fulfilling these aims, and for that purpose have appointed as their plenipotentiaries . . . who having communicated their full powers, found to be in good and due form, have agreed as follows:—

ARTICLE 1

Consistent with article 51 of the United Nations Charter the High Contracting Parties will co-operate for their security and defence. Such measures as they agree to take or give effect to this co-operation may form the subject of special agreements with each other.

ARTICLE 2

In order to ensure the realisation and effect application of the co-operation provided for in article 1 above, the competent authorities of the High Contracting Parties will determine the measures to be taken as soon as the present pact enters into force. These measures will become operative as soon as they have been approved by the Governments of the High Contracting Parties.

ARTICLE 3

The High Contracting Parties undertake to refrain from any interference whatsoever in each other's internal affairs. They will settle any dispute between themselves in a peaceful way in accordance with the United Nations Charter.

ARTICLE 4

The High Contracting Parties declare that the dispositions of the present pact are not in contradiction with any of the international obligations contracted by either of them with any third State or States. They do not derogate from and cannot be interpreted as derogating from, the said international obligations. The High Contracting Parties undertake not to enter into any international obligation incompatible with the present pact.

ARTICLE 5

This pact shall be open for accession to any member of the Arab League or any other State actively concerned with the security and peace in this region and which is fully recognised by both of the High Contracting Parties. Accession shall come into force from the date of which the instrument of accession of the State concerned is deposited with the Ministry for Foreign Affairs of Iraq.

Any acceding State party to the present pact may conclude special agreements, in accordance with article 1, with one or more States parties to the present pact. The competent authority of any acceding State may determine measures in accordance with article 2. These measures will become operative as soon as they have been approved by the Governments of the parties concerned.

ARTICLE 6

A Permanent Council at ministerial level will be set up to function within the framework of the purposes of this pact when at least four Powers become parties to the pact.

The Council will draw up its own rules of procedure.

ARTICLE 7

This pact remains in force for a period of five years renewable for other five-year periods. Any Contracting Party may withdraw from the pact by notifying the other parties in writing of its desire to do so six months before the expiration of any of the above-mentioned periods, in which case the pact remains valid for the other parties.

ARTICLE 8

This pact shall be ratified by the contracting parties and ratifications shall be exchanged at Ankara as soon as possible. Thereafter it shall come into force from the date of the exchange of ratifications.

In witness whereof, the said plenipotentiaries have signed the present pact in Arabic, Turkish and English, all three texts being equally authentic except in the case of doubt when the English text shall prevail.

Done in duplicate at Bagdad this second day of Rajab 1374 Hijri corresponding to the twenty-fourth day of February 1955.

20. United States Support for the Pact:
Department of State Press Statement, November 29, 1956

The President of Pakistan, the Prime Ministers of Iraq, Turkey and Pakistan, and the Foreign Minister of Iran in their recent meeting at Baghdad have reaffirmed their determination to further a peaceful and lasting settlement of current Middle Eastern problems.

In recent days we have indeed seen grave threats to the peace and security of the world. The action of the United Nations has brought the fighting in the Near East to an end and the world community has a new opportunity to work in accordance with the United Nations Charter to resolve serious underlying problems and to assist the nations in the area to maintain their integrity and independence.

Recent events have provided an opportunity for a new demonstration of the valuable contribution to peace and security which can be made by nations which have organized for regional cooperation under the United Nations Charter. In their dedicated efforts to maintain peace, representatives of Iran, Iraq, Pakistan and Turkey have within past weeks met, first in Tehran and then in Baghdad, in order to bring to bear both their influence and wisdom in the interest of the nations of the free world. Throughout the period of the crisis, these countries clearly revealed their faith in the Charter and their determination that the peace, not only of the area in which they find themselves, but of the whole world, must be preserved.

The United States has, from the inception of the Baghdad Pact, supported the Pact and the principles and objectives of collective security on which it is based. Through its own bilateral arrangements with Pact members in the Middle East area and its active membership in certain of the Pact's committees, the United States has revealed its readiness to assist in measures to strengthen the security of those nations.

The United States reaffirms its support for the collective efforts of these nations to maintain their independence. A threat to the territorial integrity or political independence of the members would be viewed by the United States with the utmost gravity.

21. Iranian-United States Agreement for Cooperation
in Promoting the Security and Defense of the Members
of the Baghdad Pact Organization, March 5, 1959 [1]

The Government of the United States of America and the Imperial Government of Iran,

Desiring to implement the Declaration in which they associated themselves at London on July 28, 1958; [2]

Considering that under Article I of the Pact of Mutual Cooperation signed at

---

[1] Identical agreements were signed the same day with Turkey and with Pakistan.
[2] Text in *American Foreign Policy: Current Documents, 1958*, pp. 894-895.

Baghdad on February 24, 1955,[3] the parties signatory thereto agreed to cooperate for their security and defense, and that, similarly, as stated in the above-mentioned Declaration, the Government of the United States of America, in the interest of world peace, agreed to cooperate with the Governments making that Declaration for their security and defense;

Recalling that, in the above-mentioned Declaration, the members of the Pact of Mutual Cooperation making that Declaration affirmed their determination to maintain their collective security and to resist aggression, direct or indirect;

Considering further that the Government of the United States of America is associated with the work of the major committees of the Pact of Mutual Cooperation signed at Baghdad on February 24, 1955;

Desiring to strengthen peace in accordance with the principles of the Charter of the United Nations;

Affirming their right to cooperate for their security and defense in accordance with Article 51 of the Charter of the United Nations;

Considering that the Government of the United States of America regards as vital to its national interest and to world peace the preservation of the independence and integrity of Iran;

Recognizing the authorization to furnish appropriate assistance granted to the President of the United States of America by the Congress of the United States of America in the Mutual Security Act of 1954,[4] as amended, and in the Joint Resolution to Promote Peace and Stability in the Middle East; [5] and

Considering that similar agreements are being entered into by the Government of the United States of America and the Governments of Turkey and Pakistan, respectively,

Have agreed as follows:

ARTICLE I

The Imperial Government of Iran is determined to resist aggression. In case of aggression against Iran, the Government of the United States of America, in accordance with the Constitution of the United States of America, will take such appropriate action, including the use of armed forces, as may be mutually agreed upon and is envisaged in the Joint Resolution to Promote Peace and Stability in the Middle East, in order to assist the Government of Iran at its request.

ARTICLE II

The Government of the United States of America, in accordance with the Mutual Security Act of 1954, as amended, and related laws of the United States of America, and with applicable agreements heretofore or hereafter entered into between the Government of the United States of America and the Government of Iran, reaffirms that it will continue to furnish the Government of Iran such military and economic assistance as may be mutually agreed upon between the Government of the United States of America and the Government of Iran, in order to

---

[3] Text in *American Foreign Policy, 1950-1955: Basic Documents,* pp. 1257-1259.
[4] 68 Stat. 832; 22 U.S.C. § 1751 note. [Footnote in source text.]
[5] Text in *American Foreign Policy: Current Documents, 1957,* pp. 829-831.

assist the Government of Iran in the preservation of its national independence and integrity and in the effective promotion of its economic development.

ARTICLE III

The Imperial Government of Iran undertakes to utilize such military and economic assistance as may be provided by the Government of the United States of America in a manner consonant with the aims and purposes set forth by the Governments associated in the Declaration signed at London on July 28, 1958, and for the purpose of effectively promoting the economic development of Iran and of preserving its national independence and integrity.

ARTICLE IV

The Government of the United States of America and the Government of Iran will cooperate with the other Governments associated in the Declaration signed at London on July 28, 1958, in order to prepare and participate in such defensive arrangements as may be mutually agreed to be desirable, subject to the other applicable provisions of this agreement.

ARTICLE V

The provisions of the present agreement do not affect the cooperation between the two Governments as envisaged in other international agreements or arrangements.

ARTICLE VI

This agreement shall enter into force upon the date of its signature and shall continue in force until one year after the receipt by either Government of written notice of the intention of the other Government to terminate the agreement.

Done in duplicate at Ankara, this fifth day of March, 1959.

FOR THE GOVERNMENT OF THE UNITED STATES OF AMERICA:	FOR THE IMPERIAL GOVERNMENT OF IRAN:
FLETCHER WARREN	Général HASSAN ARFA
Fletcher Warren	General Hassan Arfa
[SEAL]	[SEAL]

22. Final Communique of the Fifteenth Meeting of the Ministerial Council of the Central Treaty Organization (CENTO) April 24, 1968

The 15th Session of the Central Treaty Organization was held at Lancaster House April 23 and April 24.

Leading national delegations from five CENTO countries were: H. E. Mr. Ardeshir Zahedi (Iran), H. E. Mr. S. K. Dehlavi, S.Pk. (Pakistan), H. E. Mr.

Ihsan Sabri Caglayangil (Turkey), Rt. Hon. Michael Stewart, M.P. (U.K.), The Hon. Nicholas de B. Katzenbach (U.S.A.).

As host, the Chairman for the meeting was the United Kingdom Secretary of State for Foreign Affairs. Following an address from the Prime Minister of the United Kingdom, the Rt. Hon. Harold Wilson, in which he conveyed a message from Her Majesty, the Queen, opening statements were made by the leader of the host delegation and the Secretary General of CENTO.

Reviewing the current international situation, the Council devoted particular attention to those aspects bearing upon responsibilities of the Central Treaty Organization. They also dealt with other matters of concern to the five participating countries. They observed that despite disturbances in many parts of the world since their last meeting, maintenance of peace and stability in the CENTO region had made possible continuing increase in the pace of national development of Iran, Pakistan and Turkey. The Council reaffirmed their determination to promote and accelerate economic and social development in the CENTO region and continue to work for peace and security in the area.

The Council noted the report of the Military Committee, the progress made and the military training exercises which had taken place during the past year as well as the exercises planned for the coming year.

The Council expressed satisfaction at the steady progress maintained on CENTO road and rail projects as reported by the Economic Committee and endorsed proposals to continue emphasis on programmes concerned with agricultural development in Iran, Pakistan and Turkey. The Council also approved steps being taken to explore how CENTO might play its part in the industrial development of the region and in promoting close cooperation in the economic field.

The Council decided to hold their next meeting in Tehran next April.

E. THE EISENHOWER DOCTRINE

23. Message from President Eisenhower to Congress
January 5, 1957

First may I express to you my deep appreciation of your courtesy in giving me, at some inconvenience to yourselves, this early opportunity of addressing you on a matter I deem to be of grave importance to our country.

In my forthcoming State of the Union Message, I shall review the international situation generally. There are worldwide hopes which we can reasonably entertain, and there are worldwide responsibilities which we must carry to make certain that freedom—including our own—may be secure.

There is, however, a special situation in the Middle East which I feel I should, even now, lay before you.

Before doing so it is well to remind ourselves that our basic national objective in international affairs remains peace—a world peace based on justice. Such a peace must include all areas, all peoples of the world [,] if it is to be enduring.

There is no nation, great or small, with which we would refuse to negotiate, in mutual good faith, with patience and in the determination to secure a better understanding between us. Out of such understandings must, and eventually will, grow confidence and trust, indispensable ingredients to a program of peace and to plans for lifting from us all the burdens of expensive armaments. To promote these objectives our government works tirelessly, day by day, month by month, year by year. But until a degree of success crowns our efforts that will assure to all nations peaceful existence, we must, in the interests of peace itself, remain vigilant, alert and strong.

I.

The Middle East has abruptly reached a new and critical stage in its long and important history. In past decades many of the countries in that area were not fully self-governing. Other nations exercised considerable authority in the area and the security of the region was largely built around their power. But since the First World War there has been a steady evolution toward self-government and independence. This development the United States has welcomed and has encouraged. Our country supports without reservation the full sovereignty and independence of each and every nation of the Middle East.

The evolution to independence has in the main been a peaceful process. But the area has been often troubled. Persistent cross-currents of distrust and fear with raids back and forth across national boundaries have brought about a high degree of instability in much of the Mid East. Just recently there have been hostilities involving Western European nations that once exercised much influence in the area. Also the relatively large attack by Israel in October has intensified the basic differences between that nation and its Arab neighbors. All this instability has been heightened and, at times, manipulated by International Communism.

II.

Russia's rulers have long sought to dominate the Middle East. That was true of the Czars and it is true of the Bolsheviks. The reasons are not hard to find. They do not affect Russia's security, for no one plans to use the Middle East as a base for aggression against Russia. Never for a moment has the United States entertained such a thought.

The Soviet Union has nothing whatsoever to fear from the United States in the Middle East, or anywhere else in the world, so long as its rulers do not themselves first resort to aggression.

That statement I make solemnly and emphatically.

Neither does Russia's desire to dominate the Middle East spring from its own economic interest in the area. Russia does not appreciably use or depend upon the Suez Canal. In 1955 Soviet traffic through the Canal represented only about three fourths of 1% of the total. The Soviets have no need for, and could provide no market for, the petroleum resources which constitute the principal natural wealth of the area. Indeed, the Soviet Union is a substantial exporter of petroleum products.

The reason for Russia's interest in the Middle East is solely that of power politics. Considering her announced purpose of Communizing the world, it is easy to understand her hope of dominating the Middle East.

This region has always been the crossroads of the continents of the Eastern Hemisphere. The Suez Canal enables the nations of Asia and Europe to carry on the commerce that is essential if these countries are to maintain well-rounded and prosperous economies. The Middle East provides a gateway between Eurasia and Africa.

It contains about two thirds of the presently known oil deposits of the world and it normally supplies the petroleum needs of many nations of Europe, Asia and Africa. The nations of Europe are peculiarly dependent upon this supply, and this dependency relates to transportation as well as to production. This has been vividly demonstrated since the closing of the Suez Canal and some of the pipelines. Alternate ways of transportation and, indeed, alternate sources of power, can, if necessary, be developed. But these cannot be considered as early prospects.

These things stress the immense importance of the Middle East. If the nations of that area should lose their independence, if they were dominated by alien forces hostile to freedom, that would be both a tragedy for the area and for many other free nations whose economic life would be subject to near strangulation. Western Europe would be endangered just as though there had been no Marshall Plan, no North Atlantic Treaty Organization. The free nations of Asia and Africa, too, would be placed in serious jeopardy. And the countries of the Middle East would lose the markets upon which their economies depend. All this would have the most adverse, if not disastrous, effect upon our own nation's economic life and political prospects.

Then there are other factors, which transcend the material. The Middle East is the birthplace of three great religions—Moslem, Christian and Hebrew. Mecca and Jerusalem are more than places on the map. They symbolize religions which teach that the spirit has supremacy over matter and that the individual has a dignity and rights of which no despotic government can rightfully deprive him. It would be intolerable if the holy places of the Middle East should be subjected to a rule that glorifies atheistic materialism.

International Communism, of course, seeks to mask its purposes of domination by expressions of good will and by superficially attractive offers of political, economic and military aid. But any free nation, which is the subject of Soviet enticement, ought, in elementary wisdom, to look behind the mask.

Remember Estonia, Latvia and Lithuania. In 1939 the Soviet Union entered into mutual assistance pacts with these then independent countries; and the Soviet Foreign Minister, addressing the Extraordinary Fifth Session of the Supreme Soviet in October 1939, solemnly and publicly declared that "we stand for the scrupulous and punctilious observance of the pacts on the basis of complete reciprocity, and we declare that all the nonsensical talk about the Sovietization of the Baltic countries is only to the interest of our common enemies and of all anti-Soviet provocateurs." Yet in 1940, Estonia, Latvia and Lithuania were forcibly incorporated into the Soviet Union.

Soviet control of the satellite nations of Eastern Europe has been forcibly maintained in spite of solemn promises of a contrary intent, made during World War II.

Stalin's death brought hope that this pattern would change. And we read the pledge of the Warsaw Treaty of 1955 that the Soviet Union would follow in satellite countries "the principles of mutual respect for their independence and sovereignty and non-interference in domestic affairs." But we have just seen the subjugation of Hungary by naked armed force. In the aftermath of this Hungarian tragedy, world respect for and belief in Soviet promises have sunk to a new low. International Communism needs and seeks a recognizable success.

Thus, we have these simple and indisputable facts:

1. The Middle East, which has always been coveted by Russia, would today be prized more than ever by International Communism.

2. The Soviet rulers continue to show that they do not scruple to use any means to gain their ends.

3. The free nations of the Mid East need, and for the most part want, added strength to assure their continued independence.

III.

Our thoughts naturally turn to the United Nations as a protector of small nations. Its charter gives it primary responsibility for the maintenance of international peace and security. Our country has given the United Nations its full support in relation to the hostilities in Hungary and in Egypt. The United Nations was able to bring about a cease-fire and withdrawal of hostile forces from Egypt because it was dealing with governments and peoples who had a decent respect for the opinions of mankind as reflected in the United Nations General Assembly. But in the case of Hungary, the situation was different. The Soviet Union vetoed action by the Security Council to require the withdrawal of Soviet armed forces from Hungary. And it has shown callous indifference to the recommendations, even the censure, of the General Assembly. The United Nations can always be helpful, but it cannot be a wholly dependable protector of freedom when the ambitions of the Soviet Union are involved.

IV.

Under all the circumstances I have laid before you, a greater responsibility now devolves upon the United States. We have shown, so that none can doubt, our dedication to the principle that force shall not be used internationally for any aggressive purpose and that the integrity and independence of the nations of the Middle East should be inviolate. Seldom in history has a nation's dedication to principle been tested as severely as ours during recent weeks.

There is general recognition in the Middle East, as elsewhere, that the United States does not seek either political or economic domination over any other people. Our desire is a world environment of freedom, not servitude. On the other hand many, if not all, of the nations of the Middle East are aware of the danger that stems from International Communism and welcome closer cooperation with the United States to realize for themselves the United

Nations goals of independence, economic well-being and spiritual growth.

If the Middle East is to continue its geographic role of uniting rather than separating East and West; if its vast economic resources are to serve the well-being of the peoples there, as well as that of others; and if its cultures and religions and their shrines are to be preserved for the uplifting of the spirits of the peoples, then the United States must make more evident its willingness to support the independence of the freedom-loving nations of the area.

V.

Under these circumstances I deem it necessary to seek the cooperation of the Congress. Only with that cooperation can we give the reassurance needed to deter aggression, to give courage and confidence to those who are dedicated to freedom and thus prevent a chain of events which would gravely endanger all of the free world.

There have been several Executive declarations made by the United States in relation to the Middle East. . . .

Nevertheless, weaknesses in the present situation and the increased danger from International Communism, convince me that basic United States policy should now find expression in joint action by the Congress and the Executive. Furthermore, our joint resolve should be so couched as to make it apparent that if need be our words will be backed by action.

VI.

It is nothing new for the President and the Congress to join to recognize that the national integrity of other free nations is directly related to our own security.

We have joined to create and support the security system of the United Nations. We have reinforced the collective security system of the United Nations by a series of collective defense arrangements. Today we have security treaties with 42 other nations which recognize that their, and our, peace and security are intertwined. We have joined to take decisive action in relation to Greece and Turkey and in relations to Taiwan.

Thus, the United States through the joint action of the President and the Congress, or in the case of treaties, the Senate, has manifested in many endangered areas its purpose to support free and independent governments—and peace—against external menace, notably the menace of International Communism. Thereby we have helped to maintain peace and security during a period of great danger. It is now essential that the United States should manifest through joint action of the President and the Congress our determination to assist those nations of the Mid East area which desire that assistance.

The action which I propose would have the following features.

It would, first of all, authorize the United States to cooperate with and assist any nation or group of nations in the general area of the Middle East in the development of economic strength dedicated to the maintenance of national independence.

It would, in the second place, authorize the Executive to undertake in the same region programs of military assistance and cooperation with any nation or group of nations which desires such aid.

It would, in the third place, authorize such assistance and cooperation to include the employment of the armed forces of the United States to secure and protect the territorial integrity and political independence of such nations, requesting such aid, against overt armed aggression from any nation controlled by International Communism.

These measures would have to be consonant with the treaty obligations of the United States, including the Charter of the United Nations and with any action or recommendations of the United Nations. They would also, if armed attack occurs, be subject to the overriding authority of the United Nations Security Council in accordance with the Charter.

The present proposal would, in the fourth place, authorize the President to employ, for economic and defensive military purposes, sums available under the Mutual Security Act of 1954, as amended, without regard to existing limitations.

The legislation now requested should not include the authorization or appropriation of funds because I believe that, under the conditions I suggest, presently appropriated funds will be adequate for the balance of the present fiscal year ending June 30. I shall, however, seek in subsequent legislation the authorization of $200,000,000 to be available during each of the fiscal years 1958 and 1959 for discretionary use in the area, in addition to the other mutual security programs for the area hereafter provided for by the Congress.

VII.

This program will not solve all the problems of the Middle East. Neither does it represent the totality of our policies for the area. There are the problems of Palestine and relations between Israel and the Arab States, and the future of the Arab refugees. There is the problem of the future status of the Suez Canal. These difficulties are aggravated by International Communism, but they would exist quite apart from that threat. It is not the purpose of the legislation I propose to deal directly with these problems. The United Nations is actively concerning itself with all these matters, and we are supporting the United Nations. The United States has made clear, notably by Secretary Dulles' address of August 26, 1955, that we are willing to do much to assist the United Nations in solving the basic problems of Palistine.

The proposed legislation is primarily designed to deal with the possibility of Communist aggression, direct and indirect. There is imperative need that any lack of power in the area should be made good, not by external or alien force, but by the increased vigor and security of the independent nations of the area.

Experience shows that indirect aggression rarely if ever succeeds where there is reasonable security against direct aggression; where the government possesses loyal security forces, and where economic conditions are such as not to make Communism seem an attractive alternative. The program I suggest deals with all three aspects of this matter and thus with the problem of indirect aggression.

It is my hope and belief that if our purpose be proclaimed, as proposed by the requested legislation, that very fact will serve to halt any contemplated aggression. We shall have heartened the patriots who are dedicated to the independence of their nations. They will not feel that they stand alone, under the menace of great power. And I should add that patriotism is, throughout this area, a powerful sentiment. It is true that fear sometimes perverts true patriotism into fanaticism and to the acceptance of dangerous enticements from without. But if that fear can be allayed, then the climate will be more favorable to the attainment of worthy national ambitions.

And as I have indicated, it will also be necessary for us to contribute economically to strengthen those countries, or groups of countries, which have governments manifestly dedicated to the preservation of independence and resistance to subversion. Such measures will provide the greatest insurance against Communist inroads. Words alone are not enough.

VIII.

Let me refer again to the requested authority to employ the armed forces of the United States to assist to defend the territorial integrity and the political independence of any nation in the area against Communist armed aggression. Such authority would not be exercised except at the desire of the nation attacked. Beyond this it is my profound hope that this authority would never have to be exercised at all.

Nothing is more necessary to assure this than that our policy with respect to the defense of the area be promptly and clearly determined and declared. Thus the United Nations and all friendly governments, and indeed governments which are not friendly, will know where we stand.

If, contrary to my hope and expectation, a situation arose which called for the military application of the policy which I ask the Congress to join me in proclaiming, I would of course maintain hour-by-hour contact with the Congress if it were in session. And if the Congress were not in session, and if the situation had grave implications, I would, of course, at once call the Congress into special session.

In the situation now existing, the greatest risk, as is often the case, is that ambitious despots may miscalculate. If power-hungry Communists should either falsely or correctly estimate that the Middle East is inadequately defended, they might be tempted to use open measures of armed attack. If so, that would start a chain of circumstances which would almost surely involve the United States in military action. I am convinced that the best insurance against this dangerous contingency is to make clear now our readiness to cooperate fully and freely with our friends of the Middle East in ways consonant with the purposes and principles of the United Nations. I intend promptly to send a special mission to the Middle East to explain the cooperation we are prepared to give.

IX.

The policy which I outline involves certain burdens and indeed risks for the

United States. Those who covet the area will not like what is proposed. Already, they are grossly distorting our purpose. However, before this Americans have seen our nation's vital interests and human freedom in jeopardy, and their fortitude and resolution have been equal to the crisis, regardless of hostile distortion of our words, motives, and actions.

Indeed, the sacrifices of the American people in the cause of freedom have, even since the close of World War II, been measured in many billions of dollars and in thousands of the precious lives of our youth. These sacrifices, by which great areas of the world have been preserved to freedom, must not be thrown away.

In those momentous periods of the past, the President and the Congress have united, without partisanship, to serve the vital interests of the United States and of the free world.

The occasion has come for us to manifest again our national unity in support of freedom and to show our deep respect for the rights and independence of every nation—however great, however small. We seek not violence, but peace. To this purpose we must now devote our energies, our determination, ourselves.

DWIGHT D. EISENHOWER

THE WHITE HOUSE
January 5, 1957

24. To Promote the Peace and Stability of the Middle East: Joint Resolution of Congress, March 9, 1957

Text of Public Law 85-7 [H.J. Res. 117], 71 Stat. 5, approved March 9, 1957, as amended by the Foreign Assistance Act of 1961, P.L. 87-195 [S. 1983], 75 Stat. 424, approved September 4, 1961

JOINT RESOLUTION To promote peace and stability in the Middle East.

Resolved by the Senate and House of Representatives of the United States of America in Congress assembled, That the President be and hereby is authorized to cooperate with and assist any nation or group of nations in the general area of the Middle East desiring such assistance in the development of economic strength dedicated to the maintenance of national independence.

SEC. 2.   The President is authorized to undertake, in the general area of the Middle East, military assistance programs with any nation or group of nations of that area desiring such assistance. Furthermore, the United States regards as vital to the national interest and world peace the preservation of the independence and integrity of the nations of the Middle East. To this end, if the President determines the necessity thereof, the United States is prepared to use armed forces to assist any nation or group of such nations requesting assistance against armed aggression from any country controlled by international communism: *Provided,* That such employment shall be consonant with the treaty obligations of the United States and with the Constitution of the United States.

SEC. 3. The President is hereby authorized to use during the balance of fiscal year 1957 for economic and military assistance under this joint resolution not to exceed $200,000,000 from any appropriation now available for carrying out the provisions of the Mutual Security Act of 1954, as amended, in accord with the provisions of such Act: *Provided,* That, whenever the President determines it to be important to the security of the United States, such use may be under the authority of section 401(a) of the Mutual Security Act of 1954, as amended (except that the provisions of section 105(a) thereof shall not be waived), and without regard to the provisions of section 105 of the Mutual Security Appropriation Act, 1957: *Provided further,* That obligations incurred in carrying out the purposes of the first sentence of section 2 of this joint resolution shall be paid only out of appropriations for military assistance, and obligations incurred in carrying out the purposes of the first section of this joint resolution shall be paid only out of appropriations other than those for military assistance. This authorization is in addition to other existing authorizations with respect to the use of such appropriations. None of the additional authorizations contained in this section shall be used until fifteen days after the Committee on Foreign Relations of the Senate, the Committee on Foreign Affairs of the House of Representatives, the Committees on Appropriations of the Senate and the House of Representatives and, when military assistance is involved, the Committees on Armed Services of the Senate and the House of Representatives have been furnished a report showing the object of the proposed use, the country for the benefit of which such use is intended, and the particular appropriation or appropriations for carrying out the provisions of the Mutual Security Act of 1954, as amended, from which the funds are proposed to be derived: *Provided,* That funds available under this section during the balance of fiscal year 1957 shall, in the case of any such report submitted during the last fifteen days of the fiscal year, remain available for use under this section for the purposes stated in such report for a period of twenty days following the date of submission of such report. Nothing contained in this joint resolution shall be construed as itself authorizing the appropriations of additional funds for the purpose of carrying out the provisions of the first section or of the first sentence of section 2 of this joint resolution.

SEC. 4. The President should continue to furnish facilities and military assistance, within the provisions of applicable law and established policies, to the United Nations Emergency Force in the Middle East, with a view to maintaining the truce in that region.

SEC. 5. The President shall whenever appropriate [1] report to the Congress his action hereunder.

SEC. 6. This joint resolution shall expire when the President shall determine that the peace and security of the nations in the general area of the Middle East are reasonably assured by international conditions created by action of the United Nations or otherwise except that it may be terminated earlier by a concurrent resolution of the two Houses of Congress.

---

[1] Sec. 705 of the Foreign Assistance Act of 1961 substituted the words "whenever appropriate" in lieu of the words "within the months of January and July of each year."

25. Jordan Vital to the United States: Statement by the White House Press Secretary April 24, 1957

Press Secretary James Hagerty: "I talked to the President and to the Secretary of State, and they said I could say this: That both the President and the Secretary of State regard the independence and integrity of Jordan as vital."

Question: "Do we regard Jordan as threatened by Communist aggression?"
Answer: "I would like to discuss it more, but I cannot."
Question: "Does this mean that if Jordan asks us for military or any other sort of aid we will give it to her under the terms of the Eisenhower Doctrine?"
Answer: "I have no further comment that I can make on questions."

26. Special Message from President Eisenhower to the Congress on the Sending of United States Forces to Lebanon July 15, 1958

To the Congress of the United States:

On July 14, 1958, I received an urgent request from the President of the Republic of Lebanon that some United States Forces be stationed in Lebanon. President Chamoun stated that without an immediate showing of United States support, the government of Lebanon would be unable to survive. This request by President Chamoun was made with the concurrence of all the members of the Lebanese cabinet. I have replied that we would do this and a contingent of United States Marines has now arrived in Lebanon. This initial dispatch of troops will be augmented as required. U.S. forces will be withdrawn as rapidly as circumstances permit.

Simultaneously, I requested that an urgent meeting of the United Nations Security Council be held on July 15, 1958. At that meeting, the Permanent Representative of the United States reported to the Council the action which this Government has taken. He also expressed the hope that the United Nations could soon take further effective measures to meet more fully the situation in Lebanon. We will continue to support the United Nations to this end.

United States forces are being sent to Lebanon to protect American lives and by their presence to assist the Government of Lebanon in the preservation of Lebanon's territorial integrity and independence, which have been deemed vital to United States national interests and world peace.

About two months ago a violent insurrection broke out in Lebanon, particularly along the border with Syria which, with Egypt, forms the United Arab Republic. This revolt was encouraged and strongly backed by the official Cairo, Damascus, and Soviet radios which broadcast to Lebanon in the Arabic language. The insurrection was further supported by sizable amounts of arms, ammunition and money and by personnel infiltrated from Syria to fight against the lawful authorities. The avowed purpose of these activities was to overthrow the legally constituted government of Lebanon and to install by violence a government which would subordinate the independence of Lebanon to the policies of the United Arab Republic.

Lebanon referred this situation to the United Nations Security Council. In view of the international implications of what was occurring in Lebanon, the Security Council on June 11, 1958 decided to send observers into Lebanon for the purpose of insuring that further outside assistance to the insurrection would cease. The Secretary General of the United Nations subsequently undertook a mission to the area to reinforce the work of the observers.

It was our belief that the efforts of the Secretary General and of the United Nations observers were helpful in reducing further aid in terms of personnel and military equipment from across the frontiers of Lebanon. There was a basis for hope that the situation might be moving toward a peaceful solution, consonant with the continuing integrity of Lebanon, and that the aspect of indirect aggression from without was being brought under control.

The situation was radically changed, however, on July 14, when there was a violent outbreak in Baghdad, in nearby Iraq. Elements in Iraq strongly sympathetic to the United Arab Republic seem to have murdered or driven from office individuals comprising the lawful government of that country. We do not yet know in detail to what extent they have succeeded. We do have reliable information that important Iraqi leaders have been murdered.

We share with the Government of Lebanon the view that these events in Iraq demonstrate a ruthlessness of aggressive purpose which tiny Lebanon cannot combat without further evidence of support from other friendly nations.

After the most detailed consideration, I have concluded that, given the developments in Iraq, the measures thus far taken by the United Nations Security Council are not sufficient to preserve the independence and integrity of Lebanon. I have considered, furthermore, the question of our responsibility to protect and safeguard American citizens in Lebanon of whom there are about 2,500. Pending the taking of adequate measures by the United Nations, the United States will be acting pursuant to what the United Nations Charter recognizes is an inherent right—the right of all nations to work together and to seek help when necessary to preserve their independence. I repeat that we wish to withdraw our forces as soon as the United Nations has taken further effective steps designed to safeguard Lebanese independence.

It is clear that the events which have been occurring in Lebanon represent indirect aggression from without, and that such aggression endangers the independence and integrity of Lebanon.

It is recognized that the step now being taken may have serious consequences. I have, however, come to the considered and sober conclusion that despite the risks involved this action is required to support the principles of justice and international law upon which peace and a stable international order depend.

Our Government has acted in response to an appeal for help from a small and peaceful nation which has long had ties of closest friendship with the United States. Readiness to help a friend in need is an admirable characteristic of the American people, and I am, in this message, informing the Congress of the reasons why I believe that the United States could not in honor stand idly by in this hour of Lebanon's grave peril. As we act at the request of a friendly government to help it preserve its independence and to preserve law and order which will protect American lives, we are acting to reaffirm and strengthen principles upon which the safety and security of the United States depend.

DWIGHT D. EISENHOWER.

III.

United States Relations
With the Arab States

The documents in this chapter deal with the problems and policies concerning United States relations with the Arab states. Two major sources of problems in this area, the mutual security policies of the United States and the Arab-Israeli dispute, also vitally affect Arab-American relations, but because these also involve other Middle Eastern states they are treated elsewhere. This chapter thus examines the bilateral relations of individual Arab states with the United States and the United States involvement in the inter-Arab disputes engendered by the conflict between radical Arab nationalism, led by the United Arab Republic, and the Arab moderates, led by Saudi Arabia.

The history of United States aid to Egypt (and the UAR) in indicative of the difficulties encountered in attempting to formulate a commitment and long-range policy in this respect. The basic question has always been whether aid should be treated as an instrument of United States foreign policy. Even if the answer were in the affirmative, the matter of using this instrument by continuing aid even in the case of temporary political difficulties—or by reducing, stopping, and reinstituting it according to the political circumstances—would still remain to be resolved.

United States policies in this respect have not been thoroughly consistent. They have, in fact, fluctuated with various administrations or even within a single administration. There has also been a difference of approach between the executive branch of government and the Congress, the former often favoring flexibility—the latter more inclined to insist on limitations and conditions.

President Kennedy's press conference statement on the undesirability of tying United States aid to the UAR to the policies of President Nasser in Yemen states the case for the continuation of aid as a long-range policy despite political differences. Secretary of State Dulles' withdrawal of the United States offer to aid in the construction of the Aswan High Dam and the congressional efforts to limit food aid to the UAR after actions and speeches by President Nasser, are examples of linking aid more closely to foreign policy. Both the United States and the UAR had a mutual interest in preserving some ties so as to avoid the complete dependence of the UAR on the Soviet Union, but at times foreign policy disputes overshadowed longer-range considerations on both sides.

The Arab states had a reputation in the United States, in part justified by their own failures in public relations, for being concerned solely with the problem of Israel. Yet examination of their actual policies showed that in reality they usually were more concerned with their own internal quarrels. This "Arab Cold War" showed itself capable of erupting into serious fighting between the rival Arab camps, as was the case in Yemen.

The problems that this inter-Arab dispute raised for the United States were illustrated in Washington's policies toward radical Arab nationalism and toward Saudi Arabia. Officially, the United States attempted to remain neutral. This was demonstrated by President Johnson's statement praising the agreement "between our two friends," Saudi Arabia and the UAR, to end the Yemen civil war. The President probably considered Saudi Arabia a somewhat better friend than the UAR, but the United States did not, in fact, wish to be considered an enemy of radical Arab nationalism. In the case of Yemen the good offices of the United States as a neutral mediator were accepted by both the UAR and the Saudis and Ambassador Ellsworth Bunker led the mediating mission.

In the 1960s Yemen became for the Arab world what Spain had been for Europe in the 1930s, a civil war over rival governmental philosophies with each side being backed by larger foreign powers in sympathy with their ideological positions. Both Ambassador Bunker's mission and the Jidda agreement hailed by President Johnson proved to be abortive in solving this conflict. The Khartoum agreement of September, 1967, removed Egyptian troops supporting the republic and Saudi support for the royalists. The republicans continued to receive aid from the Soviet Union, but the crucial importance of Yemen as a potential cause of war between Saudi Arabia and the UAR was reduced.

While the United States had recognized, maintained diplomatic relations with, and even given aid to radical Arab regimes, as in Yemen, some of their policies have disturbed the stability of the Middle East, and have been harmful to American political and economic interests. United States interests have coincided more often with those of the moderate Arab states, as is demonstrated in the guarantee given by President Kennedy to support Saudi Arabia against threats to her territorial integrity and national independence, threats which came from the UAR.

A. PROBLEMS OF GIVING AND RECEIVING AID

27. The United States Supports the Aswan High Dam Project: Statement by the Department of State, December 17, 1955

Mr. Abdel Moneim El Kaissouni, Egyptian Minister of Finance, met yesterday with Acting Secretary of State Herbert Hoover, Jr., British Ambassador Sir Roger Makins and World Bank President Eugene Black for final talks before his departure for Cairo.

During their stay in Washington, Mr. Kaissouni and his colleagues have been carrying on discussions with the management of the World Bank and representatives of the United States and United Kingdom Governments concerning possible assistance in the execution of the High Aswan Dam project.

The United States and British Governments assured the Egyptian Government through Mr. Kaissouni of their support in this project, which would be of inestimable importance in the development of the Egyptian economy and in the improvement of the welfare of the Egyptian people. Such assistance would take the form of grants from the United States and the United Kingdom toward defraying foreign exchange costs of the first stages of the work. This phase, involving the Coffer Dam, foundations for the main dam, and auxiliary work will take from four to five years. Further assurance has been given to Mr. Kaissouni that the Governments of the United States and the United Kingdom would, subject to legislative authority, be prepared to consider sympathetically in the light of then existing circumstances further support toward financing the later stages to supplement World Bank financing.

Mr. Kaissouni plans to leave Washington for Egypt today, and it is understood that he will report to his Government on his talks here. Final understandings with the British and American Governments and the World Bank will await Mr. Kaissouni's consultation with the Egyptian Government.

28. United States Withdraws from the Aswan High Dam Project: Announcement by the Department of State, July 19, 1956

At the request of the Government of Egypt, the United States joined in December 1955 with the United Kingdom and with the World Bank in an offer to assist Egypt in the construction of a high dam on the Nile at Aswan. This project is one of great magnitude. It would require an estimated 12 to 16 years to complete at a total cost estimated at some $1,300,000,000, of which over $900,000,000 represents local currency requirements. It involves not merely the rights and interests of Egypt but of other states whose waters are contributory, including Sudan, Ethiopia, and Uganda.

The December offer contemplated an extension by the United States and United Kingdom of grant aid to help finance certain early phases of the work, the effects of which would be confined solely to Egypt, with the understanding that accomplishment of the project as a whole would require a satisfactory resolution of the question of Nile water rights. Another important consideration bearing upon the feasibility of the undertaking and thus the practicability of American aid was Egyptian readiness and ability to concentrate its economic resources upon this vast construction program.

Developments within the succeeding 7 months have not been favorable to the success of the project, and the U.S. Government has concluded that it is not feasible in present circumstances to participate in the project. Agreement by the riparian states has not been achieved, and the ability of Egypt to devote adequate resources to assure the project's success has become more uncertain than at the time the offer was made.

This decision in no way reflects or involves any alteration in the friendly relations of the Government and people of the United States toward the Government and people of Egypt.

The United States remains deeply interested in the welfare of the Egyptian people and in the development of the Nile. It is prepared to consider at an appropriate time and at the request of the riparian states what steps might be taken toward a more effective utilization of the water resources of the Nile for the benefit of the peoples of the region. Furthermore, the United States remains ready to assist Egypt in its effort to improve the economic condition of its people and is prepared, through its appropriate agencies, to discuss these matters within the context of funds appropriated by the Congress.

29. President Kennedy Rejects the Use of Aid as a Weapon to Force Withdrawal of UAR Troops from Yemen: News Conference November 14, 1963

Now on [the question of suspending foreign assistance to] the United Arab Republic [for failure to withdraw all of its forces from Yemen], the United States, as you know, 80 percent of its assistance consists of food, surplus food. We have been working to try to get a withdrawal, an orderly withdrawal, in the case of the Yemen. There has not been a conflict—I think a good deal as a result of effort which we and others have made—between Saudi Arabia and the UAR. I am concerned about the Yemen because the rate of the withdrawal, of course, has been quite limited.

There are going to be further withdrawals by January, but unless those withdrawals are consistent with earlier statements, I would think that the chance of increased tension between the UAR and Saudi Arabia would substantially increase. But I don't think that the language that the Senate adopted,[1] which calls upon me to make a finding which is extremely complicated to make, is particularly—strengthens our hands or our flexibility in dealing with the UAR. In fact, it will have the opposite result.

These countries are poor—I am not talking now about the UAR, most of them —these threats that the United States is going to cut off aid is a great temptation to Arabic countries to say, "Cut it off." They are nationalist, they are proud, they are in many cases radical. I don't think threats from Capitol Hill bring the results which are frequently hoped. A quiet work may not bring it. But I think there is a great temptation to say—at the time [the offer of assistance for construction of] the Aswan Dam was cut off, that produced—that did not bring the [United] Arab Republic to follow us. It produced the opposite result. I am afraid of these other threats. I think it is a very dangerous, untidy world. But we are going to have to live with it. I think one of the ways to live with it is to permit us to function. If we don't function, the voters will throw us out. But don't make it impossible for us to function by legislative restraints or inadequate appropriations.

30. "Whoever Does Not Like Our Conduct Can Go Drink Up the Sea": Speech by President Nasser (excerpts), December 23, 1964

An aggression has taken place against the Congo. American and Belgian troops landed in Stanleyville. We have condemned this aggression. For what

---

[1] Enacted by section 301(e) (3) of Public Law 88-205 (the Foreign Assistance Act of 1963), approved Dec. 16, 1963, which reads in part as follows:

"(i) No assistance shall be provided under this or any other Act, and no sales shall be made under the Agricultural Trade Development and Assistance Act of 1954, to any country which the President determines is engaging in or preparing for aggressive military efforts directed against—

"(1) the United States,

"(2) any country receiving assistance under this or any other Act, or

"(3) any country to which sales are made under the Agricultural Trade Development Act of 1954,

until the President determines that such military efforts or preparations have ceased and he reports to the Congress that he has received assurances satisfactory to him that such military efforts or preparations will not be renewed. This restriction may not be waived pursuant to any authority contained in this Act." (77 Stat. 387) is the difference between the Anglo-French aggression against Port Said in 1956 and the American-Belgian aggression against Stanleyville in 1964? Both had arms, both landed by parachute, and both killed the natives of the country. We are opposed to aggression in whatever form it may be. We are for the freedom of peoples.

Can we possibly recognize Tshombe as the representative of the Congolese people? Tshombe is a murderer. If America and Belgium had installed Tshombe as a premier, he is then a premier in the pay of America and Belgium, and we cannot under any circumstances recognize him as a premier representing the Congolese people. It is not only us who did not recognize him. You remember when Tshombe came here during the nonaligned conference? The nonaligned states did not recognize him, and not a single state agreed to allow him to attend the conference as a representative of the Congolese people.

Who then says that Tshombe represents the Congolese people? The Americans and the Belgians. We say that Tshombe is nothing but an agent of imperialism. Tshombe is an agent serving the interests of America and Belgium in the Congo. We will in no way allow this example to succeed in Africa. This example must fail in Africa, and the national forces there must succeed.

We have helped the Congolese people. They (the West—ed.) said that we have helped the Congolese people, and I say, indeed, yes, we have helped the Congolese people. We have sent arms to the Congolese people, and we will still send them arms. We do not attempt in any way to deny or hide our (few words indistinct), because we do not recognize Tshombe. We do, however, recognize him as an agent of imperialism. We consider that the national rebels in the Congo require every support from the national forces and the honorable forces in the world.

You, the people, who have resisted aggression in 1956 can in no way allow the Congolese people to be subjected to a similar aggression. This is our policy. It is a clear, well-known one. We make it clear and public. We do not hide and have never denied that we have sent arms to the Congo. We say that we have sent arms to the Congo and will still send arms to it.

This is our policy—an independent one. We have declared that we deal with the nations of the world on the basis of noninterference in the affairs of others. But if the Americans think that they are giving us a little aid to dominate us and control our policy, I would like to tell them we are sorry. We are ready to cut down in our consumption of tea, coffee, and certain commodities. But we will maintain our independence. Otherwise, we will lose it completely, and the 1956 battle will have been of no use.

I want to say that we are getting wheat from the Americans. We must disclose the matter openly. We get wheat, meat, and chicken. (laughter). We do not, by God, get factories. They do not give us factories. They give us the equivalent of about 50 million pounds per year. Our annual budget is 1.1 billion pounds. We spend some 400 million pounds or 500 million pounds on the plan. If the need arises, we could spare these 50 million pounds on our food, and it would not bother us a bit, by God.

I am saying this because the American ambassador yesterday called on the deputy premier for supply and sat with him for a few minutes, looking glum and sulky. He was supposed to talk with him about the supply material we are obtaining from America in accordance with the products law. The ambassador told the deputy premier that he cannot at present talk about this matter at all. Why? Because he does not like our conduct, that is, conduct here in Egypt. I would like him to know that whoever does not like our conduct can go drink up the sea. If the Mediterranean is not sufficient, there is the Red Sea too. We can give him that as well. What I want to say is that we cannot sell our independence for the sake of 30 or 40 or 50 million pounds. We are not ready to accept a single harsh word from any person. He who speaks a single harsh word to us will have his tongue cut off. This is how it is—clear and frank words. If nowadays we are drinking tea seven days a week, we will drink it five days a week until we build our country. If we are drinking coffee seven days a week, we will drink it five days a week. If we are eating meat four days a week, we will eat it three days a week.

What I want to say is that this incident comes at a time when they are saying that we have a supply crisis and what not. If anything, this smacks of an attempt to exert pressure on us. We are sorry. We cannot tolerate any pressure or accept insolent words and vileness. We are short-tempered people. We are born like this. We are a people with dignity. The people have their dignity and are not prepared to sell it, not even for one billion pounds, much less so for 50 or 40 or 30 million pounds.

31. President Johnson Requests Congressional Flexibility in Dealing with the UAR: News Conference, February 4, 1965

Last week, the House of Representatives adopted a proposal that would, if brought into law, by adding an amendment on the appropriation bill, prevent the United States of America from carrying out a 3-year agreement that we had made with the United Arab Republic. This agreement was to sell surplus commodities to the United Arab Republic under what is called title I of Public Law 480.

Yesterday the Senate passed a milder version of this proposal and moderated the House amendment.[1] It would permit delivery of surplus commodities if the President determined it to be in the national interest.

I judge it of the highest importance that the flexibility provided the President by the Senate version be sustained by the Congress. I hope the House of Representatives will accept the improvements made by the Senate committee and voted by the Senate. Because if we are to protect our vital interests in this part of the world where tensions are very high, then the President must have freedom of action to act in the best interest of all the people of this land.

It is of course obvious that the relations between the United States and the United Arab Republic must be improved. It will demand effort from both countries.

---

[1] The vote in the Senate was 44 to 38.

I cannot predict whether improvement can be achieved. But if we are to have any degree of success in this sensitive relationship the President must have some freedom of action. I earnestly suggest to the Congress that they consider this need which I believe is truly in the best interest of all of our people. . . .[2]

32. Congress Allows Food Aid to the UAR: Supplemental Appropriations for Fiscal Year 1965 to Finance P.L. 480 (partial text), February 11, 1965

Partial text of Public Law 89-2, 89th Congress, H.J. Res. 234, February 11, 1965.

JOINT RESOLUTION Making supplemental appropriations for the fiscal year ending June 30, 1965, for certain activities of the Department of Agriculture, and for other purposes.

*   *   *   *   *   *   *

PUBLIC LAW 480

For an additional amount for expenses during fiscal year 1965, not otherwise recoverable, and unrecovered prior years' costs, including interest thereon, under the Agricultural Trade Development and Assistance Act of 1954, as amended (7 U.S.C. 1701-1709, 1731-1736), to remain available until expended, as follows: (1) Sale of surplus agricultural commodities for foreign currencies pursuant to title I of said Act, $250,000,000; and (2) long-term supply contracts pursuant to title IV of said Act, $200,000,000: *Provided,* That no part of this appropriation shall be used during the fiscal year 1965 to finance the export of any agricultural commodity to the United Arab Republic under the provisions of title I of such Act, except when such exports are necessary to carry out the Sales Agreement entered into October 8, 1962, as amended, and if the President determines that the financing of such exports is in the national interest.

*   *   *   *   *   *   *

Approved February 11, 1965.

33. Food Aid to the UAR Is in the National Interest: Memorandum from the President to the Secretary of State December 29, 1965

In accordance with your recommendation of 17 November, I hereby determine pursuant to Section 107 of the Agricultural Trade Development and Assistance Act of 1954, as amended, that it is essential to the national interest of the United States to finance export sales of surplus agricultural commodities to the United Arab Republic under title I of that Act.

---

[2] In conference, the House accepted the Senate version, and the bill as enacted into legislation gave the President authority to carry out sales of surplus foods to the U.A.R. if he determined "that the financing of such exports is in the national interest." (Public Law 89-2; 79 Stat. 4).

B. THE PROBLEM OF RADICAL ARAB NATIONALISM

34. United States Recognition of the United Arab Republic: Statement by the Department of State, February 25, 1958

The United States Government has been officially informed of the proclamation of the United Arab Republic following the plebiscite conducted in Egypt and Syria on February 21. The United States Government, having taken note of the assurances of the United Arab Republic that it intends to respect and observe its international obligations, including all international obligations of Egypt and Syria, respectively, existing at the time of the formation of the United Arab Republic, extended recognition [today] to the Government of the United Arab Republic, with the expression of its good wishes.

35. United States Policy Respecting Arab Nationalism: Secretary of State Dulles' News Conference, July 31, 1958

. . . Let me say on Arab nationalism there is no opposition that I know of on the part of the United States to Arab nationalism. There are plenty of good reasons why there should be greater unity among the Arab nations. The United States encourages that. We were among the early nations to recognize the U.A.R. when it was formed. Some of our friends held back. We did not. We knew it had some undesirable implications, but, because we did not want to be in opposition to this increased Arab unity, we granted recognition. We were prepared to grant recognition to the Arab Union, another step toward unity. There is no opposition on the part of the United States to an increased Arab unity which expresses, and gives an opportunity to, the aspirations of the Arab peoples. That is one thing. Whether or not in this area of the world or other areas of the world processes of indirect aggression become accepted as proper instruments of national policy, that is a very different thing. That does affect the peace and security of the world.

36. Policy Toward the Iraqi Revolution: Selection from Ambassador Robert Murphy's Memoirs, August, 1958

The man who engineered this revolution, Brigadier General Abdul Karim Kassim, was now Premier, and Ambassador Gallman had arranged for us to pay him an official visit at the Defense Ministry, where he was working and sleeping in the same room which he had been occupying ever since the uprising. . . . The Premier justified the coup d'état with the explanation that only by such unconstitutional means was it possible for the impoverished people of Iraq to get rid of their corrupt royal regime. Kassim stressed the purely domestic character of the revolution, which he said had been organized for national rather than ideological reasons. He did not deplore the brutality of the accomplishment.

Changing the subject, I told Kassim that I had come to Baghdad to help my government better to understand the policies of his government, which the United States had been prompt to recognize. Coincident with the revolution in Iraq, my government had intervened militarily in neighboring Lebanon, and I had heard that Iraqi officials were suspicious of our motives. Was that true? Yes, Kassim said, he was suspicious because he believed that Americans did not intend to restrict their forces to Lebanon. He felt sure that our intervention was merely a prelude to an invasion of Iraq—which he proposed to resist. I replied that I had just flown over a good deal of Iraq and had observed that it was a vast expanse of arid country, most uninviting from a military point of view. I reminded Kassim that the President of the United States had to his credit a long and successful career as an Army officer. Kassim, I noted, was also a soldier, and I asked him to figure out one good reason why Eisenhower would want to send American troops to invade the Godforsaken stretches of Iraq. I said this with a smile, not wishing to make any reflection on his country, and after a moment Kassim smiled too. The argument seemed to make a favorable impression on him, and he expressed a desire for friendly relations with the United States and with other Western countries.

37. United States Policies in the Middle East: Letter from President Kennedy to President Nasser May 11, 1961

White House,
Washingon, 11th May, 1961
Dear Mr. President,

In recent months the world's attention has been centered on several explosive situations, the outcome of which could spell the difference between freedom and servitude, between peace and war, for many millions of people, ultimately perhaps for all mankind. I know that you have been deeply concerned about these problems, as I have been. However, I am confident that you share with me the conviction that through the dedicated efforts of men of goodwill everywhere, the storm clouds of the present can be dispersed.

Meanwhile, leaders responsive to the needs and aspirations of their peoples must, in my firm opinion, be alert to every possibility for advancing basic principles of political and economic justice. Thus, while since my inauguration on January 20 I have perforce been largely occupied with the several international issues of immediate concern, I have given considerable thought to other international issues that deserve the careful attention of us all.

My thoughts have often turned to the Middle East, an area which has contributed so much to the religious and cultural heritage of the world today, and whose potential for further rich contributions to civilization is great. As an American I am proud that the concepts of our founding patriots, of Abraham Lincoln, Woodrow Wilson and Franklin Roosevelt, have played so great a part in the emergence of vigorous, independent Arab states, respected as sovereign equals in the international community.

I am proud of the tangible encouragement which has been accorded by our Government and people to the aspirations of you and your countrymen in the past, particularly during the critical days of 1956. The United States Government, itself the product of a union of several independent states, was pleased to recognize the formation of the United Arab Republic on February 22, 1958, the Birthday Anniversary of our own first President, Washington.

In recent weeks I have noted some speculation as to the direction of the policies of the United States Administration with respect to the Middle East. Let me assure you that the concepts inherited from the men mentioned above are part of the very fibre of this nation, and that as its President I intend to uphold them. You will find us at all times and all places active in the struggle for equality. of opportunity; for Government of the people, by the people and for the people; for freedom from want and fear; and for the application of justice in the settlement of international disputes.

Translating these great precepts into United States policy in the Middle East for the next few years, I want you to know that:

1. The United States will to the best of its ability lend every appropriate assistance to all Middle Eastern states that are determined to control their own destiny, to enhance the prosperity of their people, and to allow their neighbors to pursue the same fundamental aims.

2. The United States remains ever ready to contribute both within and outside the United Nations to the search for solutions to disputes which dissipate the precious energies of the Middle Eastern states and retard the economic progress which all free peoples rightly desire.

3. With a view toward improving the welfare of the people of the Middle East, the United States is prepared to continue to support national development programs which are effectively designed, to make available American commodities under the Food for Peace Program, and to encourage educational exchanges designed to facilitate political and economic progress.

While tensions unfortunately have sharpened in certain other areas of the world, the Middle East during the past three years has been relatively tranquil. This has been due largely to statesmanship on the part of the area's leaders who have given priority to constructive programs of economic development. Secretary Rusk and I have been struck by the unanimity of views expressed to us by representatives of the various Middle Eastern states emphasizing that the present relative tranquility be preserved.

Underlying tensions do, however, remain, not the least of which is the unresolved Arab-Israel controversy. I know deep emotions are involved. No easy solution presents itself. The American Government and people believe that an honorable and humane settlement can be found and are willing to share in the labors and burdens which so difficult an achievement must entail, if the parties concerned genuinely desire such participation. We are willing to help resolve the tragic Palestine Refugee Problem on the basis of the principle of repatriation or compensation for properties, to assist in finding an equitable answer to the question of Jordan River Water resources development and to be helpful in making progress on other aspects of this complex problem.

I am pleased that the United Nations General Assembly recently underscored the necessity to implement more rapidly its previous recommendations on the refugee problem. In this connection, I wish to state unequivocally that this government's position is anchored and will continue to be anchored in the firm bedrock of support for General Assembly recommendations concerning the refugees, and of active, impartial concern that those recommendations be implemented in a way most beneficial to the refugees.

The United States, as a member of the Palestine Conciliation Commission and a nation keenly interested in the long-range advancement of the peoples of the Middle East, takes seriously the task entrusted to the Commission by the United Nations. We are determined to use our influence to assure that the Commission intensify its efforts to promote progress toward a just and peaceful solution. What precise steps the Commission may be able to take are, of course, not yet clear, but I can assure you that there will be no lack of United States interest in seeing that effective action is taken. It is my sincere hope that all the parties directly concerned will cooperate fully with whatever program is undertaken by the Commission so that the best interests and welfare of all the Arab refugees of Palestine may be protected and advanced.

With reference to relations between the United Arab Republic and the United States, I recognize that our views on important problems do not always coincide. At the same time I am pleased that mutually beneficial relations continue to exist in many spheres and that United States assistance in significant quantities has played a role in your own thorough and detailed development program. As you know, I have recently made proposals to the Congress for aiding in the preservation of Nubian monuments. We continue to welcome the hundreds of UAR students who have entered institutions in our country to further their educations. During his recent consultations in Washington, Ambassador Reinhardt told me of the significant progress which the United Arab Republic has already made in establishing an industrial base which will permit increasing prosperity and higher living standards for all your citizens. I am particularly pleased that we have been able in times past to arrange under favorable conditions the sale of substantial quantities of wheat and other commodities to the United Arab Republic since we recognize the importance of an adequately nourished population. It is my earnest hope that such mutually beneficial cooperation can continue.

I earnestly hope that these views of mine on the Middle East will prove useful to you. Given the long history of friendly relationships between the Arab people and the American people, and the interdependence of all men who wish to remain free, I want to be certain that you and other Arab leaders have no misunderstanding of our attitude towards the Arab people. It continues to be one of sincere friendship. With mutual respect for the others' points of view, mutual and active concern for the betterment of mankind, and mutual striving to eliminate the causes of international tensions, the future will bring even friendlier and more productive relationships between our countries and their freedom-loving people.

Sincerely,

JOHN F. KENNEDY

38. United States Recognition of the Yemen Arab Republic: Statement by the Department of State, December 19, 1962

In view of a number of confusing and contradictory statements which have cast doubt upon the intentions of the new regime in Yemen [1] the United States Government welcomes the reaffirmation by the Yemen Arab Republic Government of its intention to honor its international obligations, of its desire for normalization and establishment of friendly relations with its neighbors, and of its intention to concentrate on internal affairs to raise the living standards of the Yemeni people.

The United States Government also is gratified by the statesmanlike appeal of the Yemen Arab Republic to Yemenis in adjacent areas to be law-abiding citizens and notes its undertaking to honor all treaties concluded by previous Yemeni governments. This, of course, includes the Treaty of Sana'a concluded with the British Government in 1934,[2] which provides reciprocal guarantees that neither party should intervene in the affairs of the other across the existing international frontier dividing the Yemen from territory under British protection.

Further the United States Government welcomes the declaration of the United Arab Republic signifying its willingness to undertake a reciprocal disengagement and expeditious phased removal of troops from Yemen as external forces engaged in support of the Yemen royalists are removed from the frontier and as external support of the royalists is stopped.

In believing that these declarations provide a basis for terminating the conflict over Yemen and in expressing the hope that all of the parties involved in the conflict will cooperate to the end that the Yemeni peoples themselves be permitted to decide their own future, the United States has today [December 19] decided to recognize the Government of the Yemen Arab Republic and to extend to that Government its best wishes for success and prosperity. The United States has instructed its Chargé d'Affaires in Yemen to confirm this decision in writing to the Ministry of Foreign Affairs of the Yemen Arab Republic.

---

[1] On Sept. 26, 1962, revolutionary army elements rose against the ruling Imam of Yemen and proclaimed a republic.

[2] Signed Feb. 11, 1934; 137 *British and Foreign State Papers,* 212.

C. SAUDI ARABIAN-UNITED ARAB REPUBLIC DISPUTE

39. United States Support for Saudi Arabia: Letter from President Kennedy to Crown Prince Faisal October 25, 1962

YOUR HIGHNESS: As Your Highness assumes new and important responsibilities upon returning to Saudi Arabia,[1] I wish to recall your visit to the White House

---

[1] The Saudi Arabian Government announced on October 17 that King Saud had asked Prince Faisal to form a new cabinet.

on October 5. I then stated, and I want it understood clearly, that Saudi Arabia can depend upon the friendship and the cooperation of the United States in dealing with the many tasks which lie before it in the days ahead. The United States has deep and abiding interest in Saudi Arabia and in the stability and progress of Saudi Arabia. Under your firm and enlightened leadership I am confident Saudi Arabia will move ahead successfully on the path of modernization and reform which it has already charted for itself. In pursuing this course you may be assured of full United States support for the maintenance of Saudi Arabia's integrity.

I am fully aware that in order to accomplish your goals you must have the requisite tranquility—an atmosphere devoid of recriminations and instigations from within or without. I share your concern at the tensions which prevail in the area and which hamper your design to strengthen the fabric of government and society in Saudi Arabia. As I indicated to you in Washington, the United States desires to be helpful in finding means of reducing these tensions.

I foresee for our two countries not merely the continuance of the cordial relationship which began so auspiciously during the reign of your illustrious father, His Majesty Abdul Aziz Ibn Saud; rather I foresee the opening of a chapter in Saudi-United States relations in which the common bond of enlightened self-interest is firmly riveted by a common dedication to the inalienable rights of man for self-fulfillment, progress and freedom.

I wish you success and send you my warmest personal regards. May God keep you and the Saudi people and grant you peace.

Sincerely,

JOHN F. KENNEDY

40. United States Hopes for an End to the Yemeni Civil War, Supports Saudi Arabia: Department of State Press Officer's News Conference, August 4, 1965

. . . We would very strongly hope that the talks which President Nasser has indicated are taking place with Saudi Arabia would lead to a situation where the Yemenis themselves would be able to decide their own national destiny, free from any outside interference. We welcome President Nasser's July 22 statement that his Government is prepared to withdraw U.A.R. troops from the Yemen within six months or less if peace is obtained. During the course of our relations with the governments concerned we have frequently advised both sides to withdraw from their involvement in the internal affairs of Yemen. U.S. relations with Saudi Arabia have long been marked by friendship and mutual cooperation for the economic and social development of the country. We have clearly indicated our support for the maintenance of Saudi Arabia's integrity. We would deplore any extension of hostilities in the area. It has long been our stated policy that we are strongly opposed to the use of force or the threat of force in the Near East.

41. President Johnson Praises the Agreement "Between Our Two Friends" (Saudi Arabia and the UAR) to End the Yemeni Civil War: News Conference, August 29, 1965

In the Middle East, we are happy to see the statesmanlike agreement between King Faisal and President Nasser, which seems to offer great promise of a peaceful settlement in Yemen. This crisis has long been a very disruptive element in the relations between our two friends. We share their confidence that this long-festering issue is on the road to settlement by negotiation rather than force, and that is most encouraging.

IV.

United States Relations
With the Northern Tier States

The non-Arab states of the northern tier of the Middle East—Turkey and Iran—are formally linked to the United States by security agreements and are joined to each other and to the United States and Great Britain in the Central Treaty Organization (CENTO). Turkey is simultaneously a member of the North Atlantic Treaty Organization (NATO). The multiplicity of close and formal ties reflects the fact that these northern tier states are much more aware, due to their geographical position and their past history, of the danger of Russian-Soviet expansionism.

Even before the Truman Doctrine of 1947 brought about the large-scale interest of the United States in the security of the Middle East, the United States had demonstrated its interest in preserving the territorial integrity and national sovereignty of Turkey and Iran. Soviet actions and demands on these two states, even before the end of World War II, were some of the first indications that the wartime friendliness and cooperation between the Western nations and the Soviet Union would not endure in the postwar era.

In March, 1945, the Soviet Union denounced its treaty of friendship and non-aggression with Turkey, first signed in 1925. The Soviet Union demanded the cession of two provinces in eastern Turkey, Kars and Ardahan, which had been in Russian hands between 1878 and the Russian Revolution of 1917—when the Turks managed to regain them. The Kremlin also demanded a joint administration of the Turkish straits, ending the Montreux Convention, with Soviet bases on the straits. In Iran, the Soviet Union refused to honor the joint Big Three Teheran Declaration promising the withdrawal of foreign troops from Iran within six months after the end of the war. It also demanded oil concessions in northern Iran and representation of the Communist-controlled *Tudeh* (Masses) Party in the Iranian cabinet. Even more serious was the formation of two Soviet-backed "autonomous" republics in Iranian Azerbaijan and Kurdistan.

United States support, as illustrated in this collection by the remarks of Ambassador George V. Allen in Teheran and in the note delivered in Moscow by Ambassador Walter Bedell Smith, was instrumental at this juncture in strengthening the determination of the Iranian and Turkish governments to resist Soviet pressures. The Soviet Union had continued to station large combat forces in northern Iran, and had physically blocked the attempt of the Iranian army to march against the rebels in Azerbaijan. Eventually the Soviet Union withdrew its forces, partly because Iran promised oil concessions and accepted the Soviet demand for *Tudeh* Party representation in the cabinet; and partly because the United States exerted strong pressure. The Iranian *Majlis* (Parliament), however, refused to ratify the Soviet oil concessions and the Tudeh ministers were dismissed. The United States continued to maintain a small military advisory mission in Iran after the war at the invitation of the Iranian government. When the Soviet Union protested this "evidence" of American influence, Ambassador Allen frankly pointed out to the Iranian public that the Americans were present only at the invitation of the Iranian government and would leave whenever they were asked to do so; he pointed out the sharp contrast of this attitude with recent Soviet conduct in Iran.

The United States government had agreed at the Potsdam Conference that some revision of the Montreux Convention more favorable to the Soviet Union should be made, but it rejected the unilateral Soviet demands on Turkey, which included the cession of territory far from the Dardanelles and Bosphorus. The Soviet Union mounted a major propaganda campaign against Turkey, accusing her of having been pro-Nazi during the war (and conveniently forgetting its own alliance with the Nazis from August, 1939, to June, 1940). Turkey, assured now of United States support through the Truman Doctrine, ignored the Soviet demands and finally rejected them categorically in 1950.

The concession of the Anglo-Iranian Oil Company was one of the oldest in the Middle East. Because the majority of shares were owned by the British government, it was an especially sensitive concession. Despite a previous "Iranian oil crisis" in the 1930s which resulted in an agreement more favorable to Iran, the terms of the concession still lagged behind the newer concessions prevelant in the Arab states. Aside from the normal nationalist desire to gain more control over her natural resources, Iran desperately needed more oil revenue to pay for her development programs. The United States had refused to give substantial grants or loans for this purpose. The Anglo-Iranian Oil Company was nationalized—Dr. Mossadegh was named premier. The Tudeh party used the nationalist excitement and anti-imperialist agitation to make a strong recovery from its postwar depression.

Direct negotiations with the British and a series of American mediation efforts, as well as an appeal to the World Court by the British, were unable to solve the impasse. The AIOC withdrew its technicians, financial support, transportation and marketing facilities. It blocked attempts of the Iranians to sell oil by instituting law suits. For three years all production came to a virtual standstill (greatly aiding the expansion of oil production in Kuwait, Saudi Arabia, and other Arab states). The effect on the economy of Iran was catastrophic. Premier Mossadegh hoped to keep the economy going with United States aid, but this was refused as long as the oil dispute remained unsettled and Iran refused all reasonable compromises. Dr. Mossadegh had used the oil crisis in an attempt to build a "National Front" to challenge the position of the Shah of Iran. The Shah attempted to dismiss him, but Mossadegh refused, forcing the Shah to flee the country. Elements in the Iranian army, led by General Zahedi, then staged a coup d'etat against Premier Mossadegh—aided by an outpouring of popular support for the Shah. This change of government was welcomed by the United States. With Dr. Mossadegh removed it was possible for the oil crisis to be negotiated. The United States immediately extended economic aid and, in 1954, a new international consortium, with 40 percent American participation, signed a new agreement with the Iranian government on the basis of a 50-50 sharing of profits and payment of compensation to the AIOC, which retained a 40 percent share in the consortium.

Iranian and Turkish relations with the United States became closer and more formal in a series of treaties and agreements in the 1950s. As has been indicated in chapter II, these included Turkey's preliminary association and subsequent full membership in NATO, Turkish and Iranian inclusion in the Baghdad Pact, and the bilateral mutual security agreements of both with the United States concluded under the authority of the Eisenhower Doctrine in 1959.

However, in the 1960s, a new emphasis in both Iranian and Turkish relations with the United States and the Soviet Union became evident. With the growth of the "peaceful coexistence" theme of Soviet policy and the extension of a foreign aid program by the Soviet Union, its Middle Eastern neighbors came to feel less of a threat from Russia and more of the mutual advantages of economic and commercial ties. With the lessening of the immediate threat, each country became more concerned with its own local ambitions and local disputes. Iranian disputes with Iraq and with other Arab states over the future of the Persian Gulf area after Britain's impending withdrawal from the area, and Turkey's concern over the Turkish minority in Cyprus increasingly occupied their attention. The Iranian government was able to obtain substantial Soviet economic aid, and the friendly visits of Iranian and Soviet officials enhanced the prestige of the government and discouraged the Iranian opposition. Turkey also was promised Soviet economic aid, but the Cyprus dispute became a major cause of tension with the United States.

Turkey claimed the right to the full support of the United States on the Cyprus issue, but President Johnson indicated he did not feel that NATO guarantees would apply in the event of Soviet interventions on behalf of the Cyprus government of President Makarios. The mediation efforts of Cyrus Vance in the 1967 Turkish-Greek confrontation tended to restore the United States image in Turkey. United States bases and fleet visits to Turkey, however, were attacked by anti-American elements.

Both Iran and Turkey continued their association with the United States and the West. They were well aware of the long history of Russian ambitions and realized that the "era of good feelings" with the Soviet Union might be of limited duration. Both acted to take advantage of the Soviet Union's policy to obtain economic aid, as long as the Soviet Union was willing to give aid to states formally allied to the United States. Together with Pakistan, they worked within the Central Treaty Organization (CENTO) and through their own organization for Regional Cooperation and Development (RCD) to emphasize the economic-development aspects of their mutual alliance and ties to the United States and Britain.

A. IRAN

42. International Support for Iranian Independence: Declaration of the Three Powers Regarding Iran, December 1, 1943

The President of the United States, the Premier of the U. S. S. R., and the Prime Minister of the United Kingdom, having consulted with each other and with the Prime Minister of Iran, desire to declare the mutual agreement of their three Governments regarding their relations with Iran.

119

The Governments of the United States, the U. S. S. R., and the United Kingdom recognize the assistance which Iran has given in the prosecution of the war against the common enemy, particularly by facilitating the transportation of supplies from overseas to the Soviet Union.

The Three Governments realize that the war has caused special economic difficulties for Iran, and they are agreed that they will continue to make available to the Government of Iran such economic assistance as may be possible, having regard to the heavy demands made upon them by their world-wide military operation, and to the world-wide shortage of transport, raw materials, and supplies for civilian consumption.

With respect to the post-war period, the Governments of the United States, the U. S. S. R., and the United Kingdom are in accord with the Government of Iran that any economic problems confronting Iran at the close of hostilities should receive full consideration, along with those of other members of the United Nations, by conferences or international agencies held or created to deal with international economic matters.

The Governments of the United States, the U. S. S. R., and the United Kingdom are at one with the Government of Iran in their desire for the maintenance of the independence, sovereignty and territorial integrity of Iran. They count upon the participation of Iran, together with all other peace-loving nations, in the establishment of international peace, security and prosperity after the war, in accordance with the principles of the Atlantic Charter, to which all four Governments have subscribed.

WINSTON S. CHURCHILL
J. STALIN
FRANKLIN D. ROOSEVELT

43. United States Policy in Iran:
Remarks by Ambassador George V. Allen, February 4, 1948 [1]

I am particularly appreciative of the courtesy extended to me this evening by the distinguished members of the Iranian press. A free press is indispensable for the maintenance of democracy, since every totalitarian regime that I know anything about began by suppressing the opposition.

I had hoped to be able in this last meeting with you to confine my remarks to the subject of your great profession and to the field of cultural and educational exchange in which I shall be engaged upon my return to Washington. However the information carried during the past two days in the Iranian press concerning a communication which the Iranian Government has received alleging improper activities on the part of American advisers in Iran makes impossible for me to remain silent on this subject.

This communication as reported in the press seems an obvious attempt to exert influence on a matter now before the Iranian Majlis. Even if the allegations

---

[1] Delivered before the Teheran Press Club in Teheran on February 4 and released to the press in Washington on February 5, 1948. Department of State Bulletin of February 15, 1948, p. 223.

in the note were true, its delivery at this moment would constitute improper interference in the internal affairs of Iran and therefore be contrary to the dignity and independence of Iran as an equal member of the United Nations. But what makes the communication more objectionable in my view is that it includes not only misstatements of fact from start to finish but closes with an implied threat.

First and foremost, I wish to make entirely clear once more the attitude of the American Government with regard to American advisers here. We have frequently informed the Iranian Government during the past two years that American advisers in Iran will not remain here one minute longer than the Iranian Government feels they are able to perform a useful function in assisting Iran. The Iranian Government will experience no difficulty whatever in terminating the services of every one of the American advisers whenever they are no longer desired. The contracts providing for the two American military missions here are each cancelable on one month's notice by either party. The decision rests entirely in the hands of Iran.

I should also like to make our position unmistakably clear with regard to the proposed purchase of military supplies from the United States. The United States has no desire whatever to influence Iran concerning the manner in which it will spend its available funds. The funds are yours, and you must determine how you wish to allot them—whether for military supplies, farm machinery, schoolbooks, or anything else you need.

We are interested in two things. In the first place, we hope that Iran will spend what funds it has to the best possible advantage for Iran itself, because we are anxious for Iran to become strong and to remain independent. Our second and more important interest is that Iran should remain entirely free to make its own choice in this matter, unhampered by threats and menaces.

I recognize fully that an entirely honest division of opinion may exist among Iranians both as regards what military supplies you need and whether you desire American advisers. Whatever your decision may be, it will not affect in any way the friendly relations between Iran and the United States.

The communication which your Government has just received disturbs the calm atmosphere in which you will need to consider these important questions. I am confident that no self-respecting and patriotic Iranian will be deterred by this communication from doing his duty as he considers best. The allegations in the note are so clearly false that they do not require consideration in detail. I would merely ask: where are the plans for an American airport at Qum, where are the American storage tanks in southern Iran, the barracks being prepared for American troops, or any other of the things alleged in the note?

I am reminded in this connection that history repeats itself. There is considerable essential similarity between the present communication which your Government has received and one which was delivered to you in 1912 when Morgan Shuster was exerting every effort to assist Iran to become strong and independent of foreign domination. Fortunately, however, the world situation is vastly different today from what it was in 1912. Iran and all other independent countries of the world today are bound together in a world organization based on equality and respect for their sovereign independence. The entire structure of the United

Nations is built on the principle that no nation shall any longer have to stand alone as Iran did when it received the 1912 note.

I regret sincerely the injection of foreign interference in the question now before the Majlis, and I hope the deputies will consider the matter with appropriate calmness and dignity. The only important consideration is that the decision, whatever it may be, should be a free Iranian decision.

44. The Anglo-Iranian Oil Crisis: Impossibility of Increasing United States Economic Aid Pending a Settlement Message from President Eisenhower to Prime Minister Mossadegh, June 29, 1953

DEAR MR. PRIME MINISTER:

I have received your letter of May 28 in which you described the present difficult situation in Iran and expressed the hope that the United States might be able to assist Iran in' overcoming some of its difficulties. In writing my reply which has been delayed until I could have an opportunity to consult with Mr. Dulles and Ambassador [Loy] Henderson, I am motivated by the same spirit of friendly frankness as that which I find reflected in your letter.

The Government and people of the United States historically have cherished and still have deep feelings of friendliness for Iran and the Iranian people. They sincerely hope that Iran will be able to maintain its independence and that the Iranian people will be successful in realizing their national aspirations and in developing a contented and free nation which will contribute to world prosperity and peace.

It was primarily because of that hope that the United States Government during the last two years has made earnest efforts to assist in eliminating certain differences between Iran and the United Kingdom which have arisen as a result of the nationalization of the Iranian oil industry. It has been the belief of the United States that the reaching of an agreement in the matter of compensation would strengthen confidence throughout the world in the determination of Iran fully to adhere to the principles which render possible a harmonious community of free nations; that it would contribute to the strengthening of the international credit standing of Iran; and that it would lead to the solution of some of the financial and economic problems at present facing Iran.

The failure of Iran and of the United Kingdom to reach an agreement with regard to compensation has handicapped the Government of the United States in its efforts to help Iran. There is a strong feeling in the United States, even among American citizens most sympathetic to Iran and friendly to the Iranian people, that it would not be fair to the American taxpayers for the United States Government to extend any considerable amount of economic aid to Iran so long as Iran could have access to funds derived from the sale of its oil and oil products if a reasonable agreement were reached with regard to compensation whereby the large-scale marketing of Iranian oil would be resumed. Similarly, many American citizens would be deeply opposed to the purchase by the United States Government of Iranian oil in the absence of an oil settlement.

122

There is also considerable sentiment in the United States to the effect that a settlement based on the payment of compensation merely for losses of the physical assets of a firm which has been nationalized would not be what might be called a reasonable settlement and that an agreement to such a settlement might tend to weaken mutual trust between free nations engaged in friendly economic intercourse. Furthermore, many of my countrymen who have kept themselves informed regarding developments in this unfortunate dispute believe that, in view of the emotions which have been aroused both in Iran and the United Kingdom, efforts to determine by direct negotiation the amount of compensation due are more likely to increase friction than to promote understanding. They continue to adhere to the opinion that the most practicable and the fairest means of settling the question of compensation would be for that question to be referred to some neutral international body which could consider on the basis of merit all claims and counter-claims.

I fully understand that the Government of Iran must determine for itself which foreign and domestic policies are likely to be most advantageous to Iran and to the Iranian people. In what I have written, I am not trying to advise the Iranian Government on its best interests. I am merely trying to explain why, in the circumstances, the Government of the United States is not presently in a position to extend more aid to Iran or to purchase Iranian oil.

In case Iran should so desire, the United States Government hopes to be able to continue to extend technical assistance and military aid on a basis comparable to that given during the past year.

I note the concern reflected in your letter at the present dangerous situation in Iran and sincerely hope that before it is too late, the Government of Iran will take such steps as are in its power to prevent a further deterioration of that situation.

Please accept, Mr. Prime Minister, the renewed assurances of my highest consideration.

45. The Anglo-Iranian Oil Crisis: United States Gratification Over the Settlement, Message from President Eisenhower to the Shah of Iran, August 5, 1954

YOUR IMPERIAL MAJESTY: The important news that your Government, in negotiation with the British, French, Dutch and United States oil companies, has reached, in principle, a fair and equitable settlement to the difficult oil problem is indeed gratifying.

Your Majesty must take great satisfaction at the success of this significant phase in the negotiations to which you personally have made a valuable contribution. I am confident that implementation of this agreement, under Your Majesty's leadership, will mark the beginning of a new era of economic progress and stability for your country.

Like myself, all Americans have a deep concern for the well-being of Iran. With them I have watched closely your courageous efforts, your steadfastness over the past difficult years, and with them I too have hoped that you might achieve the goals you so earnestly desire. The attainment of an oil settlement along the lines which have been announced should be a significant step in the direction of the realization of your aspirations for your people.

There is concrete evidence of the friendship that exists between our two countries and of our desire that Iran prosper independently in the family of free nations. We have endeavored to be helpful in the form of economic and technical assistance and we are happy to have helped in finding a solution to the oil problem.

I can assure Your Majesty of the continued friendly interest of the United States in the welfare and progress of Iran, and of the admiration of the American people for your enlightened leadership.

With sincere best wishes for the health and happiness of Your Majesty and the people of Iran.

46. 'Soviet-Iranian Relations Are Developing Auspiciously': Joint Communique Issued at End of Visit of the Shah of Iran to the Soviet Union, July 3, 1965

His Majesty Shah Mohammed Reza Pahlevi of Iran and Her Majesty Queen Farah Pahlevi of Iran made an official visit to the U.S.S.R. from June 21 to July 3, 1965, at the invitation of the Presidium of the U.S.S.R. Supreme Soviet and the Soviet government.

During the visit in the Soviet Union, the Shah, the Queen and the persons who accompanied them visited—in addition to Moscow—Leningrad, Volgograd, Sverdlovsk, Irkutsk, Bratsk, the Baikal area, Simferopol and Yalta. In Moscow they visited the V. I. Lenin Mausoleum and laid a wreath. During the trip through the country Their Majesties had an opportunity to become acquainted with the life of the Soviet people and inspected a number of industrial enterprises and scientific and cultural institutions of the Soviet Union. The distinguished guests were given a warm reception, attesting to the friendly feelings of the Soviet people for the Iranian people.

Talks between the Shah of Iran and Soviet state leaders took place in Moscow. Participating in the talks for the Soviet side were L. I. Brezhnev, A. N. Kosygin and A. I. Mikoyan, N. G. Ignatov, Vice-Chairman of the Presidium of the U.S.S.R. Supreme Soviet; P. F. Lomako, Vice-Chairman of the U.S.S.R. Council of Ministers; A. A. Gromyko, U.S.S.R. Minister of Foreign Affairs; S. A. Skachkov, Chairman of the U.S.S.R. Council of Ministers' State Committee on Foreign Economic Relations; M. V. Zimyanin, U.S.S.R. Ambassador to Iran; G. T. Zaitsev, U.S.S.R. Ambassador to Iran; and S P. Kiktev, Chief of the Department of Middle Eastern Countries in the U.S.S.R. Ministry of Foreign Affairs.

Taking part in the talks along with the Shah of Iran were Abbas Aram, Iranian Foreign Minister; Amir Asadollah Alam, former Prime Minister and Rector of Pahlevi University; Mansur Ruhani, Minister of Water and Power; and Tahmuras Adamiyat, Iranian Ambassador to the Soviet Union.

During the talks, which proceeded in an atmosphere of mutual understanding and good will, a useful exchange of opinions on questions of further developing Soviet-Iranian relations and on certain international problems of interest to both states took place.

The talks showed that the sides have a common view regarding the need to promote in every possible way the establishment of lasting peace and the relief of international tension.

The sides jointly expressed the opinion that relations between states with different social systems must be built on the basis of principles of peaceful coexistence, which also conforms to the vital interests of the peoples of the Soviet Union and Iran.

They believe that the achievement of agreement on questions of general and complete disarmament under effective international control, including a ban on the use of atomic weapons, would play a decisive role in consolidating universal peace and would free considerable quantities of material resources for development of the countries that have recently embarked on a path of independent development.

Both sides attach great importance to strengthening the United Nations as an effective instrument for ensuring international peace and security on the basis of strict observance of the U.N. Charter.

The sides condemned colonialism in all its manifestations and persistently called for unequivocal fulfillment of the Declaration on the Granting of Independence to Colonial Countries and Peoples, adopted by the U.N. General Assembly on Dec. 14, 1960. They declared their support for countries and peoples engaged in struggle for their national liberation and political and economic independence.

The sides agreed that it is necessary to provide a just procedure in international economic relations that would give all countries the most favorable opportunities for the development of their economics. They called for the quickest possible fulfillment of the decisions of the U.N. Conference on Trade and Development and declared their support of useful steps for the purpose of enhancing the expansion of trade of developing nations.

Both sides noted with deep concern the serious deterioration of the situation in Southeast Asia and in certain other parts of the world. The sides set forth their points of view on this question, having agreed that all international issues must be resolved peaceably in accordance with the principles of the U.N. Charter.

After discussing the state of relations between the Soviet Union and Iran, the sides stated with satisfaction that Soviet-Iranian relations are developing auspiciously and that there is success in implementation of the agreement on economic and technical cooperation between the two countries, for which instruments of ratification were exchanged during the Shah's stay in Moscow.[1]

Both sides expressed readiness for further development of the friendly, neighborly relations between the two countries and for considerable expansion of

---

[1] An agreement was signed on June 25, during the Shah's visit, for construction of a dam along the Araxes River on the Soviet-Iranian border, in implementation of the economic and technical cooperation agreement between the two countries signed in July 1963. Subsequently, other agreements were reached, including one calling for construction by the Soviet Union of a steel mill in Iran.

economic, scientific-technical and cultural cooperation in the interests of both nations.

The sides also discussed questions of Soviet-Iranian trade, which has been carried out on the basis of the long-term agreement of June 20, 1964. They expressed the desire to use present possibilities for further developing mutually profitable trade.

The Iranian side expressed its satisfaction with the granting to Iran of extensive opportunities for the transit of Iranian goods through the territory of the Soviet Union, including the use of the Volgo-Balt waterway—the shortest transit route between Iran and a number of European ports.

In the interests of developing Soviet-Iranian contacts in the fields of culture, the arts and sports, it was agreed that within a very short time an agreement on cultural contacts between the two countries would be signed in Teheran.

The visit of the Shah of Iran to the Soviet Union and the exchange of opinions between the leaders of the Soviet Union and the Shah of Iran on questions of interest to both sides promotes the further strengthening of mutual understanding and neighborly relations between the two countries. The sides attach importance to the maintenance and development of personal contacts between the statesmen of the two countries.

B. TURKEY

47. The United States Position Regarding the Turkish Straits: Note from the American Ambassador to the Soviet Foreign Minister, October 9, 1946

I have the honor to inform Your Excellency that my Government has studied carefully the contents of the note of the Soviet Union to Turkey of September 24 relating to the regime of the Straits.

In pursuance of its policy of making clear to all interested parties its views on matters relating to the Straits, my Government has instructed me to inform you that after examining the note referred to above it continues to adhere to the position outlined in its note of August 19, 1946 to the Soviet Government.

It will be recalled that in the Protocol of the proceedings of the Potsdam Conference, signed by the U.S.S.R., Great Britain and the United States, the three Governments recognized that the Convention on the Straits concluded at Montreux should be revised as failing to meet present-day conditions. It was further agreed in the Protocol that as the next step the matter should be the subject of direct conversations between each of the three Governments and the Turkish Government.

It has been the understanding of my Government that the three Governments, in agreeing with one another that the regime of the Straits should be brought into accord with present-day conditions by means of a revision of the Montreux Convention, mutually recognized that all three signatories of the Protocol have an interest in the regime of the Straits and in any changes which might be made in that regime. My Government furthermore informed the Soviet Government in its note of August 19, that in its view the regime of the Straits is a matter of concern not only to the Black Sea powers but also to other powers, including the United States. The Soviet Government, nevertheless, in its note of September 24, apparently continues to take the position set forth in its note of August 7 to Turkey that "the establishment of a regime of the Straits . . . should come under the competence of Turkey and the other Black Sea powers." My Government does not consider that it was contemplated at the Potsdam Conference that the direct conversations which might take place between any one of the three signatory governments and the Turkish Government with regard to the regime of the Convention of the Straits concluded at Montreux should have the effect of prejudicing the participation of the other two signatory powers in the revision of the regime of the Straits. On the contrary, my Government considers that the Potsdam Agreement definitely contemplated only an exchange of views with the Turkish Government as a useful preliminary to a conference of all of the interested powers, including the United States, to consider the revision of the Montreux Convention. As stated in its note of August 19, my Government stands ready to participate in such a conference.

My Government also feels that it would be lacking in frankness if it should fail to point out again at this time, in the most friendly spirit, that in its opinion the Government of Turkey should continue to be primarily responsible for the defense of the Straits and that should the Straits become the object of attack or threat of attack by an aggressor, the resulting situation would be a matter for action on the part of the Security Council of the United Nations.

48. United States and Turkish Views on NATO Obligations and the Cyprus Crisis: Correspondence Between President Johnson and Prime Minister Inonu June 5 and 13, 1964

WHITE HOUSE STATEMENT

At the request of the Government of Turkey, the White House is today releasing the texts of letters exchanged on June 5, 1964, between President Johnson and the then Prime Minister of Turkey Ismet Inonu on the Cyprus crisis. Steps subsequent to this exchange of letters led to the visit of Prime Minister Inonu to Washington later in that month and constructive discussions by the President and the Prime Minister of the issues involved.

A joint communiqué released at the conclusion of those discussions welcomed the opportunity for a full exchange of views by the two leaders and the occasion to consider ways in which the two countries could strengthen the efforts of the United Nations with respect to the safety and security of Cyprus. The communiqué noted that "the cordial and candid conversations of the two leaders strengthened the broad understanding already existing between Turkey and the United States."

The United States continues to value highly the close and friendly relations we maintain with Turkey.

Dear Mr. Prime Minister:

I am gravely concerned by the information which I have had through Ambassador Hare from you and your Foreign Minister that the Turkish Government is contemplating a decision to intervene by military force to occupy a portion of Cyprus. I wish to emphasize, in the fullest friendship and frankness, that I do not consider that such a course of action by Turkey, fraught with such far-reaching consequences, is consistent with the commitment of your Government to consult fully in advance with us. Ambassador Hare has indicated that you have postponed your decision for a few hours in order to obtain my views. I put to you personally whether you really believe that it is appropriate for your Government, in effect, to present a unilateral decision of such consequence to an ally who has demonstrated such staunch support over the years as has the United States for Turkey. I must, therefore, first urge you to accept the responsibility for complete consultation with the United States before any such action is taken.

It is my impression that you believe that such intervention by Turkey is permissible under the provisions of the Treaty of Guarantee of 1960. I must call your attention, however, to our understanding that the proposed intervention by Turkey would be for the purpose of effecting a form of partition of the Island, a solution which is specifically excluded by the Treaty of Guarantee. Further, that Treaty requires consultation among the Guarantor Powers. It is the view of the United States that the possibilities of such consultation have by no means been exhausted in this situation and that, therefore, the reservation of the right to take unilateral action is not yet applicable.

I must call to your attention, also, Mr. Prime Minister, the obligations of NATO. There can be no question in your mind that a Turkish intervention in Cyprus would lead to a military engagement between Turkish and Greek forces. Secretary of State Rusk declared at the recent meeting of the Ministerial Council of NATO in The Hague that war between Turkey and Greece must be considered as "literally unthinkable." Adhesion to NATO, in its very essence, means that NATO countries will not wage war on each other. Germany and France have buried centuries of animosity and hostility in becoming NATO allies; nothing less can be expected from Greece and Turkey. Furthermore, a military intervention in Cyprus by Turkey could lead to a direct involvement by the Soviet Union. I hope you will understand that your NATO allies have not had a chance to consider whether they have an obligation to protect Turkey against the Soviet Union if Turkey takes a step which results in Soviet intervention without the full consent and understanding of its NATO Allies.

Further, Mr. Prime Minister, I am concerned about the obligations of Turkey as a member of the United Nations. The United Nations has provided forces on the Island to keep the peace. Their task has been difficult but, during the past several weeks, they have been progressively successful in reducing the incidents of violence on that Island. The United Nations Mediator has not yet completed his work. I have no doubt that the general membership of the United Nations would react in the strongest terms to unilateral action by Turkey which

128

would defy the efforts of the United Nations and destroy any prospect that the United Nations could assist in obtaining a reasonable and peaceful settlement of this difficult problem.

I wish also, Mr. Prime Minister, to call your attention to the bilateral agreement between the United States and Turkey in the field of military assistance. Under Article IV of the Agreement with Turkey of July 1947, your Government is required to obtain United States consent for the use of military assistance for purposes other than those for which such assistance was furnished. Your Government has on several occasions acknowledged to the United States that you fully understand this condition. I must tell you in all candor that the United States cannot agree to the use of any United States supplied military equipment for a Turkish intervention in Cyprus under present circumstances.

Moving to the practical results of the contemplated Turkish move, I feel obligated to call to your attention in the most friendly fashion the fact that such a Turkish move could lead to the slaughter of tens of thousands of Turkish Cypriots on the Island of Cyprus. Such an action on your part would unleash the furies and there is no way by which military action on your part could be sufficiently effective to prevent wholesale destruction of many of those whom you are trying to protect. The presence of United Nations forces could not prevent such a catastrophe.

You may consider that what I have said is much too severe and that we are disregardful of Turkish interests in the Cyprus situation. I should like to assure you that this is not the case. We have exerted ourselves both publicly and privately to assure the safety of Turkish Cypriots and to insist that a final solution of the Cyprus problem should rest upon the consent of the parties most directly concerned. It is possible that you feel in Ankara that the United States has not been sufficiently active in your behalf. But surely you know that our policy has caused the liveliest resentments in Athens (where demonstrations have been aimed against us) and has led to a basic alienation between the United States and Archbishop Makarios. As I said to your Foreign Minister in our conversation just a few weeks ago, we value very highly our relations with Turkey. We have considered you as a great ally with fundamental common interests. Your security and prosperity have been a deep concern of the American people and we have expressed that concern in the most practical terms. You and we have fought together to resist the ambitions of the Communist world revolution. This solidarity has meant a great deal to us and I would hope that it means a great deal to your Government and to your people. We have no intention of lending any support to any solution of Cyprus which endangers the Turkish Cypriot community. We have not been able to find a final solution because this is, admittedly, one of the most complex problems on earth. But I wish to assure you that we have been deeply concerned about the interests of Turkey and of the Turkish Cypriots and will remain so.

Finally, Mr. Prime Minister I must tell you that you have posed the gravest issues of war and peace. These are issues which go far beyond the bilateral relations between Turkey and the United States. They not only will certainly involve war between Turkey and Greece but could involve wider hostilities because of the

unpredictable consequences which a unilateral intervention in Cyprus could produce. You have your responsibilities as Chief of the Government of Turkey; I also
have mine as President of the United States. I must, therefore, inform you in the
deepest friendship that unless I can have your assurance that you will not take
such action without further and fullest consultation I cannot accept your injunction
to Ambassador Hare of secrecy and must immediately ask for emergency meetings
of the NATO Council and of the United Nations Security Council.

I wish it were possible for us to have a personal discussion of this situation.
Unfortunately, because of the special circumstances of our present Constitutional
position, I am not able to leave the United States. If you could come here for a
full discussion I would welcome it. I do feel that you and I carry a very heavy
responsibility for the general peace and for the possibilities of a sane and peaceful
resolution of the Cyprus problem. I ask you, therefore, to delay any decisions
which you and your colleagues might have in mind until you and I have had the
fullest and frankest consultation.

Sincerely,

LYNDON B. JOHNSON

PRIME MINISTER INONU'S RESPONSE TO THE PRESIDENT *June 13, 1964*

Dear Mr. President,

I have received your message of June 5, 1964 through Ambassador Hare. We
have, upon your request, postponed our decision to exercise our right of unilateral
action in Cyprus conferred to us by the Treaty of Guarantee. With due regard
to the spirit of candour and friendship in which your message is meant to be
written, I will, in my reply, try also to explain to you in full frankness my views
about the situation.

Mr. President,

Your message, both in wording and content has been disappointing for an ally
like Turkey who has always been giving the most serious attention to its relations
of alliance with the United States and has brought to the fore substantial divergences
of opinion in various fundamental matters pertaining to these relations.

It is my sincere hope that both these divergences and the general tone of your
message are due to the haste in which a representation made in good-will was,
under pressure of time, based on data hurriedly collected.

In the first place, it is being emphasized in your message that we have failed
to consult with the United States when a military intervention in Cyprus was
deemed indispensable by virtue of the Treaty of Guarantee. The necessity of a
military intervention in Cyprus has been felt four times since the closing days of
1963. From the outset we have taken a special care to consult the United States
on this matter. Soon after the outbreak of the crisis, on December 25, 1963, we
have immediately informed the United States of our contacts with the other
guaranteeing powers only to be answered that the United States was not a party

130

to this issue. We then negotiated with the United Kingdom and Greece for intervention and, as you know, a tri-partite military administration under British command was set-up on December 26, 1963. Upon the failure of the London conference and of the joint Anglo-American proposals, due to the attitude of Makarios and in the face of continuing assaults in the island against the Turkish Cypriots, we lived through very critical days in February and taking advantage of the visit of Mr. George Ball to Ankara, we informed again the United States of the gravity of the situation. We tried to explain to you that the necessity of intervention to restore order in the island might arise in view of the vacuum caused by the rejection of the Anglo-American proposals and we informed you that we might have to intervene at any time. We even requested guarantees from you on specific issues and your answers were in the affirmative. However, you asked us not to intervene and assured us that Makarios would get at the United Nations a severe lesson while all the Turkish rights and interests would be preserved.

We complied with your request without any satisfactory result being secured at the United Nations. Moreover the creation of the United Nations force, decided upon by the Security Council, became a problem. The necessity for intervention was felt for the third time to protect the Turkish community against the assaults of the terrorists in Cyprus who were encouraged by the doubts as to whether the United Nations forces would be set up immediately after the adoption of the Security Council resolution of March 4, 1964. But assuring us that the force would be set up very shortly, you insisted again that we refrain from intervening. Thereupon we postponed our intervention once again, awaiting the United Nations forces to assume their duty.

Dear Mr. President,

The era of terror in Cyprus has a particular character which rendered ineffective all measures taken so far. From the very outset, the negotiations held to restore security and the temporary set-ups have all helped only to increase the aggressiveness and the destructiveness of the Makarios administration. The Greek Cypriots have lately started to arm themselves overtly and considered the United Nations as an additional instrument to back up their ruthless and unconstitutional rule. It has become quite obvious that the United Nations have neither the authority nor the intent to intervene for the restoration of constitutional order and to put an end to aggression. You are well aware of the instigative attitude of the Greek Government towards the Greek Cypriots. During the talks held in your office, in the United States, we informed you that under the circumstances we would eventually be compelled to intervene in order to put an end to the atrocities in Cyprus. We also asked your Secretary of State at The Hague whether the United States would support us in such an eventuality and we received no answer. I think, I have thus reminded you how many times and under what circumstances we informed you of the necessity for intervention in Cyprus. I do remember having emphasized to your high level officials our due appreciation of the special responsibilities incumbent upon the United States within the alliance and of the necessity to be particularly careful and helpful to enable her to maintain solidarity within the alliance. As you see, we never had the intention to confront you with a unilateral decision on our part. Our grievance stems from our inability to explain to you a problem which caused us for months utmost distress and from your refusal to take a frank and firm stand on the issue as to which party is on the right side in the dispute between two allies, namely, Turkey and Greece.

Mr. President,

In your message you further emphasized the obligation of Turkey, under the provisions of the Treaty, to consult with the other two guaranteeing powers, before taking any unilateral action. Turkey is fully aware of this obligation. For the past six months we have indeed complied with the requirements of this obligation. But Greece has not only thwarted all the attempts made by Turkey to seek jointly the ways and means to stop Greek Cypriots from repudiating international treaties, but has also supported their unlawful and inhuman acts and has even encouraged them.

The Greek Government itself has not hesitated to declare publicly that the international agreements it signed with us were no longer in force. Various examples to that effect were, in due course, communicated in detail, orally and in writing, to your State Department.

We have likewise fulfilled our obligation of constant consultation with the Government of the United Kingdom, the other guaranteeing power.

In several instances we have, jointly with the Government of the United Kingdom, made representations to the Greek Cypriots with a view to restoring constitutional order. But unfortunately, these representations were of no avail due to the negative attitude of the Greek Cypriot authorities.

As you see, Turkey has earnestly explored every avenue of consulting continuously and acting jointly with the other two guaranteeing powers. This being the fact, it can not be asserted that Turkey has failed to abide by her obligation of consulting with the other two guaranteeing powers before taking unilateral action.

I put it to you, Mr. President, whether the United States Government which has felt the need to draw the attention of Turkey to her obligation of consultation, yet earnestly and faithfully fulfilled by the latter, should not have reminded Greece, who repudiates treaties signed by herself, of the necessity to abide by the precept "pacta sunt servanda" which is the fundamental rule of international law. This precept which, only a fortnight ago, was most eloquently characterized as "the basis of survival" by your Secretary of State himself in his speech at the "American Law Institute," is now being completely and contemptuously ignored by Greece, our NATO ally and by the Greek Cypriots.

Dear Mr. President,

As implied in your message, by virtue of the provisions of Article 4 of the Treaty of Guarantee, the three guaranteeing powers have, in the event of a breach of the provisions of that Treaty, the right to take concerted action and, if that proves impossible, unilateral action with the sole aim of re-establishing the state of affairs created by the said Treaty. The Treaty of Guarantee was signed with this understanding being shared by all parties thereto. The "Gentleman's Agree-

132

ment" signed on February 19, 1959 by the Foreign Ministers of Turkey and Greece, is an evidence of that common understanding.

On the other hand, at the time of the admission of the Republic of Cyprus to the United Nations, the members of the organization were fully acquainted with all the international commitments and obligations of the said Republic and no objections were raised in this respect.

Furthermore, in the course of the discussions on Cyprus leading to the resolution adopted on March 4, 1964 by the Security Council, the United States Delegate, among others, explicitly declared that the United Nations had no power to annul or amend international treaties.

The understanding expressed in your message that the intervention by Turkey in Cyprus would be for the purposes of effecting the partition of the island has caused me great surprise and profound sorrow. My surprise stems from the fact that the data furnished to you about the intentions of Turkey could be so remote from the realities repeatedly proclaimed by us. The reason of my sorrow is that our ally, the Government of the United States, could think that Turkey might lay aside the principle constituting the foundation of her foreign policy, i.e., absolute loyalty to international law, commitments and obligations, as factually evidenced in many circumstances well known to the United States.

I would like to assure you most categorically and most sincerely that if ever Turkey finds herself forced to intervene militarily in Cyprus this will be done in full conformity with the provisions and aims of international agreements.

In this connection, allow me to stress, Mr. President, that the postponement of our decision does naturally, in no way affect the rights conferred to Turkey by Article 4 of the Treaty of Guarantee.

Mr. President,

Referring to NATO obligations, you state in your message that the very essence of NATO requires that allies should not wage war on each other and that a Turkish intervention in Cyprus would lead to a military engagement between Turkish and Greek forces.

I am in full agreement with the first part of your statement, but the obligation for the NATO allies to respect international agreements concluded among themselves as well as their mutual treaty rights and commitments is an equally vital requisite of the alliance. An alliance among states which ignore their mutual contractual obligations and commitments is unthinkable.

As to the concern you expressed over the outbreak of a Turco-Greek war in case of Turkey's intervention in Cyprus in conformity with her rights and obligations stipulated in international agreements, I would like to stress that Turkey would undertake a "military operation" in Cyprus exclusively under the conditions and for the purpose set forth in the agreements. Therefore, a Turco-Greek war so properly described as "literally unthinkable" by the Honorable Dean Rusk could only occur in case of Greece's aggression against Turkey. Our view, in case of such an intervention, is to invite to an effective collaboration, with the aim of restoring the constitutional order in Cyprus, both Greece and the United Kingdom in their capacity as guaranteeing powers. If despite this invitation and its contractual obligations Greece were to attack Turkey, we could in no way be held responsible of the consequences of such an action. I would like to hope that you have already seriously drawn the Greek Government's attention on these matters.

The part of your message expressing doubts as to the obligation of the NATO allies to protect Turkey in case she becomes directly involved with the USSR as a result of an action intiated in Cyprus, gives me the impression that there are as between us wide divergence of views as to the nature and basic principles of the North Atlantic Alliance. I must confess that this has been to us the source of great sorrow and grave concern. Any aggression against a member of NATO will naturally call from the aggressor an effort of justification. If NATO's structure is so weak as to give credit to the aggressor's allegations, then it means that this defect of NATO needs really to be remedied. Our understanding is that the North Atlantic Treaty imposes upon all member states the obligation to come forthwith to the assistance of any member victim of an aggression. The only point left to the discretion of the member states is the nature and the scale of this assistance. If NATO members should start discussing the right and wrong of the situation of their fellow-member victim of a Soviet aggression, whether this aggression was provoked or not and if the decision on whether they have an obligation to assist the member should be made to depend on the issue of such a discussion, the very foundations of the Alliance would be shaken and it would lose its meaning. An obligation of assistance, if it is to carry any weight, should come into being immediately upon the observance of aggression. That is why Article 5 of the North Atlantic Treaty considers an attack against one of the member states as an attack against them all and makes it imperative for them to assist the party so attacked by taking forthwith such action as they deem necessary. In this connection I would like to further point out that the agreements on Cyprus have met with the approval of the North Atlantic Council, as early as the stage of the United Nations debate on the problem, i.e., even prior to the establishment of the Republic of Cyprus, hence long before the occurrence of the events of December 1963.

As you will recall, at the meeting of the NATO Ministerial Council held three weeks ago at The Hague, it was acknowledged that the treaties continued to be the basis for legality as regards the situation in the island and the status of Cyprus. The fact that these agreements have been violated as a result of the flagrantly unlawful acts of one of the parties on the island should in no way mean that the said agreements are no longer in force and that the rights and obligations of Turkey by virtue of those agreements should be ignored. Such an understanding would mean that as long as no difficulties arise, the agreements are considered as valid and they are no longer in force when difficulties occur. I am sure you will agree with me that such an understanding of law cannot be accepted. I am equally convinced that there could be no shadow of doubt about the obligation to protect Turkey within the NATO Alliance in a situation that can, by no means, be attributed to an arbitrary act of Turkey. An opposite way of thinking would lead to the repudiation and denial of the concept of law and of Article 51 of the United Nations Charter.

In your message, concern has been expressed about the commitments of Turkey as a member of the United Nations. I am sure, Mr. President, you will agree with me if I say that such a concern, which I do not share, is groundless especially for the following reasons: Turkey has distinguished herself as one of the most loyal members of the United Nations ever since its foundation. The Turkish people has spared no effort to safeguard the principles of the United Nations Charter, and has even sacrificed her sons for this cause. Turkey has never failed in supporting this organization and, in order to secure its proper functioning, has borne great moral and material sacrifices even when she had most pressing financial difficulties. Despite the explicit rights conferred to Turkey by the Treaty of Guarantee, my Government's respect for and adherence to the United Nations have recently been demonstrated once more by its acceptance of the Security Council resolution of March 4, 1964 as well as by the priority it has given to the said resolution.

Should the United Nations have been progressively successful in carrying out their task as pointed out in your message, a situation which is of such grave concern for both you and I, would never have arisen. It is a fact that the United Nations operations in the island have proved unable to put an end to the oppression.

The relative calm which has apparently prevailed in the island for the past few weeks marks the beginning of preparations of the Greek Cypriots for further tyranny. Villages are still under siege. The United Nations forces, assuaging Turkish Cypriots, enable the Greeks to gather their crops; but they do not try to stop the Greeks when the crops of Turks are at stake and they act as mere spectators to Greek assaults. These vitally important details may not well reach you, whereas we live in the atmosphere created by the daily reports of such tragic events.

The report of the Secretary-General will be submitted to the United Nations on June 15, 1964. I am seriously concerned that we may face yet another defeat similar to the one we all suffered on March 4, 1964. The session of March 4th had further convinced Makarios that the Treaty of Guarantee did not exist for him and thereupon he took the liberty of actually placing the United Nations forces under his control and direction. From then on the assassination of hostages and the besieging of villages have considerably increased.

Dear Mr. President,

Our allies who are in a position to arbiter in the Cyprus issue and to orient it in the right direction have so far been unable to disentangle the problem from a substantial error. The Cyprus tragedy has been engendered by the deliberate policy of the Republic of Cyprus aimed at annulling the treaties and abrogating the constitution. Security can be established in the island only through the proper functioning of an authority above the Government of Cyprus. Yet only the measures acceptable to the Cypriot Government are being sought to restore security in Cyprus. The British administration set up following the December events, the Anglo-American proposals and finally the United Nations command have all been founded on this unsound basis and consequently every measure acceptable to Makarios has proved futile and has, in general, encouraged oppression and aggression.

Dear Mr. President,

You put forward in your message the resentment caused in Greece by the policy pursued by your Government. Within the content of the Cyprus issues, the nature of the Greek policy and the course of action undertaken by Greece indicate that she is apt to resort to every means within her power to secure the complete annulment of the existing treaties. We are at pains to make our allies understand the sufferings we bear in our rightful cause and the irretrievable plight in which the Turkish Cypriots are living. On the other hand, it is not the character of our nation to exploit demonstrations of resentment. I assure you that our distress is deeply rooted since we can not make you understand our rightful position and convince you of the necessity of spending every effort and making use of all your authority to avert the perils inherent in the Cyprus problem by attaching to it the importance it well deserves.

That France and Germany have buried their animosity is indeed a good example. However, our nation had.already given such an example forty years ago by establishing friendly relations with Greece, right after the ruthless devastation of the whole Anatolia by the armies of that country.

Dear Mr. President,

As a member of the Alliance our nation is fully conscious of her duties and rights. We do not pursue any aim other than the settlement of the Cyprus problem in compliance with the provisions of the existing treaties. Such a settlement is likely to be reached if you lend your support and give effect with your supreme authority to the sense of justice inherent in the character of the American nation. Mr. President,

I thank you for your statement emphasizing the value attached by the United States to the relations of alliance with Turkey and for your kind words about the Turkish nation. I shall be happy to come to the United States to talk the Cyprus problem with you. The United Nations Security Council will meet on June the 17th. In the meantime, Mr. Dirk Stikker, Secretary General of NATO, will have paid a visit to Turkey. Furthermore, the United Nations mediator Mr. Tuomioja will have submitted his report to the Secretary-General. These developments may lead to the emergence of a new situation. It will be possible for me to go abroad to join you, at a date convenient for you, immediately after June 20th.

It will be most helpful for me if you would let me know of any defined views and designs you may have on the Cyprus question so that I may be able to study them thoroughly before my departure for Washington.

Finally, I would like to express my satisfaction for the frank, fruitful and promising talks we had with Mr. G. Ball in Ankara just before forwarding this message to you.

Sincerely,

ISMET INONU,
Prime Minister of Turkey.

C. EMPHASIS ON ECONOMIC DEVELOPMENT AND REGIONALISM

49. Regional Cooperation for Development: Joint Communique Issued by the Presidents of Pakistan and Turkey and the Shah of Iran, July 21, 1964

Document VII-7

The heads of state of Iran, Pakistan, and Turkey, Iran's Shah-in-Shah Mohammed Reza Shah Pahlavi, Pakistani President Field Marshall Mohammed Ayub Kahn, and Turkey President Cemal Gursel met in Istanbul on 20 and 21 July 1964. The heads of state reiterated their belief that regional cooperation is a basic factor in accelerating the pace of national development and contributing to peace and stability. They expressed the belief that the strong cultural and historic ties which link the peoples of their respective countries, and which already constitute a strong basis for cooperation, should be further reinforced in the common interests of all peoples of the region. For this purpose the heads of state have decided that all appropriate steps should be taken to further broaden and develop existing cooperation in all fields.

They unanimously expressed their belief that this new cooperation should be implemented in a spirit of regional cooperation without harming their existing activities within other regional organizations of which they are a member. The three countries will be pleased to study the participation of other countries in the region in this cooperation. The heads of state, who reviewed the practical measures taken in connection with cooperation among the three countries by their foreign ministers at the meeting held on 3 and 4 July 1964 in Ankara, expressing their great appreciation of the progress already achieved in this direction.

The heads of state declared that they support the proposals on common and regional interests drawn up on 18 and 19 July at the ministerial meeting in Ankara which preceded the three countries heads of state conference. They noted with [satisfaction?] the setting up of a ministerial council, composed of foreign ministers and other ministers of their governments, to adopt and implement appropriate decisions on matters of common interest. They noted with satisfaction the decision of their heads of government to set up a regional planning committee which will be composed of the heads of the planning organizations of the three countries, and which will work to harmonize regional cooperation and development projects. They agreed to make arrangements for a secretariat to assist the regional planning committee and the ministerial council.

Accord was reached in principle on the following points:

1—To promote free or freer exchange of goods through all kinds of practical means, such as the conclusion of trade agreements.

2—To establish closer cooperation between existing chambers of commerce and eventually to establish a joint chamber of commerce.

3—To implement projects with joint aims.

4—To reduce postal fees among the three countries to the level of domestic postal fees.

5—To develop air transport services within the region and eventually to set up a strong and competitive international air line establishment among the three countries.

6—To set up a joint marine transport establishment in the field of marine transport or to seek means of closer cooperation, including the holding of conferences.

7—To carry out the work necessary to construct and develop railway and highway links.

8—To conclude an agreement in the near future between the three countries for the development of tourism.

9—To abolish visa formalities on travel between the three countries.

10—To provide mutual technical aid in the procurement of experts and educational facilities.

The heads of state have also asked that all opportunities be sought to expand cultural development between the regional countries. The program on cultural relations, among other things, particularly proposes joint activities designed to create among the people of the region a desire to acquire a common heritage, to create seats in universities, to exchange students, to grant scholarships, to establish cultural centers, and to set up an institute to carry out studies and research on the common cultural heritage of the peoples in the region.

The activities falling within the scope of this cooperation will be carried out under the title "Regional Cooperation for Development." The heads of state have expressed the hope that the spirit of excellent harmony and regional solidarity, which from the start prevailed in the Istanbul talks, will insure the attainment of the objectives and aims declared at the conference. They are confident that the joint efforts which will be exerted by their peoples for this purpose will unfold before them new horizons of hope and new opportunities, and that in this way they will contribute to world peace and the prosperity of the whole region.

V.

The Palestine Problem
and
the Arab-Israeli Dispute

The second world war, which brought the United States so many new responsibilities in the area of mutual security in the Middle East, had no less a profound effect on United States policy in Palestine. As the British before them, United States policymakers were caught in the clash of competing nationalisms—Zionist and Arab—each claiming precisely the same territory. By 1939 the British had seen the importance of having Arab goodwill in the forthcoming war against the Axis. They agreed to the limitation of Jewish immigration and land purchases in Palestine. This would eventually have led to an independent Palestine with an Arab majority and a Jewish minority with guaranteed rights. On its part, the Zionist movement shifted its hopes from Britain to the United States, and in its "Biltmore Program" of 1942 demanded a fully sovereign Jewish state for all of Palestine (which still had a substantial Arab majority) instead of the Balfour Declaration's ambiguous formula of a Jewish national home in Palestine.

The United States attempted to find some mutually acceptable solution. This involved promises to the Arabs as well as pro-Zionist pressure on the British, who still exercised the mandatory power in Palestine, the mandate having been transferred from the League of Nations to the United Nations. During the course of the war President Roosevelt met with King Abdul Aziz Ibn Saud of Saudi Arabia on board an American warship in Egyptian waters. He expressed sympathy for the Arab position on the Palestine issue, and in one of his last letters reassured King Ibn Saud that the Arabs would be "fully consulted" prior to any solution of the Palestine question. However, with the conclusion of the war in Europe and the revelations of the magnitude of the Nazis' genocide of European Jews, the demand for unrestricted immigration of Jewish displaced persons to Palestine intensified and attracted the sympathy of American policymakers. The United States successfully pressed Britain to announce a special quota of 100,000 immigrants. Two Anglo-American groups investigated the problem, but no solution palatable to both Zionists and Arabs could be found.

In the meantime, anti-British agitation and terrorism by elements among the Zionists in Palestine increased daily. The British finally turned the whole problem over to the United Nations, announcing that regardless of the circumstances they would give up the mandate the following year (1948). The United Nations appointed a committee to suggest a solution, but even it could not reach agreement. Two plans were put forward. The majority plan provided for the partition of Palestine into Jewish and Arab states, together with an economic union and the internationalization of Jerusalem. The minority called for a single bi-national state with guarantees to protect the rights of the Jewish minority within Palestine. The majority report was strongly supported by the United States, which used its influence to get other United Nations members to back the plan. In the end, on November 29, 1947, the partition plan received the necessary two-thirds majority in the General Assembly. Both the United States and the Soviet Union favored it, while the British abstained.

The support of the United States did not, however, go to the length of supplying the military force necessary to impose this solution on Palestine. The Arabs made it clear that they would not accept the partition plan, especially as some areas of almost exclusive Arab population, such as the Negev, were assigned to the Jewish state. The United States knew that it would require either a large American army or an international force which would necessarily have to include Soviet troops to enforce the partition. The administration could accept neither of these alternatives. Before the termination of British rule the United States proposed a temporary United Nations trusteeship, but soon withdrew this plan under attack from both sides. When the mandate ended at midnight, May 14, 1948, both Arabs and Jews knew that the final shape of Palestine would be determined by force of arms.

The first Palestine war broke out even before the British left. There were confused guerrilla and terrorist attacks by both sides. Israel proclaimed its independence and the Arab states came to the aid of the Palestinian Arabs. The United States immediately recognized Israel's independence. The United Nations succeeded, after several attempts, in obtaining a series of armistice agreements between Israel and the Arab states signed on the island of Rhodes in 1949, but these did not lead to any formal peace. During the fighting Israel had succeeded in significantly enlarging her borders, but the Jordanians and Palestinians had held onto a substantial Arab territory in the center of the country.

The Palestine Conciliation Commission was created by the United Nations in an attempt to reach a permanent peace settlement. Its mandate established certain principles, such as the right of the Arab refugees to be repatriated or compensated and the international status of Jerusalem. These principles have continued to be a part of the position of the United Nations. The United Nations admitted Israel to membership, thus confirming her right to national existence. The right of unhindered passage for Israeli shipping through the Suez Canal was subsequently endorsed by the United Nations Security Council, but like the larger issue of a peaceful settlement this was not enforced.

The policy of the United States supported the efforts of the United Nations to reach a peace in the area. A major international effort to stabilize the territorial status quo achieved in the armistice agreements was made in 1950 through the Tripartite Declaration of the United States, Great Britain, and France. This declaration also called for the limitation of arms supplied to states in the area. The United States demonstrated its continuing support for the international status of Jerusalem by refusing to transfer its embassy in Israel from Tel Aviv when the Israelis moved their Foreign Ministry to Jerusalem.

The Tripartite Declaration of 1950 proved to be ineffective in stabilizing the Arab-Israeli dispute. This was partly because it did not include the Soviet Union, which became the major arms supplier to Egypt after 1955, and partly because Egypt supported anti-imperialist revolutions and nationalized the Suez Canal, which brought the interests of Britain and France into alignment with those of Israel in opposition to Egypt.

The Suez War of 1956 demonstrated that the United States was capable of taking a strong stand against the use of force to settle Middle Eastern problems, even when the use of force was initiated by Israel and by America's closest allies—Britain and France—against the far-from-friendly government of Egypt. Although Egyptian actions had been provocative and Egyptian relations with the Soviet Union had been close, the naked aggression by Washington's friends and allies was not condoned. The full extent of the prior collusion between Israel, France, and Britain was not known for several years, but the United States joined with the Soviet Union in condemning the attack.

After these strong pressures forced Britain, France, and Israel to end their campaign against Egypt, the United States and the United Nations became involved in the delicate task of eliminating the consequences of the war. The United Nations Emergency Force (UNEF) was created as a major instrument in international peace keeping to separate the combatants. The British and French soon withdrew their forces from the Canal Zone, but Israel refused to withdraw from all of the Sinai Peninsula and the Gaza Strip until she received adequate international guarantees of her security. Eventually, United States pressure on Israel, symbolized by the withdrawal of economic aid and coupled with American moves aimed at assuring the freedom of navigation of the Gulf of Aqaba, caused Israel to agree to withdraw her troops from Sinai and Gaza. However, Israeli Foreign Minister Golda Meir, in a speech to the General Assembly, clearly warned that any new attempt to close the Gulf of Aqaba would be regarded by Israel as an act of war.

Israel's compliance with the United Nations injunction to withdraw did not extend, however, to Israel's acceptance of the United Nations Emergency Force on her territory. Premier Ben-Gurion, in fact, made it clear in a speech to the Knesset that Israel would not tolerate the presence of any foreign troops on her soil. By contrast, Egypt accepted the UNEF, but there was question as to its permanent status. On one hand, Egypt was a sovereign state and United Nations troops could not remain on her territory against her desires. On the other hand, Secretary General Dag Hammarskjold evidently had reached a secret gentleman's agreement that Egypt would only ask for the withdrawal of the UNEF through the General Assembly and thus would avoid precipitate withdrawal.

Tensions between the Arab states and Israel were somewhat quiescent during the next few years. The Arabs were absorbed in their own disputes, and the UNEF acted as an effective buffer between the two major antagonists—Israel and the United Arab Republic. The United States, as indicated in the two statements of President Kennedy included in this collection, hoped that this status quo would continue. Washington opposed the upsetting of this balance, either by the introduction of nuclear weapons into the area or by the use of force on either side. United States policy supported the security of both Israel and her Arab neighbors.

The American position regarding the dispute between the Arabs and Israelis has not been as one-sided as some Arab sources have contended. The Suez war and its solution attested to this. The excerpt from a speech by Assistant Secretary of State Byroade, which aroused critical comment in Israeli and Zionist circles, gives a frank exposition of the United States finding that both parties were at fault for failing to reach a more permanent settlement. Byroade was particularly critical of the basic Zionist ideological view of Israel as the home for all the

143

world's Jews, a concept that the Arabs feel indicated Israeli expansionist aims. In an early example of an even-handed policy he also criticized the Arabs' refusal to give up their "belligerent rights" against Israel, despite their signing of formal armistice agreements.

A. THE PALESTINE PROBLEM

50. United States Attitude Toward the Palestine Problem: Letter From President Roosevelt to the King of Saudi Arabia April 5, 1945

GREAT AND GOOD FRIEND:

I have received the communication which Your Majesty sent me under date of March 10, 1945, in which you refer to the question of Palestine and to the continuing interest of the Arabs in current developments affecting that country.

I am gratified that Your Majesty took this occasion to bring your views on this question to my attention and I have given the most careful attention to the statements which you make in your letter. I am also mindful of the memorable conversation which we had not so long ago and in the course of which I had an opportunity to obtain so vivid an impression of Your Majesty's sentiments on this question.

Your Majesty will recall that on previous occasions I communicated to you the attitude of the American Government toward Palestine and made clear our desire that no decision be taken with respect to the basic situation in that country without full consultation with both Arabs and Jews. Your Majesty will also doubtless recall that during our recent conversation I assured you that I would take no action in my capacity as Chief of the Executive Branch of this Government which might prove hostile to the Arab people.

It gives me pleasure to renew to Your Majesty the assurances which you have previously received regarding the attitude of my Government and my own, as Chief Executive, with regard to the question of Palestine and to inform you that the policy of this Government in this subject is unchanged.

I desire also at this time to send you my best wishes for Your Majesty's continued good health and for the welfare of your people.

Your Good Friend,

FRANKLIN D. ROOSEVELT

His Majesty

ABDUL AZIZ IBN ABDUR RAHMAN AL FAISAL AL SAUD
King of Saudi Arabia
Riyadh

51. The Partition of Palestine: Resolution of the United Nations General Assembly (excerpts), November 29, 1947

At the 128th plenary meeting of the General Assembly on 29 November 1947, the General Assembly considered the report of the *ad hoc* Committee and adopted the resolution on the future government of Palestine by thirty-three votes in favour, thirteen against, with ten abstentions, as follows:

In favour: Australia, Belgium, Bolivia, Brazil, Byelorussian Soviet Socialist Republic, Canada, Costa Rica, Czechoslovakia, Denmark, Dominican Republic, Ecuador, France, Guatemala, Haiti, Iceland, Liberia, Luxembourg, Netherlands, New Zealand, Nicaragua, Norway, Panama, Paraguay, Peru, Philippines, Poland, Sweden, Ukraian Soviet Socialist Republic, Union of South Africa, Union of Soviet Socialist Republics, United States of America, Uruguay, Venezuela.

Against: Afghanistan, Cuba, Egypt, Greece, India, Iran, Iraq, Lebanon, Pakistan, Saudi Arabia, Syria, Turkey, Yemen.

Abstained: Argentina, Chile, China, Colombia, El Salvador, Ethiopia, Honduras, Mexico, United Kingdom, Yugoslavia.

At the same meeting the General Assembly elected Bolivia, Czechoslovakia, Denmark, Panama and the Philippines as members of the United Nations Palestine Commission charged with implementing the resolution. It also authorized the Secretary-General to draw from the Working Capital Fund a sum not to exceed $2,000,000 for the purposes set forth in the last paragraph of the resolution on the future government of Palestine.

RESOLUTION ADOPTED ON THE REPORT OF THE AD HOC COMMITTEE ON THE PALESTINIAN QUESTION

A

The General Assembly,

Having met in special session at the request of the mandatory Power to constitute and instruct a special committee to prepare for the consideration of the question of the future government of Palestine at the second regular session;

Having constituted a Special Committee and instructed it to investigate all questions and issues relevant to the problem of Palestine, and to prepare proposals for the solution of the problem, and

Having received and examined the report of the Special Committee (document A/364)[1] including a number of unanimous recommendations and a plan of partition with economic union approved by the majority of the Special Committee,

Considers that the present situation in Palestine is one which is likely to impair the general welfare and friendly relations among nations;

Takes note of the declaration by the mandatory Power that it plans to complete its evacuation of Palestine by 1 August 1948;

Recommends to the United Kingdom, as the mandatory Power for Palestine, and to all other Members of the United Nations the adoption and implementation, with regard to the future government of Palestine, of the Plan of Partition with Economic Union set out below;

Requests that

(*a*) The Security Council take the necessary measures as provided for in the plan for its implementation;

---

[1] See *Official Records of the second session of the General Assembly,* Supplement No. 11, Volumes I-IV.

(*b*) The Security Council consider, if circumstances during the transitional period require such consideration, whether the situation in Palestine constitutes a threat to the peace. If it decides that such a threat exists, and in order to maintain international peace and security, the Security Council should supplement the authorization of the General Assembly by taking measures, under Articles 39 and 41 of the Charter, to empower the United Nations Commission, as provided in this resolution, to exercise in Palestine the functions which are assigned to it by this resolution;

(*c*) The Security Council determine as a threat to the peace, breach of the peace or act of aggression, in accordance with Article 39 of the Charter, any attempt to alter by force the settlement envisaged by this resolution;

(*d*) The Trusteeship Council be informed of the responsibilities envisaged for it in this plan;

Calls upon the inhabitants of Palestine to take such steps as may be necessary on their part to put this plan into effect;

Appeals to all Governments and all peoples to refrain from taking any action which might hamper or delay the carrying out of these recommendations, and

Authorizes the Secretary-General to reimburse travel and subsistence expenses of the members of the Commission referred to in Part I, Section B, paragraph 1 below, on such basis and in such form as he may determine most appropriate in the circumstances, and to provide the Commission with the necessary staff to assist in carrying out the functions assigned to the Commission by the General Assembly.

B [2]

The General Assembly

Authorizes the Secretary-General to draw from the Working Capital Fund a sum not to exceed $2,000,000 for the purposes set forth in the last paragraph of the resolution on the future government of Palestine.

PLAN OF PARTITION WITH ECONOMIC UNION

PART I

FUTURE CONSTITUTION AND GOVERNMENT OF PALESTINE

A. Termination of Mandate Partition and Independence

1. The Mandate for Palestine shall terminate as soon as possible but in any case not later than 1 August 1948.

2. The armed forces of the mandatory Power shall be progressively withdrawn from Palestine, the withdrawal to be completed as soon as possible but in any case not later than 1 August 1948.

The mandatory Power shall advise the Commission, as far in advance as possible, of its intention to terminate the Mandate and to evacuate each area.

The mandatory Power shall use its best endeavours to ensure that an area situated in the territory of the Jewish State, including a seaport and hinterland

---

[2] This resolution was adopted without reference to a Committee.

adequate to provide facilities for a substantial immigration, shall be evacuated at the earliest possible date and in any event not later than 1 February 1948.

3. Independent Arab and Jewish States and the Special International Regime for the City of Jerusalem, set forth in part III of this plan, shall come into existence in Palestine two months after the evacuation of the armed forces of the mandatory Power has been completed but in any case not later than 1 October 1948. The boundaries of the Arab State, the Jewish State, and the City of Jerusalem shall be as described in parts II and III below.

4. The period between the adoption by the General Assembly of its recommendation on the question of Palestine and the establishment of the independence of the Arab and Jewish States shall be a transitional period.

B. *Steps Preparatory to Independence*

1. A Commission shall be set up consisting of one representative of each of five Member States. The Members represented on the Commission shall be elected by the General Assembly on as broad a basis, geographically and otherwise, as possible.

2. The administration of Palestine shall, as the mandatory Power withdraws its armed forces, be progressively turned over to the Commission, which shall act in conformity with the recommendations of the General Assembly, under the guidance of the Security Council. The mandatory Power shall to the fullest possible extent co-ordinate its plans for withdrawal with the plans of the Commission to take over and administer areas which have been evacuated.

In the discharge of this administrative responsibility the Commission shall have authority to issue necessary regulations and take other measures as required.

The mandatory Power shall not take any action to prevent, obstruct or delay the implementation by the Commission of the measures recommended by the General Assembly.

3. On its arrival in Palestine the Commission shall proceed to carry out measures for the establishment of the frontiers of the Arab and Jewish States and the City of Jerusalem in accordance with the general lines of the recommendations of the General Assembly on the partition of Palestine. Nevertheless, the boundaries as described in part II of this plan are to be modified in such a way that village areas as a rule will not be divided by state boundaries unless pressing reasons make that necessary.

4. The Commission, after consultation with the democratic parties and other public organizations of the Arab and Jewish States, shall select and establish in each State as rapidly as possible a Provisional Council of Government. The activities of both the Arab and Jewish Provisional Councils of Government shall be carried out under the general direction of the Commission.

If by 1 April 1948 a Provisional Council of Government cannot be selected for either of the States, or, if selected, cannot carry out its functions, the Commission shall communicate that fact to the Security Council for such action with respect to that State as the Security Council may deem proper, and to the Secretary-General for communication to the Members of the United Nations.

5. Subject to the provisions of these recommendations, during the transitional period the Provisional Councils of Government, acting under the Commission, shall have full authority in the areas under their control, including authority over matters of immigration and land regulation.

6. The Provisional Council of Government of each State, acting under the Commission, shall progressively receive from the Commission full responsibility for the administration of that State in the period between the termination of the Mandate and the establishment of the State's independence.

7. The Commission shall instruct the Provisional Councils of Government of both the Arab and Jewish States, after their formation, to proceed to the establishment of administrative organs of government, central and local.

8. The Provisional Council of Government of each State shall, within the shortest time possible, recruit an armed militia from the residents of that State, sufficient in number to maintain internal order and to prevent frontier clashes.

This armed militia in each State shall, for operational purposes, be under the command of Jewish or Arab officers resident in that State, but general political and military control, including the choice of the militia's High Command, shall be exercised by the Commission.

9. The Provisional Council of Government of each State shall, not later than two months after the withdrawal of the armed forces of the mandatory Power, hold elections to the Constituent Assembly which shall be conducted on democratic lines.

The election regulations in each State shall be drawn up by the Provisional Council of Government and approved by the Commission. Qualified voters for each State for this election shall be persons over eighteen years of age who are: (a) Palestinian citizens residing in that State and (b) Arabs and Jews residing in the State, although not Palestinian citizens, who, before voting, have signed a notice of intention to become citizens of such State.

Arabs and Jews residing in the City of Jerusalem who have signed a notice of intention to become citizens, the Arabs of the Arab State and the Jews of the Jewish State, shall be entitled to vote in the Arab and Jewish States respectively.

Women may vote and be elected to the Constituent Assemblies.

During the transitional period no Jew shall be permitted to establish residence in the area of the proposed Arab State, and no Arab shall be permitted to establish residence in the area of the proposed Jewish State, except by special leave of the Commission.

10. The Constituent Assembly of each State shall draft a democratic constitution for its State and choose a provisional government to succeed the Provisional Council of Government appointed by the Commission. The constitutions of the States shall embody chapters 1 and 2 of the Declaration provided for in section C below and include *inter alia* provisions for:

> (a) Establishing in each State a legislative body elected by universal suffrage and by secret ballot on the basis of proportional representation, and an executive body responsible to the legislature;

(*b*) Settling all international disputes in which the State may be involved by peaceful means in such a manner that international peace and security, and justice, are not endangered;

(*c*) Accepting the obligation of the State to refrain in its international relations from the threat or use of force against the territorial integrity or political independence of any State, or in any other manner inconsistent with the purposes of the United Nations;

(*d*) Guaranteeing to all persons equal and nondiscriminatory rights in civil, political, economic and religious matters and the enjoyment of human rights and fundamental freedoms, including freedom of religion, language, speech and publication, education, assembly and association;

(*e*) Preserving freedom of transit and visit for all residents and citizens of the other State in Palestine and the City of Jerusalem, subject to considerations of national security, provided that each State shall control residence within its borders.

11. The Commission shall appoint a preparatory economic commission of three members to make whatever arrangements are possible for economic co-operation, with a view to establishing, as soon as practicable, the Economic Union and the Joint Economic Board, as provided in section D below.

12. During the period between the adoption of the recommendations on the question of Palestine by the General Assembly and the termination of the Mandate, the mandatory Power in Palestine shall maintain full responsibility for administration in areas from which it has not withdrawn its armed forces. The Commission shall assist the mandatory Power in the Carrying out of these functions. Similarly the mandatory Power shall co-operate with the Commission in the execution of its functions.

13. With a view to ensuring that there shall be continuity in the functioning of administrative services and that, on the withdrawal of the armed forces of the mandatory Power, the whole administration shall be in the charge of the Provisional Councils and the Joint Economic Board, respectively, acting under the Commission, there shall be a progressive transfer, from the mandatory Power of the Commission, of responsibility for all the functions of government, including that of maintaining law and order in the areas from which the forces of the mandatory Power have been withdrawn.

14. The Commission shall be guided in its activities by the recommendations of the General Assembly and by such instructions as the Security Council may consider necessary to issue.

The measures taken by the Commission, within the recommendations of the General Assembly, shall become immediately effective unless the Commission has previously received contrary instructions from the Security Council.

The Commission shall render periodic monthly progress reports, or more frequently if desirable, to the Security Council.

15. The Commission shall make its final report to the next regular session of the General Assembly and to the Security Council simultaneously.

C. Declaration

A declaration shall be made to the United Nations by the provisional government of each proposed State before independence. It shall contain *inter alia* the following clauses:

General provision

The stipulations contained in the declaration are recognized as fundamental laws of the State and no law, regulation or official action shall conflict or interfere with these stipulations, nor shall any law, regulation or official action prevail over them.

CHAPTER 1

Holy Places, religious buildings and sites

1. Existing rights in respect of Holy Places and religious buildings or sites shall not be denied or impaired.

2. In so far as Holy Places are concerned, the liberty of access, visit and transit shall be guaranteed, in conformity with existing rights, to all residents and citizens of the other State and of the City of Jerusalem, as well as to aliens, without distinction as to nationality, subject to requirements of national security, public order and decorum.

Similarly, freedom of worship shall be guaranteed in conformity with existing rights, subject to the maintenance of public order and decorum.

3. Holy Places and religious buildings or sites shall be preserved. No act shall be permitted which may in any way impair their sacred character. If at any time it appears to the Government that any particular Holy Place, religious building or site is in need of urgent repair, the Government may call upon the community or communities concerned to carry out such repair. The Government may carry it out itself at the expense of the community or communities concerned if no action is taken within a reasonable time.

4. No taxation shall be levied in respect to any Holy Place, religious building or site which was exempt from taxation on the date of the creation of the State.

No change in the incidence of such taxation shall be made which would either discriminate between the owners or occupiers of Holy Places, religious buildings or sites, or would place such owners or occupiers in a position less favourable in relation to the general incidence of taxation than existed at the time of the adoption of the Assembly's recommendations.

5. The Governor of the City of Jerusalem shall have the right to determine whether the provisions of the Constitution of the State in relation to Holy Places, religious buildings and sites within the borders or the State and the religious rights appertaining thereto, are being properly applied and respected, and to make decisions on the basis of existing rights in cases of disputes which may arise between the different religious communities or the rites of a religious community with repect to such places, buildings and sites. He shall receive full cooperation and such privileges and immunities as are necessary for the exercise of his functions in the State.

CHAPTER 2

Religious and minority rights

1. Freedom of conscience and the free exercise of all forms of worship, subject only to the maintenance of public order and morals, shall be ensured to all.

2. No discrimination of any kind shall be made between the inhabitants on the ground of race, religion, language or sex.

3. All persons within the jurisdiction of the State shall be entitled to equal protection of the laws.

4. The family law and personal status of the various minorities and their religious interests, including endowments, shall be respected.

5. Except as may be required for the maintenance of public order and good government, no measure shall be taken to obstruct or interfere with the enterprise of religious or charitable bodies of all faiths or to discriminate against any representative or member of these bodies on the ground of his religion or nationality.

6. The State shall ensure adequate primary and secondary education for the Arab and Jewish minority, respectively, in its own language and its cultural traditions.

The right of each community to maintain its own schools for the education of its own members in its own language, while conforming to such educational requirements of a general nature as the State may impose, shall not be denied or impaired. Foreign educational establishments shall continue their activity on the basis of their existing rights.

7. No restriction shall be imposed on the free use by any citizen of the State of any language in private intercourse, in commerce, in religion, in the Press or in publications of any kind, or at public meetings.[3]

8. No expropriation of land owned by an Arab in the Jewish State (by a Jew in the Arab State)[4] shall be allowed except for public purposes. In all cases of expropriation full compensation as fixed by the Supreme Court shall be paid previous to dispossession.

CHAPTER 3

Citizenship, international conventions and financial obligations

1. *Citizenship.* Palestinian citizens residing in Palestine outside the City of Jerusalem, as well as Arabs and Jews who, not holding Palestinian citizenship, reside in Palestine outside the City of Jerusalem shall, upon the recognition of independence, become citizens of the State in which they are resident and enjoy full civil and political rights. Persons over the age of eighteen years may opt, within one year from the date of recognition of independence of the State in which they reside, for citizenship of the other State, providing that no Arab residing in the

---

[3] The following stipulation shall be added to the declaration concerning the Jewish State: "In the Jewish State adequate facilities shall be given to Arabic-speaking citizens for the use of their language, either orally or in writing, in the legislature, before the Courts and in the Administration."

[4] In the declaration concerning the Arab State, the words "by an Arab in the Jewish State" should be replaced by the words "by a Jew in the Arab State."

proposed Arab State shall have the right to opt for citizenship in the proposed Jewish State and no Jew residing in the proposed Jewish State shall have the right to opt for citizenship in the proposed Arab State. The exercise of this right of option will be taken to include the wives and children under eighteen years of age of persons so opting.

Arabs residing in the area of the proposed Jewish State and Jews residing in the area of the proposed Arab State who have signed a notice of intention to opt for citizenship of the other State shall be eligible to vote in the elections to the Constituent Assembly of that State, but not in the elections to the Constituent Assembly of the State in which they reside.

2. *International conventions.* (*a*) The State shall be bound by all the international agreements and conventions, both general and special, to which Palestine has become a party. Subject to any right of denunciation provided for therein, such agreements and conventions shall be respected by the State throughout the period for which they were concluded.

(*b*) Any dispute about the applicability and continued validity of international conventions or treaties signed or adhered to by the mandatory Power on behalf of Palestine shall be referred to the International Court of Justice in accordance with the provisions of the Statute of the Court.

3. *Financial obligations.* (*a*) The State shall respect and fulfill all financial obligations of whatever nature assumed on behalf of Palestine by the mandatory Power during the exercise of the Mandate and recognized by the State. This provision includes the right of public servants to pensions, compensations or gratuities.

(*b*) These obligations shall be fulfilled through participation in the Joint Economic Board in respect of those obligations applicable to Palestine as a whole, and individually in respect of those applicable to, and fairly apportionable between, the States.

(*c*) A Court of Claims, affiliated with the Joint Economic Board, and composed of one member appointed by the United Nations, one representative of the United Kingdom and one· representative of the State concerned, should be established. Any dispute between the United Kingdom and the State respecting claims not recognized by the latter should be referred to that Court.

(*d*) Commercial concessions granted in respect of any part of Palestine prior to the adoption of the resolution by the General Assembly shall continue to be valid according to their terms, unless modified by agreement between the concession-holder and the State.

CHAPTER 4

Miscellaneous provisions

1. The provisions of chapters 1 and 2 of the declaration shall be under the guarantee of the United Nations, and no modifications shall be made in them without the assent of the General Assembly of the United Nations. Any Member of the United Nations shall have the right to bring to the attention of the General

Assembly any infraction or danger of infraction of any of these stipulations, and the General Assembly may thereupon make such recommendations as it may deem proper in the circumstances.

2. Any dispute relating to the application or the interpretation of this declaration shall be referred, at the request of either party, to the International Court of Justice, unless the parties agree to another mode of settlement.

D. Economic Union and Transit

1. The Provisional Council of Government of each State shall enter into an undertaking with respect to Economic Union and Transit. This undertaking shall be drafted by the Commission provided for in section B, paragraph 1, utilizing to the greatest possible extent the advice and co-operation of representative organizations and bodies from each of the proposed States. It shall contain provisions to establish the Economic Union of Palestine and provide for other matters of common interest. If by 1 April 1948 the Provisional Councils of Government have not entered into the undertaking, the undertaking shall be put into force by the Commission.

The Economic Union of Palestine

2. The objectives of the Economic Union of Palestine shall be:

(*a*) A customs union;

(*b*) A joint currency system providing for a single foreign exchange rate;

(*c*) Operation in the common interest on a non-discriminatory basis of railways; inter-State highways; postal, telephone and telegraphic services, and ports and airports involved in international trade and commerce;

(*d*) Joint economic development, especially in respect of irrigation, land reclamation and soil conservation;

(*e*) Access for both States, and for the City of Jerusalem on a non-discriminatory basis to water and power facilities.

3. There shall be established a Joint Economic Board, which shall consist of three representatives of each of the two States and three foreign members appointed by the Economic and Social Council of the United Nations. The foreign members shall be appointed in the first instance for a term of three years; they shall serve as individuals and not as representatives of States.

4. The functions of the Joint Economic Board shall be to implement either directly or by delegation the measures necessary to realize the objectives of the Economic Union. It shall have all powers of organization and administration necessary to fulfill its functions.

5. The States shall bind themselves to put into effect the decisions of the Joint Economic Board. The Board's decisions shall be taken by a majority vote.

6. In the event of failure of a State to take the necessary action the Board may, by a vote of six members, decide to withhold an appropriate portion of that part of the customs revenue to which the State in question is entitled under the Economic Union. Should the State persist in its failure to cooperate, the Board may decide by a simple majority vote upon such further sanctions, including disposition of funds which it has withheld, as it may deem appropriate.

7. In relation to economic development, the functions of the Board shall be the planning, investigation and encouragement of joint development projects, but it shall not undertake such projects except with the assent of both States and the City of Jerusalem, in the event that Jerusalem is directly involved in the development project.

8. In regard to the joint currency system the currencies circulating in the two States and the City of Jerusalem shall be issued under the authority of the Joint Economic Board, which shall be the sole issuing authority and which shall determine the reserves to be held against such currencies.

9. So far as is consistent with paragraph 2(b) above, each State may operate its own central bank, control its own fiscal and credit policy, its foreign exchange receipts and expenditures, the grant of import licenses, and may conduct international financial operations on its own faith and credit. During the first two years after the termination of the Mandate, the Joint Economic Board shall have the authority to take such measures as may be necessary to ensure that—to the extent that the total foreign exchange revenues of the two States from the export of goods and services permit, and provided that each State takes appropriate measures to conserve its own foreign exchange resources—each State shall have available, in any twelve months' period, foreign exchange sufficient to assure the supply of quantities of imported goods and services for consumption in its territory equivalent to the quantities of such goods and services consumed in that territory in the twelve months' period ending 31 December 1947.

10. All economic authority not specifically vested in the Joint Economic Board is reserved to each State.

11. There shall be a common customs tariff with complete freedom of trade between the States, and between the States and the City of Jerusalem.

12. The tariff schedules shall be drawn up by a Tariff Commission, consisting of representatives of each of the States in equal numbers, and shall be submitted to the Joint Economic Board for approval by a majority vote. In case of disagreement in the Tariff Commission, the Joint Economic Board shall arbitrate the points of difference. In the event that the Tariff Commission fails to draw up any schedule by a date to be fixed, the Joint Economic Board shall determine the tariff schedule.

13. The following items shall be a first charge on the customs and other common revenue of the Joint Economic Board:

(a) The expenses of the customs service and of the operation of the joint services;

(b) The administrative expenses of the Joint Economic Board;

(c) The financial obligations of the Administration of Palestine consisting of:

(i) The service of the outstanding public debt;

(ii) The cost of superannuation benefits, now being paid or falling due in the future, in accordance with the rules and to the extent established by paragraph 3 of chapter 3 above.

14. After these obligations have been met in full, the surplus revenue from the customs and other services shall be divided in the following manner: not less than 5 per cent and not more than 10 per cent to the City of Jerusalem; the residue shall be allocated to each State by the Joint Economic Board equitably, with the objective of maintaining a sufficient and suitable level of government and social services in each State, except that the share of either State shall not exceed the amount of that State's contribution to the revenues of the Economic Union by more than approximately four million pounds in any year. The amount granted may be adjusted by the Board according to the price level in relation to the prices prevailing at the time of the establishment of the Union. After five years, the principles of the distribution of the joint revenues may be revised by the Joint Economic Board on a basis of equity.

15. All international conventions and treaties affecting customs tariff rates, and those communications services under the jurisdiction of the Joint Economic Board, shall be entered into by both States. In these matters, the two States shall be bound to act in accordance with the majority vote of the Joint Economic Board.

16. The Joint Economic Board shall endeavour to secure for Palestine's exports fair and equal access to world markets.

17. All enterprises operated by the Joint Economic Board shall pay fair wages on a uniform basis.

Freedom of transit and visit

18. The undertaking shall contain provisions preserving freedom of transit and visit for all residents or citizens of both States and of the City of Jerusalem, subject to security considerations; provided that each State and the City shall control residence within its borders.

Termination, modification and interpretation of the undertaking

19. The undertaking and any treaty issuing therefrom shall remain in force for a period of ten years. It shall continue in force until notice of termination, to take effect two years thereafter, is given by either of the parties.

20. During the initial ten-year period, the undertaking and any treaty issuing therefrom may not be modified except by consent of both parties and with the approval of the General Assembly.

21. Any dispute relating to the application or the interpretation of the undertaking and any treaty issuing therefrom shall be referred, at the request of either party, to the International Court of Justice, unless the parties agree to another mode of settlement.

E. *Assets*

1. The movable assets of the Administration of Palestine shall be allocated to the Arab and Jewish States and the City of Jerusalem on an equitable basis. Allocations should be made by the United Nations Commission referred to in section B, paragraph 1, above. Immovable assets shall become the property of the government of the territory in which they are situated.

2. During the period between the appointment of the United Nations Commis-

sion and the termination of the Mandate, the mandatory Power shall, except in respect of ordinary operations, consult with the Commission on any measure which it may contemplate involving the liquidation, disposal or encumbering of the assets of the Palestine Government, such as the accumulated treasury surplus, the proceeds of Government bond issues, State lands or any other asset.

F. *Admission to membership in the United Nations*

When the independence of either the Arab or the Jewish State as envisaged in this plan has become effective and the declaration and undertaking, as envisaged in this plan, have been signed by either of them, sympathetic consideration should be given to its application for admission to membership in the United Nations in accordance with Article 4 of the Charter of the United Nations.

*   *   *

PART III

CITY OF JERUSALEM

A. *Special Regime*

The City of Jerusalem shall be established as a *corpus separatum* under a special international regime and shall be administered by the United Nations. The Trusteeship Council shall be designated to discharge the responsibilities of the Administering Authority on behalf of the United Nations.

B. *Boundaries of the City*

The City of Jerusalem shall include the present municipality of Jerusalem plus the surrounding villages and towns, the most eastern of which shall be Abu Dis; the most southern, Bethlehem; the most western, Ein Karim (including also the built-up area of Motsa); and the most northern Shu'fat, as indicated on the attached sketch-map (annex B).

C. *Statute of the City*

The Trusteeship Council shall, within five months of the approval of the present plan, elaborate and approve a detailed Statute of the City which shall contain *inter alia* the substance of the following provisions:

1. *Government machinery; special objectives.* The Administering Authority in discharging its administrative obligations shall pursue the following special objectives:

   (*a*) To protect and to preserve the unique spiritual and religious interests located in the city of the three great monotheistic faiths throughout the world, Christian, Jewish and Moslem; to this end to ensure that order and peace, and especially religious peace, reign in Jerusalem;

   (*b*) To foster co-operation among all the inhabitants of the city in their own interests as well as in order to encourage and support the peaceful development of the mutual relations between the two Palestinian peoples, throughout the Holy Land; to promote the security, well-being and any constructive measures of development of the residents, having regard to the special circumstances and customs of the various peoples and communities.

156

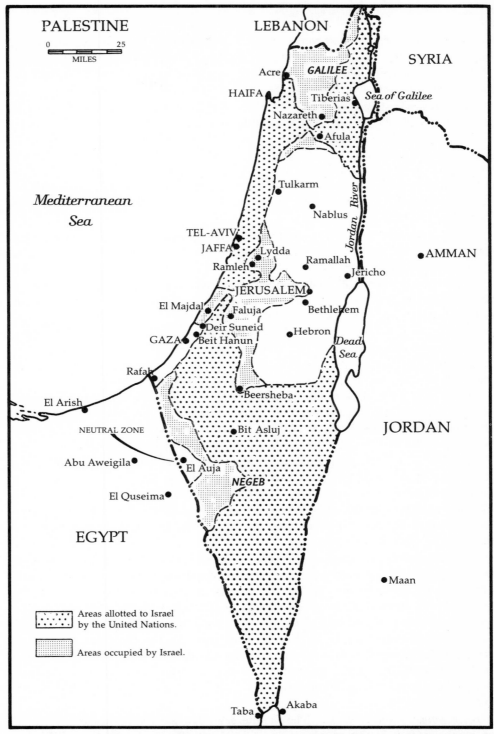

PALESTINE

0   25
MILES

LEBANON

SYRIA

GALILEE

Acre

HAIFA

Tiberias   *Sea of Galilee*

Nazareth

Afula

Mediterranean Sea

Tulkarm

Nablus

Jordan River

AMMAN

TEL-AVIV

JAFFA

Lydda

Ramallah

Ramleh

Jericho

JERUSALEM

El Majdal

Faluja

Bethlehem

Deir Suneid

Hebron

GAZA

Beit Hanun

Dead Sea

Rafah

El Arish

Beersheba

NEUTRAL ZONE

JORDAN

Bit Asluj

Abu Aweigila

El Auja

NEGEB

El Quseima

EGYPT

Maan

Areas allotted to Israel
by the United Nations.

Areas occupied by Israel.

Taba   Akaba

Map adapted from George Lenczowski, *The Middle East in World Affairs,* 3d edition (Ithaca: Cornell University Press, 1962).

157

2. *Governor and administrative staff.* A Governor of the City of Jerusalem shall be appointed by the Trusteeship Council and shall be responsible to it. He shall be selected on the basis of special qualifications and without regard to nationality. He shall not, however, be a citizen of either State in Palestine.

The Governor shall represent the United Nations in the City and shall exercise on their behalf all powers of administration, including the conduct of external affairs. He shall be assisted by an administrative staff classed as international officers in the meaning of Article 100 of the Charter and chosen whenever practicable from the residents of the city and of the rest of Palestine on a non-discriminatory basis. A detailed plan for the organization of the administration of the city shall be submitted by the Governor to the Trusteeship Council and duly approved by it.

3. *Local autonomy.* (*a*) The existing local autonomous units in the territory of the city (villages, townships and municipalities) shall enjoy wide powers of local government and administration.

(*b*) The Governor shall study and submit for the consideration and decision of the Trusteeship Council a plan for the establishment of special town units consisting, respectively, of the Jewish, and Arab sections of new Jerusalem. The new town units shall continue to form part of the present municipality of Jerusalem.

4. *Security measures.* (*a*) The City of Jerusalem shall be demilitarized; its neutrality shall be declared and preserved, and no para-military formations, exercises or activities shall be permitted within its borders.

(*b*) Should the administration of the City of Jerusalem be seriously obstructed or prevented by the non-co-operation or interference of one or more sections of the population, the Governor shall have authority to take such measures as may be necessary to restore the effective functioning of the administration.

(*c*) To assist in the maintenance of internal law and order and especially for the protection of the Holy Places and religious buildings and sites in the city, the Governor shall organize a special police force of adequate strength, the members of which shall be recruited outside of Palestine. The Governor shall be empowered to direct such budgetary provision as may be necessary for the maintenance of this force.

5. *Legislative organization.* A Legislative Council, elected by adult residents of the city irrespective of nationality on the basis of universal and secret suffrage and proportional representation, shall have powers of legislation and taxation. No legislative measures shall, however, conflict or interfere with the provisions which will be set forth in the Statute of the City, nor shall any law, regulation, or official action prevail over them. The Statute shall grant to the Governor a right of vetoing bills inconsistent with the provisions referred to in the preceding sentence. It shall also empower him to promulgate temporary ordinances in case the Council fails to adopt in time a bill deemed essential to the normal functioning of the administration.

6. *Administration of justice.* The Statute shall provide for the establishment of an independent judiciary system, including a court of appeal. All the inhabitants of the City shall be subject to it.

7. *Economic union and economic regime.* The City of Jerusalem shall be included in the Economic Union of Palestine and be bounded by all stipulations of the undertaking and of any treaties issued therefrom, as well as by the decisions of the Joint Economic Board. The headquarters of the Economic Board shall be established in the territory of the City.

The Statute shall provide for the regulation of economic matters not falling within the regime of the Economic Union, on the basis of equal treatment and non-discrimination for all Members of the United Nations and their nationals.

8. *Freedom of transit and visit: control of residents.* Subject to considerations of security, and of economic welfare as determined by the Governor under the directions of the Trusteeship Council, freedom of entry into, and residence within, the borders of the City shall be guaranteed for the residents or citizens of the Arab and Jewish States. Immigration into, and residence within, the borders of the city for nationals of other States shall be controlled by the Governor under the directions of the Trusteeship Council.

9. *Relations with the Arab and Jewish States.* Representatives of the Arab and Jewish States shall be accredited to the Governor of the City and charged with the protection of the interests of their States and nationals in connexion with the international administration of the City.

10. *Official languages.* Arabic and Hebrew shall be the official languages of the city. This will not preclude the adoption of one or more additional working languages, as may be required.

11. *Citizenship.* All the residents shall become *ipso facto* citizens of the City of Jerusalem unless they opt for citizenship of the State of which they have been citizens or, if Arabs or Jews, have filed notice of intention to become citizens of the Arab or Jewish State respectively, according to part I, section B, paragraph 9, of this plan.

The Trusteeship Council shall make arrangements for consular protection of the citizens of the City outside its territory.

12. *Freedoms of citizens.* (*a*) Subject only to the requirements of public order and morals, the inhabitants of the City shall be ensured the enjoyment of human rights and fundamental freedoms, including freedom of conscience, religion and worship, language, education, speech and press, assembly and association, and petition.

(*b*) No discrimination of any kind shall be made between the inhabitants on the grounds of race, religion, language or sex.

(*c*) All persons within the City shall be entitled to equal protection of the laws.

(*d*) The family law and personal status of the various persons and communities and their religious interests, including endowments, shall be respected.

(*e*) Except as may be required for the maintenance of public order and good government, no measure shall be taken to obstruct or interfere with the enterprise of religious or charitable bodies of all faiths or to discriminate against any representative or member of these bodies on the ground of his religion or nationality.

(*f*) The City shall ensure adequate primary and secondary education for the

Arab and Jewish communities respectively, in their own languages and in accordance with their cultural traditions.

The right of each community to maintain its own schools for the education of its own members in its own language, while conforming to such educational requirements of a general nature as the City may impose, shall not be denied or impaired. Foreign educational establishments shall continue their activity on the basis of their existing rights.

(*g*) No restriction shall be imposed on the free use by any inhabitant of the City of any language in private intercourse, in commerce, in religion, in the Press or in publications of any kind, or at public meetings.

13. *Holy Places.* (*a*) Existing rights in respect of Holy Places and religious buildings or sites shall not be denied or impaired.

(*b*) Free access to the Holy Places and religious buildings or sites and the free exercise of worship shall be secured in conformity with existing rights and subject to the requirements of public order and decorum.

(*c*) Holy Places and religious buildings or sites shall be preserved. No act shall be permitted which may in any way impair their sacred character. If at any time it appears to the Governor that any particular Holy Place, religious building or site is in need of urgent repair, the Governor may call upon the community or communities concerned to carry out such repair. The Governor may carry it out himself at the expense of the community or communities concerned if no action is taken within a reasonable time.

(*d*) No taxation shall be levied in respect of any Holy Place, religious building or site which was exempt from taxation on the date of the creation of the City. No change in the incidence of such taxation shall be made which would either discriminate between the owners or occupiers of Holy Places, religious buildings or sites, or would place such owners or occupiers in a position less favourable in relation to the general incidence of taxation than existed at the time of the adoption of the Assembly's recommendations.

14. *Special powers of the Governor in respect of the Holy Places, religious buildings and sites in the City and in any part of Palestine.* (*a*) The protection of the Holy Places, religious buildings and sites located in the City of Jerusalem shall be a special concern of the Governor.

(*b*) With relation to such places, buildings and sites in Palestine outside the city, the Governor shall determine, on the ground of powers granted to him by the Constitutions of both States, whether the provisions of the Constitutions of the Arab and Jewish States in Palestine dealing therewith and the religious rights appertaining thereto are being properly applied and respected.

(*c*) The Governor shall also be empowered to make decisions on the basis of existing rights in cases of disputes which may arise between the different religious communities or the rites of a religious community in respect of the Holy Places, religious buildings and sites in any part of Palestine.

In this task he may be assisted by a consultative council of representatives of different denominations acting in an advisory capacity.

D. *Duration of the Special Regime*

The Statute elaborated by the Trusteeship Council on the aforementioned principles shall come into force not later than 1 October 1948. It shall remain in force in the first instance for a period of ten years, unless the Trusteeship Council finds it necessary to undertake a re-examination of these provisions at an earlier date. After the expiration of this period the whole scheme shall be subject to re-examination by the Trusteeship Council in the light of the experience acquired with its functioning. The residents of the City shall be then free to express by means of a referendum their wishes as to possible modifications of the regime of the City.

PART IV

CAPITULATIONS

States whose nationals have in the past enjoyed in Palestine the privileges and immunities of foreigners, including the benefits of consular jurisdiction and protection, as formerly enjoyed by capitulation or usage in the Ottoman Empire, are invited to renounce any right pertaining to them to the re-establishment of such privileges and immunities in the proposed Arab and Jewish States and the City of Jerusalem.

52. Creation of the Palestine Conciliation Commission: Resolution of the United Nations General Assembly, December 11, 1948

THE GENERAL ASSEMBLY,

HAVING CONSIDERED FURTHER the situation in Palestine,

1. *Expresses* its deep appreciation of the progress achieved through the good offices of the late United Nations Mediator in promoting a peaceful adjustment of the future situation of Palestine, for which cause he sacrificed his life; and

Extends its thanks to the Acting Mediator and his staff for their continued efforts and devotion to duty in Palestine;

2. *Establishes* a Conciliation Commission consisting of three States Members of the United Nations which shall have the following functions:

(a) To assume, insofar as it considers necessary in existing circumstances, the functions given to the United Nations Mediator on Palestine by the resolution of the General Assembly of 14 May 1948;

(b) To carry out the specific functions and directives given to it by the present resolution and such additional functions and directives as may be given to it by the General Assembly or by the Security Council;

(c) To undertake, upon the request of the Security Council, any of the functions now assigned to the United Nations Mediator on Palestine or to the United Nations Truce Commission by resolutions of the Security Council; upon such requests to the Conciliation Commission by the Security Council with respect to all the remaining functions of the United Nations Mediator on Palestine under Security Council resolutions, the office of the Mediator shall be terminated;

161

3. *Decides* that a Committee of the Assembly, consisting of China, France, the Union of Soviet Socialist Republics, the United Kingdom and the United States of America, shall present, before the end of the first part of the present session of the General Assembly, for the approval of the Assembly, a proposal concerning the names of the three States which will constitute the Conciliation Commission;

4. *Requests* the Commission to begin its functions at once, with a view to the establishment of contact between the parties themselves and the Commission at the earliest possible date;

5. *Calls upon* the Governments and authorities concerned to extend the scope of the negotiations provided for in the Security Council's resolution of 16 November 1948 and to seek agreement by negotiations conducted either with the Conciliation Commission or directly with a view to the final settlement of all questions outstanding between them;

6. *Instructs* the Conciliation Commission to take steps to assist the Governments and authorities concerned to achieve a final settlement of all questions outstanding between them;

7. *Resolves* that the Holy Places—including Nazareth—religious building and sites in Palestine should be protected and free access to them assured, in accordance with existing rights and historical practice; that arrangements to this end should be under effective United Nations supervision; that the United Nations Conciliation Commission, in presenting to the fourth regular session of the General Assembly its detailed proposal for a permanent international regime for the territory of Jerusalem, should include recommendations concerning the Holy Places in that territory; that with regard to the Holy. Places in the rest of Palestine the Commission should call upon the political authorities of the areas concerned to give appropriate formal guarantees as to the protection of the Holy Places and access to them; and that these undertakings should be presented to the General Assembly for approval;

8. *Resolves* that, in view of its association with three world religions, the Jerusalem area, including the present municipality of Jerusalem *plus* the surrounding villages and towns, the most Eastern of which shall be Avu Dis; the most Southern, Bethlehem; the most· Western, Ein Karim (including also the built-up area of Motsa); and the most Northern, Shufat, should be accorded special and separate treatment from the rest of Palestine and should be placed under effective United Nations control;

Requests the Security Council to take further steps to ensure the demilitarization of Jerusalem at the earliest possible date;

Instructs the Conciliation Commission to present to the fourth regular session of the General Assembly detailed proposals for a permanent international regime for the Jerusalem area which will provide for the maximum local autonomy for distinctive groups consistent with the special international status of the Jerusalem area;

The Conciliation Commission is authorized to appoint a United Nations representative who shall co-operate with the local authorities with respect to the interim administration of the Jerusalem area;

9. *Resolves* that, pending agreement on more detailed arrangements among the

Governments and authorities concerned, the freest possible access to Jerusalem by road, rail or air should be accorded to all inhabitants of Palestine;

Instructs the Conciliation Commission to report immediately to the Security Council, for appropriate action by that organ, any attempt by any party to impede such access;

10. *Instructs* the Conciliation Commission to seek arrangements among the Governments and authorities concerned which will facilitate the economic development of the area, including arrangements for access to ports and airfields and the use of transportation and communication facilities;

11. *Resolves* that the refugees wishing to return to their homes and live at peace with their neighbors should be permitted to do so at the earliest practicable date, and that compensation should be paid for the property of those choosing not to return and for loss of or damage to property which, under principles of international law or in equity, should be made good by the Governments or authorities responsible;

Instructs the Conciliation Commission to facilitate the repatriation, resettlement and economic and social rehabilitation of the refugees and the payment of compensation, and to maintain close relations with the Director of the United Nations Relief for Palestine Refugees and, through him, with the appropriate organs and agencies of the United Nations;

12. *Authorizes* the Conciliation Commission to appoint such subsidiary bodies and to employ such technical experts, acting under its authority, as it may find necessary for the effective discharge of its functions and responsibilities under the present resolution;

The Conciliation Commission will have its official headquarters at Jerusalem. The authorities responsible for maintaining order in Jerusalem will be responsible for taking all measures necessary to ensure the security of the Commission. The Secretary-General will provide a limited number of guards for the protection of the staff and premises of the Commission;

13. *Instructs* the Conciliation Commission to render progress reports periodically to the Secretary-General for transmission to the Security Council and to the Members of the United Nations;

14. *Calls* upon all Governments and authorities concerned to cooperate with the Conciliation Commission and to take all possible steps to assist in the implementation of the present resolution;

15. *Requests* the Secretary-General to provide the necessary staff and facilities and to make appropriate arrangements to provide the necessary funds required in carrying out the terms of the present resolution.

B. AFTER ISRAEL'S INDEPENDENCE

53. Peace and Stability in the Middle East: Tripartite Declaration of the United States, the United Kingdom and France
May 25, 1950

The Governments of the United Kingdom, France, and the United States, having had occasion during the recent Foreign Ministers meeting in London to review certain questions affecting the peace and stability of the Arab states and of Israel, and particularly that of the supply of arms and war material to these states, have resolved to make the following statements:

1. The three Governments recognize that the Arab states and Israel all need to maintain a certain level of armed forces for the purposes of assuring their internal security and their legitimate self-defense and to permit them to play their part in the defense of the area as a whole. All applications for arms or war material for these countries will be considered in the light of these principles. In this connection the three Governments wish to recall · and reaffirm the terms of the statements made by their representatives on the Security Council on August 4, 1949, in which they declared their opposition to the development of an arms race between the Arab states and Israel.

2. The three Governments declare that assurances have been received from all the states in question, to which they permit arms to be supplied from their countries, that the purchasing state does not intend to undertake any act of aggression against any other state. Similar assurances will be requested from any other state in the area to which they permit arms to be supplied in the future.

3. The three Governments take this opportunity of declaring their deep interest in and their desire to promote the establishment and maintenance of peace and stability in the area and their unalterable opposition to the use cf force or threat between any of the states in that area. The three Governments, should they find that any of these states was preparing to violate frontiers or armistice lines, would, consistently with their obligations as members of the United Nations, immediately take action, both within and outside the United Nations, to prevent such violation.

54. Passage of Israeli Ships Through the Suez Canal: Resolution of the United Nations Security Council, September 1, 1951

The Security Council

1. *Recalling* that in its resolution of 11 August 1949, (S/1376) relating to the conclusion of Armistice Agreements between Israel and the neighboring Arab States it drew attention to the pledges, in these Agreements "against any further acts of hostility between the Parties";

2. *Recalling* further that in its resolution of 17 November 1950 (S/1907) it reminded the States concerned that the Armistice Agreements to which they were parties contemplated "the return of permanent peace in Palestine," and therefore urged them and the other States in the area to take all such steps as would lead to the settlement of the issues between them;

3. *Noting* the report of the Chief of Staff of the Truce Supervision Organization to the Security Council of 12 June 1951 (S/2194);

4. *Further noting* that the Chief of Staff of the Truce Supervision Organization recalled the statement of the senior Egyptian delegate in Rhodes on 13 January 1949, to the effect that his delegation was "inspired with every spirit of co-opera-

tion, conciliation and a sincere desire to restore peace in Palestine," and that the Egyptian Government has not complied with the earnest plea of the Chief of Staff made to the Egyptian delegate on 12 June 1951, that it desist from the present practice of interfering with the passage through the Suez Canal of goods destined for Israel;

5. *Considering* that since the Armistice regime, which has been in existence for nearly two and a half years, is of a permanent character, neither party can reasonably assert that it is actively a belligerent or requires to exercise the right of visit, search, and seizure for any legitimate purpose of self-defense;

6. *Finds* that the maintenance of the practice mentioned in paragraph 4 above is inconsistent with the objectives of a peaceful settlement between the parties and the establishment of a permanent peace in Palestine set forth in the Armistice Agreement;

7. *Finds further* that such practice is an abuse of the exercise of the right of visit, search and seizure;

8. *Further finds* that practice cannot in the prevailing circumstances be justified on the ground that it is necessary for self-defense;

9. *And further noting* that the restrictions on the pàssage of goods through the Suez Canal to Israel ports are denying to nations at no time connected with the conflict in Palestine valuable supplies required for their economic reconstruction, and that these restrictions together with sanctions applied by Egypt to certain ships which have visited Israel ports represent unjustified interference with the rights of nations to navigate the seas and to trade freely with one another, including the Arab States and Israel;

10. *Calls upon* Egypt to terminate the restrictions on the passage of international commercial shipping and goods through the Suez Canal wherever bound and to cease all interference with such shipping beyond that essential to the safety of shipping in the Canal itself and to the observance of international conventions in force.

55. United States Regret Over the Removal of the Israeli Foreign Ministry to Jerusalem: Statement by the Secretary of State, July 28, 1953

The United States regrets that the Israeli Government has seen fit to move its Foreign Office from Tel Aviv to Jerusalem.

We have made known our feelings on that subject to the Government of Israel on two prior occasions. It was done in July 1952 and again in March 1953, when our Ambassador, hearing rumors that this was in contemplation, called upon the Israeli Government and requested them not to transfer their Foreign Ministry to Jerusalem.

We feel that way because we believe that it would embarrass the United Nations, which has a primary responsibility for determining the future status of Jerusalem. You may recall that the presently standing U.N. resolution about Jerusalem contemplates that it should be to a large extent at least an international city. Also, we feel that this particular action by the Government of Israel at this particular time is inopportune in relation to the tensions which exist in the Near East, tensions which are rather extreme, and that this will add to rather than to relax any of these tensions.

The views that I express here are, we know, shared by a considerable number of other governments who have concern with the development of an atmosphere of peace and good will in that part of the world.

We have notified the Government of Israel that we do not intend to move our own Embassy to Jerusalem.

56. Retention of the American Embassy in Tel Aviv: Statement Issued by the Department of State, November 3, 1954

The ranking diplomatic representatives of Jordan, Lebanon, Iraq, Yemen, Saudi Arabia, Libya, Syria, and Egypt called on the Secretary of State on November 3 to make known the views of their Governments with respect to the plans for presentation of credentials in Jerusalem by the appointed American Ambassador to Israel, Edward B. Lawson.

In the course of the conversation the Secretary recalled the policy of the U.S. Government to look to the United Nations as primarily responsible for determining the future status of Jerusalem. Following normal practice, the presentation of credentials would be effected by Ambassador Lawson at the place where the Chief of State actually is. The fact that this means that the presentation will take place in Jerusalem implies no change in our attitude regarding Jerusalem nor does it imply any change in the location of the American Embassy in Israel, which is at Tel Aviv.

57. Reaffirmation of the Tripartite Declaration by the United States: Statement by the President, November 9, 1955

All Americans have been following with deep concern the latest developments in the Near East. The recent outbreak of hostilities has led to a sharp increase in tensions. These events inevitably retard our search for world peace. Insecurity in one region is bound to affect the world as a whole.

While we continue willing to consider requests for arms needed for legitimate self-defense, we do not intend to contribute to an arms competition in the Near East because we do not think such a race would be in the true interest of any of the participants. The policy which we believed would best promote the interests and the security of the peoples of the area was expressed in the Tripartite Declaration of May 25, 1950. This still remains our policy.

I stated last year that our goal in the Near East as elsewhere is a just peace. Nothing has taken place since which invalidates our fundamental policies, policies based on friendship for all of the peoples of the area.

We believe that true security must be based upon a just and reasonable settlement. The Secretary of State outlined on August 26th the economic and security contributions which this country was prepared to make toward such a solution. On that occasion I authorized Mr. Dulles to state, that given a solution of the other related problems, I would recommend that the United States join in formal treaty engagements to prevent or thwart any effort by either side to alter by force the boundaries between Israel and its Arab neighbors.

Recent developments have made it all the more imperative that a settlement be found. The United States will continue to play its full part and will support firmly the United Nations, which has already contributed so markedly to minimize violence in the area. I hope that other nations of the world will cooperate in this endeavor, thereby contributing significantly to world peace.

58. A Direct Appeal to the Israelis and Arabs: Speech by Assistant Secretary of State Byroade, April 9, 1954

To the Israelis I say that you should come to truly look upon yourselves as a Middle Eastern state and see your own future in that context rather than as a headquarters, or nucleus so to speak, of worldwide groupings of peoples of a particular religious faith who must have special rights within and obligations to the Israeli state. You should drop the attitude of the conqueror and the conviction that force and a policy of retaliatory killings is the only policy that your neighbors will understand. You should make your deeds correspond to your frequent utterances of the desire for peace.

To the Arabs I say you should accept this state of Israel as an accomplished fact. I say further that you are deliberately attempting to maintain a state of affairs delicately suspended between peace and war, while at present desiring neither. This is a most dangerous policy and one which world opinion will increasingly condemn if you continue to resist any move to obtain at least a less dangerous *modus vivendi* with your neighbor.

C. THE SUEZ WAR AND ITS AFTERMATH

59. Nationalization of the Suez Canal: Decree of the Egyptian Government, July 26, 1956

In the Name of the Nation

The President of the Republic,

Considering the two firmans issued on November 30, 1854 and January 5, 1856 (respectively) concerning the preferential rights relating to the administration of the Suez Canal Transit Service and the establishment of an Egyptian joint-stock company to operate it;

and Law No. 129 of 1947 concerning public utility concessions;

and Law No. 317 of 1952 concerning individual labor contracts;

and Law No. 26 of 1954 concerning joint-stock companies, limited partnerships by shares and limited liability companies;

with the advice of the State Council;

has issued the following law;

Article I

The Universal Company of the Suez Maritime Canal (Egpytian joint-stock company) is hereby nationalized. All its assets, rights and obligations are transferred to the Nation and all the organizations and committees that now operate its management are hereby dissolved.

Stockholders and holders of founders shares shall be compensated for the ordinary or founders shares they own in accordance with the value of the shares shown in the closing quotations of the Paris Stock Exchange on the day preceding the effective date of the present law.

The payment of said indemnity shall be effected after the Nation has taken delivery of all the assets and properties of the nationalized company.

Article II

An independent organization endowed with juristic personality and annexed to the Ministry of Commerce, shall take over the management of the Suez Canal Transit Service. The composition of the organization and the remuneration of its members shall be fixed in an order of the President of the Republic. In so far as managing the Transit Service is concerned the organization shall have all the necessary powers required for the purpose without being restricted by Government regulations and procedures.

Without prejudice to the auditing of its final accounts by the State Audit Department, the organization shall have an independent budget prepared in accordance with the rules in force for commercial concerns. Its financial year shall begin on July 1 and end on June 30 each year. The budget and final accounts shall be approved by an order of the President of the Republic. The first financial year shall begin on the effective date of the present law and end with June 30, 1957.

The organization may delegate one or several of its members to implement its decisions or to discharge any duty assigned to these members.

It may also set up from among its own members or from among other people, a technical committee to assist it in its own research work and studies.

The chairman of the organization shall represent it before the courts, government agencies, and other places, and in its dwellings with third parties.

Article III

The assets and rights of the nationalized company in the Republic of Egypt and abroad, are hereby frozen. Without specific permission obtained in advance from the organization provided for in Article II above, banks, organizations and private persons are hereby prohibited from disposing of those assets or making any payment requested them or due by them.

Article IV

The organization shall retain all the present officials, employees and laborers of the nationalized company at their posts; they shall have to continue with the discharge of their duties; no one will be allowed to leave his work or vacate his post in any manner and for any reason whatsoever except with the permission of the organization provided for in Article II above.

Article V

All violations of the provisions of Article III above shall be punished by imprisonment and a fine equal to three times the value of the amount involved in the offense. All violations of the provisions of Article IV shall be punished by imprisonment in addition to the forfeiture by the offender of all rights to compensation, pension or indemnity.

Article VI

The present order shall be published in the Official Gazette and shall have the force of law. It shall come into force on the date of its publication. The Minister of Commerce shall issue the necessary administrative orders for its implementation.

It shall bear the Seal of the State and be implemented as one of the State laws. Given this 18th day of Zul Heggah, 1375 A. H. (July 26, 1956)

GAMAL ABDEL NASSER

60. The United States Rejects the Use of Force: Speech by President Eisenhower (excerpts), October 31, 1956

My Fellow Americans:

Tonight I report to you as your President.

We all realize that the full and free debate of a political campaign surrounds us. But the events and issues I wish to place before you this evening have no connection whatsoever with matters of partisanship. They are concerns of every American—his present and his future.

I wish, therefore, to give you a report of essential facts so that you—whether belonging to either one of our two great parties, or to neither—may give thoughtful and informed consideration to this swiftly changing world scene.

The changes of which I speak have come in two areas of the world—Eastern Europe and the Mid-East.

* * * * * * *

[At this point the President spoke of events in Eastern Europe.]

I now turn to that other part of the world where, at this moment, the situation is somber. It is not a situation that calls for extravagant fear or hysteria. But it invites our most serious concern.

I speak, of course, of the Middle East. This ancient crossroads of the world was, as we all know, an area long subject to colonial rule. This rule ended after World War II, when all countries there won full independence. Out of the Palestinian mandated territory was born the new State of Israel.

169

These historic changes could not, however, instantly banish animosities born of the ages. Israel and her Arab neighbors soon found themselves at war with one another. And the Arab nations showed continuing anger toward their former colonial rulers, notably France and Great Britain.

The United States—through all the years since the close of World War II—has labored tirelessly to bring peace and stability to this area.

We have considered it a basic matter of United States policy to support the new State of Israel and—at the same time—to strengthen our bonds both with Israel and with the Arab countries. But, unfortunately through all these years, passion in the area threatened to prevail over peaceful purposes, and in one form or another, there has been almost continuous fighting.

This situation recently was aggravated by Egyptian policy including rearmament with Communist weapons. We felt this to be a misguided policy on the part of the Government of Egypt. The State of Israel, at the same time, felt increasing anxiety for its safety. And Great Britain and France feared more and more that Egyptian policies threatened their "life line" of the Suez Canal.

These matters came to a crisis on July 26th of this year, when the Egyptian Government seized the Universal Suez Canal Company. For ninety years—ever since the inauguration of the Canal—that Company has operated the Canal, largely under British and French technical supervision.

Now there were some among our allies who urged an immediate reaction to this event by use of force. We insistently urged otherwise, and our wish prevailed —through a long succession of conferences and negotiations for weeks—even months—with participation by the United Nations. And there, in the United Nations, only a short while ago, on the basis of agreed principles, it seemed that an acceptable accord was within our reach.

But the direct relations of Egypt with both Israel and France kept worsening to a point at which first Israel—then France—and Great Britain also—determined that, in their judgment, there could be no protection of their vital interests without resort to force.

Upon this decision, events followed swiftly. On Sunday [October 28] the Israeli Government ordered total mobilization. On Monday, their armed forces penetrated deeply into Egypt and to the vicinity of the Suez Canal, nearly one hundred miles away. And on Tuesday, the British and French Governments delivered a 12-hour ultimatum to Israel and Egypt—now followed up by armed attack against Egypt.

The United States was not consulted in any way about any phase of these actions. Nor were we informed of them in advance.

As it is the manifest right of any of these nations to take such decisions and actions, it is likewise our right—if our judgment so dictates—to dissent. We believe these actions to have been taken in error. For we do not accept the use of force as a wise or proper instrument for the settlement of international disputes.

To say this—in this particular instance—is in no way to minimize our friendship with these nations—nor our determination to maintain those friendships.

And we are fully aware of the grave anxieties of Israel, of Britain and of France. We know that they have been subjected to grave and repeated provocations.

The present fact, nonetheless, seems clear: the action taken can scarcely be reconciled with the principles and purposes of the United Nations to which we have all subscribed. And, beyond this, we are forced to doubt that resort to force and war will for long serve the permanent interest of the attacking nations.

Now—we must look to the future.

In the circumstances I have described, there will be no United States involvement in these present hostilities. I therefore have no plan to call the Congress in Special Session. Of course, we shall continue to keep in contact with Congressional leaders of both parties.

I assure you, your government will remain alert to every possibility of this situation, and keep in close contact and coordination with the Legislative Branch of this government.

At the same time it is—and it will remain—the dedicated purpose of your government to do all in its power to localize the fighting and to end the conflict.

We took our first measure in this action yesterday. We went to the United Nations with a request that the forces of Israel return to their own land and that hostilities in the area be brought to a close. This proposal was not adopted —because it was vetoed by Great Britain and by France.

The processes of the United Nations, however, are not exhausted. It is our hope and intent that this matter will be brought before the United Nations General Assembly. There—with no veto operating—the opinion of the world can be brought to bear in our quest for a just end to this tormenting problem. In the past the United Nations has proved able to find a way to end bloodshed. We believe it can and that it will do so again.

My fellow citizens, as I review the march of world events in recent years, I am ever more deeply convinced that the processes of the United Nations represents the soundest hope for peace in the world. For this very reason, I believe that the processes of the United Nations need further to be developed and strengthened. I speak particularly of increasing its ability to secure justice under international law.

In all the recent troubles in the Middle East, there have indeed been injustices suffered by all nations involved. But I do not believe that another instrument of injustice—war—is the remedy for these wrongs.

There can be no peace—without law. And there can be no law—if we were to invoke one code of international conduct for those who oppose us—and another for our friends.

The society of nations has been slow in developing means to apply this truth.

But the passionate longing for peace—on the part of all peoples of the earth— compels us to speed our search for new and more effective instruments of justice.

The peace we seek and need means much more than mere absence of war. It means the acceptance of law, and the fostering of justice, in all the world.

To our principles guiding us in this quest we must stand fast. In so doing we can honor the hopes of all men for a world in which peace will truly and justly reign.

61. The Establishment of the United Nations Emergency Force: Resolution of the United Nations General Assembly,[1] November 5, 1956

The General Assembly

Having requested the Secretary-General, in its resolution 998 (ES-I) of 4 November 1956, to submit to it a plan for an emergency international United Nations Force, for the purposes stated,

Noting with satisfaction the first report of the Secretary-General on the plan, and having in mind particularly paragraph 4 of that report,

1. *Establishes* a United Nations Command for an emergency international Force to secure and supervise the cessation of hostilities in accordance with all the terms of General Assembly resolution 997 (ES-I) of 2 November 1956;

2. *Appoints,* on an emergency basis, the Chief of Staff of the United Nations Truce Supervision Organization, Major-General E. L. M. Burns, as Chief of the Command;

3. *Authorizes* the Chief of the Command immediately to recruit, from the observer corps of the United Nations Truce Supervision Organization, a limited number of officers who shall be nationals of countries other than those having permanent membership in the Security Council, and further authorizes him, in consultation with the Secretary-General, to undertake the recruitment directly, from various Member States other than the permanent members of the Security Council, of the additional number of officers needed;

4. *Invites* the Secretary-General to take such administrative measures as may be necessary for the prompt execution of the actions envisaged in the present resolution.

565th plenary meeting,
5 November 1956.

62. Presence and Functions of the UNEF: Report of the Secretary General, November 20, 1956

1. After the adoption, 7 November 1956, by the General Assembly of resolution 1001 (ES-1) concerning the establishment of the United Nations Emergency Force, the Government of Egypt was immediately approached by the Secretary-General through the Commander of the Force, Major General E.L.M. Burns, in order to prepare the ground for a prompt implementation of the resolution.

2. The Government of Egypt had, prior to the final decision of the General Assembly, accepted the Force in principle by formally accepting the preceding resolution 1000 (ES-1) on the establishment of a United Nations Command. Before consenting to the arrival of the Force, the Government of Egypt wished to have certain points in the resolutions of the General Assembly clarified. An exchange of views took place between the Secretary-General and the Government of Egypt in which the Secretary-General, in reply to questions addressed to him by the Government of Egypt, gave his interpretations of the relevant General

---

[1] Introduced by Canada, Colombia, and Norway as draft resolution A/3290 (Nov. 4, 1956).

Assembly resolutions, in respect of the character and functions of the Force. At the end of the exchange, he gave to the Advisory Committee set up by General Assembly resolution 1001 (ES-1), a full account of the interpretations given. Approving these interpretations, the Advisory Committee recommended that the Secretary-General should proceed to start the transfer of the United Nations Emergency Force.

3. On the basis of the resolutions, as interpreted by the Secretary-General, the Government of Egypt consented to the arrival of the United Nations Force in Egypt. The first transport of troops took place on 15 November 1956.

4. While the Secretary-General found that the exchange of views which had taken place was sufficient as a basis for the sending of the first units, he felt, on the other hand, that a firmer foundation had to be laid for the presence and functioning of the Force in Egypt and for the continued co-operation with the Egyptian authorities. For that reason, and also because he considered it essential personally to discuss with the Egyptian authorities certain questions which flowed from the decision to send the Force, after visiting the staging area of the Force in Naples, he went to Cairo, where he stayed from 16 until 18 November. On his way to Cairo he stopped briefly at the first staging area in Egypt, at Abu Suweir.

5. In Cairo he discussed with the President and the Foreign Minister of Egypt basic points for the presence and functioning of the Force in Egypt. Time obviously did not permit a detailed study of the various legal, technical and administrative arrangements which would have to be made and the exchange of views was therefore related only to questions of principle.

6. The Secretary-General wishes to inform the General Assembly of the main results of these discussions. They are summarized in an *"Aide-mémoire on the basis for presence and functioning of the United Nations Emergency Force in Egypt,"* submitted as an annex to this report.

7. The text of this *Aide-mémoire,* if noted with approval by the General Assembly, with the concurrence of Egypt, would establish an understanding between the United Nations and Egypt, on which the co-operation could be developed and necessary agreements on various details be elaborated. The text, as it stands, is presented on the responsibility of the Secretary-General. It has the approval of the Government of Egypt.

*   *   *

ANNEX

AIDE-MEMOIRE ON THE BASIS FOR THE PRESENCE AND FUNCTIONING OF THE UNITED NATIONS EMERGENCY FORCE IN EGYPT

Noting that by telegram of 5 November 1956 addressed to the Secretary-General the Government of Egypt, in exercise of its sovereign rights, accepted General Assembly resolution 1000 (ES-1) of the same date establishing "a United Nations Command for an emergency international Force to secure and supervise the cessation of hostilities in accordance with all the terms of resolution 997 (ES-1) of the General Assembly of 2 November 1956";

Noting that the General Assembly in its resolution 1001 (ES-1) of 7 November 1956 approved the principle that it could not request the Force "to be stationed or operate on the territory of a given country without the consent of the Government of that country" (A/3302, para. 9);

Having agreed on the arrival in Egypt of the United Nations Emergency Force (UNEF);

Noting that advance groups of UNEF have already been received in Egypt,

The Government of Egypt and the Secretary-General of the United Nations have stated their understanding on the basic points for the presence and functioning of UNEF as follows:

1. The Government of Egypt declares that, when exercising its sovereign rights on any matter concerning the presence and functioning of UNEF, it will be guided, in good faith, by its acceptance of General Assembly resolution 1000 (ES-1) of 5 November 1956.

2. The United Nations takes note of this declaration of the Government of Egypt and declares that the activities of UNEF will be guided, in good faith, by the task established for the Force in the aforementioned resolutions; in particular, the United Nations, understanding this to correspond to the wishes of the Government of Egypt, reaffirms its willingness to maintain UNEF until its task is completed.

3. The Government of Egypt and the Secretary-General declare that it is their intention to proceed forthwith, in the light of points 1 and 2 above, to explore jointly concrete aspects of the functioning of UNEF, including its stationing and the question of its lines of communication and supply; the Government of Egypt, confirming its intention to facilitate the functioning of UNEF, and the United Nations are agreed to expedite in co-operation the implementation of guilding principles arrived at as a result of that joint exploration on the basis of the resolutions of the General Assembly.

63. Israel Refuses to Permit Stationing of UNEF in Israel: Statement by Prime Minister Ben-Gurion to Knesset (excerpts), November 7, 1956

The glorious military operation which lasted a week and conquered the entire Sinai Peninsula of 60,000 square kilometers is an unprecedented feat in Jewish history and is rare in the world's history. The Army did not make an effort to occupy enemy territory in Egypt proper and limited its operations to free the area from northern Sinai to the tip of the Red Sea.

This heroic advance is a focal point not only for the consolidation of the State's security and internal tranquility but also for our external relations on the world scene. Our forces did not attack Egypt proper and I hope the Egyptian dictator won't compel Israelis to violate the Biblical injunction never to return to that country.

* * *

I know that I express the feeling of the entire nation and the Jewish people throughout the world when I say that our love and admiration go out to the

174

Israeli army on land, sea, and air. The whole nation is proud of you. You enhanced the prestige of our people in the world and powerfully reinforced Israeli's security.

During the fighting I was profoundly concerned with the fate of the cities which might be bombed by Egyptian bombers, and we took special precautions to decrease the danger.

Referring to the international situation, I will not ask the United Nations why it did not take equally prompt action when the Arab countries invaded our country in 1948 which we revived in accordance with the General Assembly's own recommendations.

There is not a people in the world so deeply concerned for the principles of peace and justice contained in the United Nations Charter than [as] the Jewish people, not only because these principles are part of our ancient spiritual heritage and were passed on by us to the civilized world, but because the entire future of our people depends largely on the rule of peace and justice in the world.

Israel will not consent, under any circumstances, that a foreign force—called whatever it may—take up positions whether on Israeli soil or in any area held by Israel. The armistice with Egypt is dead, as are the armistice lines, and no wizards or magicians can resurrect these lines which cloaked Egyptian murders and sabotage.

*   *   *

[Mr. Ben-Gurion, summarizing his speech, presented a seven-point declaration which he offered the world "with full moral force and unflinching determination." The seven points were as follows:

1. The armistice agreement with Egypt is dead and buried and cannot be restored to life.

2. In consequence, the armistice lines between Israel and Egypt have no more validity.

3. There is no dispute whatever between the people of Israel and the Egyptian people.

4. We do not wish our relations with Egypt to continue in the present anarchic state and we are ready to enter into negotiations for a stable peace, cooperation and good, neighborly relations with Egypt on condition that they are direct negotiations without prior conditions on either side and are not under duress from any quarter whatever.

5. We hope that all peace-loving nations will support our desire for such negotiations with each of the Arab States, but even if they are unprepared for a permanent peace, so long as they observe the armistice agreements, Israel, on her part will do so, too.

6. On no account will Israel agree to the stationing of a foreign force, no matter how it is called, in her territory or in any of the area occupied by her.

7. Israel will not fight against any Arab country or against Egypt unless it is attacked by them.]

64. Presence and Functions of the UNEF:
Secret Aide Memoire of Secretary General Hammarskjold
August 5, 1957

Special to The New York Times

WASHINGTON, June 18—Following is the text of an aide-mémoire prepared Aug. 5, 1957, by Dag Hammarskjold, then Secretary General, for his files on negotiations covering the presence of United Nations troops in the United Arab Republic. Before his death, Mr. Hammarskjold gave a copy of the memorandum to a friend, Ernest A. Gross, former United States representative at the United Nations, who has agreed to its publication this week by the American Society of International Law.

As the decision on the U.N.E.F. [United Nations Emergency Force] was taken under Chapter VI [of the Charter] it was obvious from the beginning that the resolution did in no way limit the sovereignty of the host state. This was clear both from the resolution of the General Assembly and from the second and final report on the emergency force. Thus, neither the General Assembly nor the Secretary General, acting for the General Assembly, created any right for Egypt, or gave any right to Egypt, in accepting consent as a condition for the presence and functioning of the U.N.E.F. on Egyptian territory. Egypt had the right, and the only problem was whether that right in this context should and could in some way be limited.

Cable From Burns

My starting point in the consideration of this last-mentioned problem—the limitation of Egypt's sovereign right in the interest of political balance and stability in the U.N.E.F. operation—was the fact that Egypt had spontanously endorsed the General Assembly resolution of 5 November [creating the force] and by endorsing that resolution had consented to the presence of the U.N.E.F. for certain tasks. They could thus not ask the U.N.E.F. to withdraw before the completion of the tasks without running up against their own acceptance of the resolution on the force and its tasks.

The question arose in relation to Egypt first in a cable received 9 November from Burns [E.L.M. Burns, Canadian lieutenant general who was chief of staff of the United Nations Truce Supervision Organization in Palestine and who became in November, 1956, commander of the United Nations Emergency Force and is now adviser on disarmament to the Canadian Government] covering an interview the same day with Fawzi [Mahmoud Fawzi, Egyptian Foreign Minister in 1956 and now Deputy Premier for Foreign Affairs of the United Arab Republic]. In that interview Egypt had requested clarification of the question how long it was contemplated that the force would stay in the demarcation line area. To this I replied the same day: "A definite reply is at present impossible, but the emergency character of the force links it to the immediate crisis envisaged in the resolution of 2 November [calling for truce] and its liquidation. In case of different views as to when the crisis does not any longer warrant the presence of the troops, the

176

matter will have to be negotiated with the parties." In a further cable to Burns the same day I said, however, also that "as the United Nations force would come with Egypt's consent, they cannot stay nor operate unless Egypt continues to consent."

On 10 November Ambassador Loutfi [Omar Loutfi, chief Egyptian delegate at the United Nations in 1956, later an Under Secretary of the United Nations, who died in 1963], under instruction, asked me "whether it was recognized that an agreement is necessary for their (U.N.E.F.'s) remaining in the canal area" once their task in the area had been completed. I replied that it was my view that such an agreement would then be necessary.

On 11 November Ambassador Loutfi saw me again. He then said that it must be agreed that when the Egyptian consent is no more valid, the U.N. force should withdraw. To this I replied that I did not find that a withdrawal of consent could be made before the tasks which had justified the entry, had been completed; if, as might happen, different views on the degree of completion of the tasks prescribed proved to exist, the matter should be negotiated.

The view expressed by Loutfi was later embodied in an aide-mémoire, dated the same day, where it was said: "The Egyptian Government takes note of the following: A. It being agreed that consent of Egypt is indispensable for entry and presence of the U.N. forces in any part of its territory, if such consent no longer persists, these forces shall withdraw."

I replied to this in a memo dated 12 November in which I said: "I have received your aide-mémoire setting out the understanding on the basis of which the Egyptian Government accepts my announcing today that agreement on the arrival in Egypt of the United Nations force has been reached. I wish to put on record my interpretation of two of these points." Regarding the point quoted above in the Egyptian aide-mémoire, I then continued: "I want to put on record that the conditions which motivate the consent to entry and presence, are the very conditions to which the tasks established for the force in the General Assembly resolution [requesting preparations for establishment of the force], 4 November, are directed. Therefore, I assume it to be recognized that as long as the task, thus prescribed, is not completed, the reasons for the consent of the government remain valid, and that a withdrawal of this consent before completion of the task would run counter to the acceptance by Egypt of the decision of the General Assembly. I read the statement quoted in the light of these considerations. If a difference should develop, whether or not the reasons for the arrangements are still valid, the matter should be brought up for negotiation with the United Nations."

Message From Fawzi

This explanation of mine was sent to the Egyptian mission after my telephone conversation in the morning of the 12th with Dr. Fawzi where we agreed on publication of our agreement on the entry of the U.N.E.F. into Egypt. In view of the previous exchanges, I had no reason to believe that my statement would introduce any new difficulty. I also counted on the fact that Egypt probably by then was so committed as to be rather anxious not to reopen the discussion. However, I recognized to myself that there was an element of gambling involved which I felt I simply had to take in view of the danger that further delays might cause Egypt to change its mind, accept volunteers and throw our approaches overboard.

However, the next morning, 13 November, I received a message from Dr. Fawzi to the effect that the Government of Egypt could not subscribe to my interpretation of the question of consent and withdrawal, as set out on 12 November, and therefore, in the light of my communication of that date, "felt impelled to consider that the announced agreements should remain inoperative until all misunderstandings were cleared up." The Government reiterated in this context its view that if its consent no longer persisted, the U.N.E.F. should withdraw.

I replied to this communication—which caused a further delay of the transportation of troops to Egypt by at least 24 hours—in a cable sent immediately on receipt of the communication. In drafting my reply I had a feeling that it now was a must to get the troops in and that I would be in a position to find a formula, saving the face of Egypt while protecting the U.N. stand, once I would discuss the matter personally with President Nasser.

In the official reply 13 November I said that my previous statements had put forward my personal opinion that "the reasons" for consent remained valid as long as the task was not completed. I also said that for that reason a withdrawal of consent leading to the withdrawal of the force before the task was completed (as previously stated) in my view, "although within the rights of the Egyptian Government would go against its acceptance of the basic resolution of the General Assembly." I continued by saying that my reference to negotiation was intended to indicate only that the question of withdrawal should be a matter of discussion to the extent that different views were held as to whether the task of the General Assembly was fulfilled or not. I referred in this respect to my stand as explained already in my message of 9 November, as quoted above.

'Freedom of Action'

I commented upon the official reply in a special personal message to Fawzi, sent at the same time, where I said that we "both had to reserve our freedom of action, but that, all the same, we could go ahead, hoping that a controversial situation would not arise." "If arrangements would break down on this issue" (withdrawal only on completion of the tasks), "I could not avoid going to the General Assembly" (with the conflict which had developed between us on this question of principle) "putting it to their judgment to decide what could or could not be accepted as an understanding. This situation would be a most embarrassing one for all but I would fear the political repercussions, as obviously very few would find it reasonable that recognition of your freedom of action should mean that you, after having permitted the force to come, might ask it to withdraw at a time when the very reasons which had previously prompted you to accept were still obviously valid." I ended by saying that I trusted that Fawzi on the basis of this personal message could help me by "putting the stand I had to take on my own rights, in the right perspective." The letter to Fawzi thus made it clear that if the Government did not accept my stand on withdrawal as a precondition for further steps, the matter would be raised in the Assembly.

On the basis of these two final communications from me, Egypt gave green lights for the arrival of the troops, thus, in fact, accepting my stand and letting it supersede their own communication 13 November.

In my effort to follow up the situation, which prevailed after the exchange in which different stands had been maintained by Egypt and by me, I was guided by the consideration that Egypt constitutionally had an undisputed right to request the withdrawal of the troops, even if initial consent had been given, but that, on the other hand, it should be possible on the basis of my own stand as finally tacitly accepted, to force them into an agreement in which they limited their freedom of action as to withdrawal by making a request for withdrawal dependent upon the completion of the task—a question which, in the U.N., obviously would have to be submitted to interpretation by the General Assembly.

Obstacles to Solution

The most desirable thing, of course, would have been to tie Egypt by an agreement in which they declared, that withdrawal should take place only if so decided by the General Assembly. But in this naked form, however, the problem could never have been settled. I felt that the same was true of an agreement to the effect that withdrawal should take place upon "agreement on withdrawal" between the U.N. and the Egyptian Government. However, I found it worthwhile to try a line, very close to the second one, according to which Egypt would declare to the United Nations that it would exert all its sovereign rights with regard to the troops on the basis of a good faith interpretation of the tasks of the force. The United Nations should make a reciprocal commitment to maintain the force as long as the task was not completed. If such a dual statement was introduced in an agreement between the parties, it would be obvious that the procedure in case of a request from Egypt for the withdrawal of U.N.E.F. would be as follows. The matter would at once be brought before the General Assembly. If the General Assembly found that the task was completed, everything would be all right. If they found that the task was not completed and Egypt, all the same, maintained its stand and enforced the withdrawal, Egypt would break the agreement with the United Nations. Of course Egypt's freedom of action could under no circumstances be limited but by some kind of agreement. The device I used meant only that instead of limiting their rights by a basic understanding requesting an agreement *directly concerning withdrawal,* we created an obligation to reach agreement on the fact that the tasks were completed, and thus, *the conditions for a withdrawal established.*

I elaborated a draft text for an agreement along the lines I had in mind during the night between 15 and 16 November in Capodichino [Italy] I showed the text to Fawzi at our first talk on 16 November and I discussed practically only this issue with Nasser for seven hours in the evening and night of 17 November. Nasser, in this final discussion, where the text I had proposed was approved with some amendments, showed that he very fully understood that, by limiting their freedom of action in the way I proposed, they would take a very serious step, as it would mean that the question of the extent of the task would become decisive for the relations between Egypt and the United Nations and would determine Egypt's political freedom of action. He felt, not without justification, that the definition given of the task in the U.N. texts was very loose and that, tying the freedom of action of Egypt to the concept of the task—which had to be interpreted also by the General Assembly—and doing so in a written agreement, meant that he accepted a far-reaching and unpredictable restriction. To shoot the text through in spite of Nasser's strong wish to avoid this, and his strong suspicion of the legal construction—especially of the possible consequences of differences of views regarding the task—I felt obliged, in the course of the discussion, to threaten three times, that unless an agreement of this type was made, I would have to propose the immediate withdrawal of the troops. If any proof would be necessary for how the text of the agreement was judged by President Nasser, this last mentioned fact tells the story.

It is obvious that, with a text of the content mentioned approved by Egypt, the whole previous exchange of views was superseded by a formal and explicit recognition by Egypt of the stand I had taken all through, in particular on 9 and 12 November. The previous exchange of cables cannot any longer have any interpretative value as only the text of the agreement was put before the General Assembly and approved by it with the concurrence of Egypt and as its text was self-contained and conclusive. All further discussion, therefore, has to start from the text of the agreement, which is to be found in document A/3375. The interpretation of the text must be the one set out above.

65. The United States Urges Israeli Withdrawal from Sinai: Aide Memoire from Secretary of State Dulles to Ambassador Eban, February 11, 1957

The United Nations General Assembly has sought specifically, vigorously, and almost unanimously, the prompt withdrawal from Egypt of the armed forces of Britain, France and Israel. Britain and France have complied unconditionally. The forces of Israel have been withdrawn to a considerable extent but still hold Egyptian territory at Sharm el Shaikh at the entrance to the Gulf of Aqaba. They also occupy the Gaza Strip which is territory specified by the Armistice arrangements to be occupied by Egypt.

We understand that it is the position of Israel that (1) it will evacuate its military forces from the Gaza Strip provided Israel retains the civil administration and police in some relationship to the United Nations; and (2) it will withdraw from Sharm el Shaikh if continued freedom of passage through the Straits is assured.

With respect to (1) the Gaza Strip—it is the view of the United States that the United Nations General Assembly has no authority to require of either Egypt or Israel a substantial modification of the Armistice Agreement, which, as noted, now gives Egypt the right and responsibility of occupation. Accordingly, we believe that Israeli withdrawal from Gaza should be prompt and unconditional, leaving the future of the Gaza Strip to be worked out through the efforts and good offices of the United Nations.

We recognize that the area has been a source of armed infiltration and reprisals back and forth contrary to the Armistice Agreement and is a source of great potential danger because of the presence there of so large a number of Arab refugees—about 200,000. Accordingly, we believe that the United Nations General Assembly and the Secretary-General should seek that the United Nations Emergency Force, in the exercise of its mission, move into this area and be on the boundary between Israel and the Gaza Strip.

The United States will use its best efforts to help to assure this result, which we believe is contemplated by the Second Resolution of February 2, 1957.

With respect to (2) the Gulf of Aqaba and access thereto—the United States believes that the Gulf comprehends international waters and that no nation has the right to prevent free and innocent passage in the Gulf and through the Straits giving access thereto. We have in mind not only commercial usage, but the passage of pilgrims on religious missions which should be fully respected.

The United States recalls that on January 28, 1950, the Egyptian Ministry of Foreign Affairs informed the United States that the Egyptian occupation of the two islands of Tiran and Senafir at the entrance of the Gulf of Aqaba was only to protect the islands themselves against possible damage or violation and that "this occupation being in no way conceived in a spirit of obstructing in any way innocent passage through the stretch of water separating these two islands from the Egyptian coast of Sinai, it follows that this passage, the only practicable one, will remain free as in the past, in conformity with international practice and recognized principles of the law of nations."

In the absence of some overriding decision to the contrary, as by the International Court of Justice, the United States, on behalf of vessels of United States registry, is prepared to exercise the right of free and innocent passage and to join with others to secure general recognition of this right.

It is of course clear that the enjoyment of a right of free and innocent passage by Israel would depend upon its prior withdrawal in accordance with the United Nations Resolutions. The United States has no reason to assume that any littoral state would under these circumstances obstruct the right of free and innocent passage.

The United States believes that the United Nations General Assembly and the Secretary-General should, as a precautionary measure seek that the United Nations Emergency Force move into the Straits area as the Israeli forces are withdrawn. This again we believe to be within the contemplation of the Second Resolution of February 2, 1957.

(3) The United States observes that the recent resolutions of the United Nations General Assembly call not only for the prompt and unconditional withdrawal of Israel behind the Armistice lines but call for other measures.

We believe, however, that the United Nations has properly established an order of events and an order of urgency and that the first requirement is that forces of invasion and occupation should withdraw.

The United States is prepared publicly to declare that it will use its influence, in concert with other United Nations members, to the end that, following Israel's withdrawal, these other measures will be implemented.

We believe that our views and purposes in this respect are shared by many other nations and that a tranquil future for Israel is best assured by reliance upon that fact, rather than by an occupation in defiance of the overwhelming judgment of the world community.

66. Israel Agrees to Withdraw from Sinai: Statement by Israeli Foreign Minister Meir in the United Nations General Assembly, March 1, 1957

The Government of Israel is now in a position to announce its plans for full and prompt withdrawal from the Sharm el-Sheikh area and the Gaza Strip, in compliance with resolution I of 2 February 1957.

We have repeatedly stated that Israel has no interest in the strip of land overlooking the western coast of the Gulf of Aqaba. Our sole purpose has been to ensure that, on the withdrawal of Israel forces, continued freedom of navigation will exist for Israel and international shipping in the Gulf of Aqaba and the Straits of Tiran. Such freedom of navigation is a vital national interest for Israel, but it is also of importance and legitimate concern to the maritime Powers and to many States whose economies depend upon trade and navigation between the Red Sea and the Mediterranean Sea.

There has recently been an increasingly wide recognition that the Gulf of Aqaba comprehends international waters in which the right of free and innocent passage exists.

On 11 February 1957, the Secretary of State of the United States of America handed to the Ambassador of Israel in Washington a memorandum dealing, among other things, with the subject of the Gulf of Aqaba and the Straits of Tiran.

This statement discusses the rights of nations in the Gulf of Aqaba and declares the readiness of the United States to exercise those rights on its own behalf and to join with others in securing general recognition of those rights.

My Government has subsequently learned with gratification that other leading maritime Powers are prepared to subscribe to the doctrine set out in the United States memorandum of 11 February and have a similar intention to exercise their rights of free and innocent passage in the Gulf and the Straits.

The General Assembly's resolution (II) of 2 February 1957 contemplates that units of the United Nations Emergency Force will move into the Straits of Tiran area on Israel's withdrawal. It is generally recognized that the function of the United Nations Emergency Force in the Straits of Tiran area includes the prevention of belligerent acts.

In this connection, my Government recalls the statements by the representative of the United States in the General Assembly on 28 January and 2 February 1957, with reference to the function of the United Nations Emergency Force units which are to move into the Straits of Tiran area on Israel's withdrawal. The statement of 28 January, repeated on 2 February, said:

"It is essential that units of the United Nations Emergency Force be stationed at the Straits of Tiran in order to achieve there the separation of Egyptian and

Israeli land and sea forces. This separation is essential until it is clear that the non-existence of any claimed belligerent rights has established in practice the peaceful conditions which must govern navigation in waters having such an international interest."

My Government has been concerned with the situation which would arise if the United Nations Emergency Force, having taken up its position in the Straits of Tiran area for the purpose of assuring non-belligerency, were to be withdrawn, in conditions which might give rise to interference with free and innocent navigation and, therefore, to the renewal of hostilities. Such a premature cessation of the precautionary measures taken by the United Nations for the prevention of belligerent acts would prejudice important international interests and threaten peace and security. My Government has noted the assurance embodied in the Secretary-General's report of 26 February 1957, that any proposal for the withdrawal of the United Nations Emergency Force from the Gulf of Aqaba area would first come to the Advisory Committee, which represents the General Assembly in the implementation of its resolution of 2 November 1956. This procedure will give the General Assembly an opportunity to ensure that no precipitate changes are made which would have the effect of increasing the possibility of belligerent acts. We have reason to believe that in such a discussion many Members of the United Nations would be guided by the view expressed by Ambassador Lodge on 2 February in favor of maintaining the United Nations Emergency Force in the Straits of Tiran until peaceful conditions were in practice assured.

In the light of these doctrines, policies and arrangements by the United Nations and the maritime Powers, my Government is confident that free and innocent passage for international and Israel shipping will continue to be fully maintained after Israel's withdrawal.

It remains for me now to formulate the policy of Israel both as a littoral State and as a country which intends to exercise its full rights of free passage in the Gulf of Aqaba and through the Straits of Tiran.

The Government of Israel believes that the Gulf of Aqaba comprehends international waters and that no nation has the right to prevent free and innocent passage in the Gulf and through the Straits giving access thereto, in accordance with the generally accepted definition of those terms in the law of the sea.

In its capacity as a littoral State, Israel will gladly offer port facilities to the ships of all nations and all flags exercising free passage in the Gulf of Aqaba. We have received with gratification the assurances of leading maritime Powers that they foresee a normal and regular flow of traffic of all cargoes in the Gulf of Aqaba.

Israel will do nothing to impede free and innocent passage by ships of Arab countries bound to Arab posts or to any other destination.

Israel is resolved on behalf of vessels of Israel registry to exercise the right of free and innocent passage and is prepared to join with others to secure universal respect of this right.

Israel will protect ships of its own flag exercising the right of free and innocent passage on the high seas and in international waters.

Interference, by armed forces, with ships of Israel flag exercising free and innocent passage in the Gulf of Aqaba and through the Straits of Tiran, will be regarded by Israel as an attack entitling it to exercise its inherent right of self-defense under Article 51 of the Charter and to take all such measures as are necessary to ensure the free and innocent passage of its ships in the Gulf and in the Straits.

We make this announcement in accordance with the accepted principles of international law under which all States have an inherent right to use their forces to protect their ships and their rights against interference by armed force. My Government naturally hopes that this contingency will not occur.

In a public address on 20 February, President Eisenhower stated:

"We should not assume that if Israel withdraws, Egypt will prevent Israel shipping from using the Suez Canal or the Gulf of Aqaba."

This declaration has weighed heavily with my Government in determining its action today.

Israel is now prepared to withdraw its forces from the Gulf of Aqaba and the Straits of Tiran in the confidence that there will be continued freedom of navigation for international and Israeli shipping in the Gulf of Aqaba and through the Straits of Tiran.

We propose that a meeting be held immediately between the Chief of Staff of the Israel Defense Army and the Commander of the United Nations Emergency Force in order to arrange for the United Nations to take over its responsibilities in the Sharm el-Sheikh area.

The Government of Israel announces that it is making a complete withdrawal from the Gaza strip in accordance with General Assembly resolution (I) of 2 February 1957 (A/RES/460). It makes this announcement on the following assumptions:

(a) That on its withdrawal the United Nations Forces will be deployed in Gaza and that the takeover of Gaza from the military and civilian control of Israel will be exclusively by the United Nations Emergency Force.

(b) It is further Israel's expectation that the United Nations will be the agency to be utilized for carrying out the functions enumerated by the Secretary-General, namely:

"safeguarding life and property in the area by providing efficient and effective police protection; as will guarantee good civilian administration; as will assure maximum assistance to the United Nations refugee programme; and as will protect and foster the economic development of the territory and its people."

(c) It is further Israel's expectation that the aforementioned responsibility of the United Nations in the administration of Gaza will be maintained for a transitory period from the takeover until there is a peace settlement, to be sought as rapidly as possible, or a definitive agreement on the future of the Gaza strip.

It is the position of Israel that if conditions are created in the Gaza strip which indicate a return to the conditions of deterioration which existed previously, Israel would reserve its freedom to act to defend its rights.

Accordingly, we propose that a meeting be held immediately between the Chief of Staff of the Israel Defense Army and the Commander of the United Nations Emergency Force in order to arrange for the United Nations to take over its responsibilities in the Gaza area.

For many weeks, amidst great difficulty, my Government has sought to ensure that on the withdrawal from the Sharm el-Sheikh and the Gaza areas, circumstances would prevail which would prevent the likelihood of belligerent acts.

We record with gratitude the sympathetic efforts of many Governments and delegations to help bring about a situation which would end the insecurity prevailing for Israel and her neighbours these many years. In addition, to the considerations to which I have referred, we place our trust in the vigilant resolve of the international community that Israel, equally with all Member States, enjoy its basic rights of freedom from fear of attack; freedom to sail the high seas and international waterways in peace, freedom to pursue its national destiny in tranquillity without the constant peril which has surrounded it in recent years.

In this reliance we are embarking upon the course which I have announced today.

May I now add these few words to the States in the Middle East area and, more specifically, to the neighbours of Israel:

We all come from an area which is a very ancient one. The hills and the valleys of the region have been witnesses to many wars and many conflicts. But that is not the only thing which characterizes that part of the world from which we come. It is also a part of the world which is of an ancient culture. It is that part of the world which has given to humanity three great religions. It is also that part of the world which has given a code of ethics to all humanity. In our countries, in the entire region, all our peoples are anxious for and in need of a higher standard of living, of great programmes of development and progress.

Can we, from now on—all of us—turn a new leaf and, instead of fighting with each other, can we all, united, fight poverty and disease and illiteracy? Is it possible for us to put all our efforts and all our energy into one single purpose, the betterment and progress and development of all our lands and all our peoples?

I can here pledge the Government and the people of Israel to do their part in this united effort. There is no limit to what we are prepared to contribute so that all of us, together, can live to see a day of happiness for our peoples and see again from that region a great contribution to peace and happiness for all humanity.

D. THE SECOND TRUCE: CONTINUED TENSIONS

67. United States Opposition to the Introduction or Manufacture of Nuclear Weapons in the Middle East: President Kennedy's News Conference, April 3, 1963

As you know, the German Government itself has indicated its displeasure, and there is some question of whether it may be a breach of the law, the German scientists who are working on missiles, air engines, and air frames for the U.A.R. There is not a great number of them, but there are some of them, and of course they do affect the tensions of the Middle East. So I think this matter has been very strongly brought to the attention by the Israeli Government and by other interested parties who are seeking to diminish rather than increase the arms race in the Middle East.[1]

Now, on the question of what military assistance we would give the Israelis: as you know, the United States has never been a supplier of military equipment directly to the Israelis. We have given economic assistance. The Israelis themselves have bought equipment, a good deal of it from France. We will just have to see what the balance of the military power may be in the Middle East, as time goes on. We are anxious to see it diminished rather than participate in encouraging it.

On the other hand, we would be reluctant to see a military balance of power in the Middle East which was such as to encourage aggression rather than discourage it. So this is a matter which we will have to continue to observe. We have expressed our strong opposition to the introduction or manufacture of nuclear weapons in the Middle East, and we have indicatd that strongly to all of the countries. So we have to wait and see as the time goes on. At the present time, there is a balance which I think would discourage military action on either side. I would hope it will continue.

68. United States Supports Security of Both Israel and Her Neighbors: President Kennedy's News Conference, November 14, 1963

I don't think that the balance of military power has been changed in the Middle East in recent days. Obviously there are political changes in the Middle East which still do not show a precise pattern and on which we are unable to make any final judgments. The United States supports social and economic and political progress in the Middle East. We support the security of both Israel and her neighbors. We seek to limit the Near East arms race which obviously takes resources from an area already poor and puts them into an increasing race which does not really bring any great security.

We strongly oppose the use of force or the threat of force in the Near East, and we also seek to limit the spread of communism in the Middle East which would, of course, destroy the independence of the people. This Government has been and remains strongly opposed to the use of force or the threat of force in the Near East. In the event of aggression or preparation for aggression, whether direct or indirect, we would support appropriate measures in the United Nations, adopt other courses of action on our own to prevent or to put a stop to such aggression, which, of course, has been the policy which the United States has followed for some time.

---

[1] Reference to protests by the Israel Foreign Minister (Meir) and the Israel Knesset of Mar. 20, and by the Zionist Organization of America of Mar. 31, 1963.

186

VI.

The June War
and
Its Aftermath

The roots of the June war of 1967 are, of course, as old as the Arab-Israeli dispute itself. However, a new factor which greatly increased tension appeared in the area in 1965. The Palestinian Arabs, despairing of ever getting unified and effective support from Arab governments for their efforts to regain their homeland, began to form their own independent guerrilla organizations to harass Israel. These received support mainly from Syria—the most radical of all Arab regimes then in power. Jordan was apprehensive of Israeli retaliation, but was reluctant to stop the guerrilla organizations, which enjoyed great popular appeal— particularly among the ranks of Arab youth.

The guerrillas' growing effectiveness and popularity in the Arab states caused Israel to react with her customary policy of retaliation by regular forces against the Arab states in which the small commando and terrorist attacks originated. The inability of the Arab governments effectively to resist these Israeli raids weakened their standing with their people, but, more importantly, they greatly embarrassed President Nasser of the United Arab Republic. He claimed to be the leader of the Arab world, but in reality his forces were being sheltered behind the shield of the UNEF (a force stationed with his consent on Egypt's soil, but excluded by Israel) while others bore the burdens of the struggle. As tension on the Syrian-Israeli border mounted in the spring of 1967, President Nasser dramatically demanded and then secured the removal of the UNEF. United Nations Secretary General U Thant explained that the force was there with the consent of Egypt, and could not remain if Cairo demanded its withdrawal. The delaying procedures of the Hammarskjold Memorandum (see document number 64, chapter V, above) were not applied by U Thant. Nasser then announced that the Gulf of Aqaba would be closed to Israeli shipping and reinforced his troops in the border area. He also formed a joint military command with his erstwhile enemies, King Hussein of Jordan and the Syrian Ba'ath Party regime.

The UAR had thus regained, with virtually no effort, the leadership of the Arab nationalist cause and had presented Israel with a *fait accompli*. The United States attempted to dampen the build-up of tensions and to secure freedom of navigation in the Gulf of Aqaba. On May 23, 1967, President Johnson stated that the United States was firmly opposed to aggression and supported the political independence and territorial integrity of all nations in the area.

The Israelis, however, refused to accept the *fait accompli* presented to them by President Nasser in the form of new-found Arab unity and his announced but still untested blockade of the Gulf of Aqaba. The war began with an Israeli attack on the Sinai Peninsula on June 5. When Jordan and Syria joined the conflict they were in turn defeated. After intense diplomatic activity in the United Nations, cease-fires were finally secured between the combatants—the last between Syria and Israel coming on June 11. In six days the Israeli armed forces had been uniformly successful, and they were in occupation of all of Palestine. They had also added the Golan Heights of Syria and the entire Sinai Peninsula, as far as the banks of the Suez Canal, to their conquests.

The United States and the Soviet Union had shown themselves reluctant to become involved in the conflict. The Soviet Union gave full diplomatic support to the actions of the Arabs, maintaining that the sole cause of the war was Israeli aggression. The United States pointed out that provocations from the Arab side had been serious and continuous. In the shock of defeat certain Arab states shunned all ties with the United States and Great Britain, but they were also disappointed at the lack of effective Soviet support. Cairo and Amman tried for a time to claim that British and American planes had aided the Israelis, but this charge was eventually dropped. An Arab embargo on oil exports was soon abandoned by decision of the Arab Summit Conference at Khartoum in August-September, 1967.

Israeli occupation of Arab territories then emerged as the most pressing issue in Arab-Israeli relations. Israel insisted that her troops could only be withdrawn as part of a formal peace treaty signed with the Arab states. The Arabs argued that they could not negotiate until the Israelis had withdrawn from Arab lands. Hundreds of thousands of new refugees appeared as Arabs fled from the West Bank territory of Jordan, across the Jordan River to old Trans-Jordan.

The Glassboro Summit Conference was an important indication that both the United States and the Soviet Union had no intention of becoming active participants in the Arab-Israeli war. It was far from successful, however, in reaching an agreement leading to peace in the area. President Johnson pointed out that all nations in the area had a right to national existence and that Israeli troops should be withdrawn under "the right circumstances." Premier Kosygin stated that the main problem was the withdrawal of troops, without indicating any prior conditions for this withdrawal.

One major territorial gain for Israel was her conquest of the old Arab city of Jerusalem. She made prompt efforts to annex and integrate the former Jordanian sector into Israeli Jerusalem, and Israeli leaders repeatedly announced they would never give up this territory. The United States continued to maintain its traditional objection that no unilateral action of any state could change the international status of Jerusalem. However, in deference to Israel, the United States abstained from the strongly-worded United Nations General Assembly resolution condemning Israel's action. This resolution was passed by a vote of 99 to 0, with 20 abstentions.

In the aftermath of the war a number of peace plans were proposed by the United States, the Soviet Union, the Israelis, and the Arabs. United States policy has been to support a balanced plan, one which would assure Israel's right to live in peace and security, but which would also solve the Arab refugee problem and secure the territorial integrity of all states. The United States has also continually emphasized the importance of reducing the arms race in the area as a step towards the lessening of tensions. President Johnson's speech of September 10, 1968, made a further clarification of the policy of supporting the territorial intergity of all states in the area. He held that the precise position of the borders between Israel and her Arab neighbors must be a matter of negotiation, but that they "cannot and should not reflect the weight of conquest."

The most significant of the peace plans was the unanimous United Nations Security Council Resolution of November 22, 1967, passed unanimously. It was a carefully balanced set of principles, with points made for each side. More importantly, the British-originated resolution was approved by both the United States and the Soviet Union, showing their desire to reach a settlement of this explosive issue. However, the efforts of the United Nations special representative, Gunnar Jarring, were unable to shake either side from its initial bargaining position. The Israelis insisted on direct negotiations with the Arab states and a formal peace treaty guaranteeing their borders before agreeing to withdraw from occupied Arab territory. They have pointed to their withdrawal in 1957 following the Suez war on the strength of promises of international support for their rights to the navigation of the Gulf of Aqaba, promises which proved to be ineffective when President Nasser demanded the removal of the UNEF. The Arabs continue to insist that they cannot negotiate until after "the consequences of aggression"—the Israeli occupation of Arab territory—have been eliminated. The interviews with President Nasser and Prime Minister Eshkol included in this collection illustrate these basic positions. Opinion in Israel is itself divided over the wisdom of giving up any of the conquered territory. When the late Prime Minister Eshkol indicated in his *Newsweek* interview that Arab territory, with the exception of Jerusalem, might be returned to secure peace he was faced with criticism in Israel. This led to a Knesset motion of no-confidence, which was voted down. President Nasser's indication that the Arabs would be willing to end their state of belligerency with Israel showed that the Arab states were prepared to allow Israeli navigation of the Suez Canal and to end their boycott of companies doing business with Israel, since this state of belligerency was the legal justification for these measures. This was confirmed in King Hussein's six-point peace plan, which he presented, with Nasser's endorsement, during his visit to the United States in April, 1969. (See document number 82.)

The United Nations cease fire which went into effect after the end of the June war was broken repeatedly by both sides, following much the same pattern as that which led up to the crisis of 1967. Guerrilla raids by Arab commandos and terrorist bombings were countered by Israeli army and air strikes aimed at both the Arab guerrillas and at the Arab governments, which Israel charged with protecting the guerrillas. The United States joined in United Nations condemnation of the large-scale Israeli raids, but also condemned truce violations by the Arab side.

After the Nixon Administration took over, there were new initiatives by the United States and the Soviet Union to reach a settlement of the Arab-Israeli dispute. Former Governor Scranton's fact-finding visit to the Middle East and subsequent statements at a New York press conference indicated the Nixon Administration's desire to move away from an excessively close identification of United States interests with Israeli policy. President Nixon tried new approaches, principally through four-power talks of the United States, Britain, France, and the Soviet Union within the framework of the United Nations. These sought to implement the principles of the November 22 Security Council peace plan.

Israel was especially critical of these efforts by outside powers, fearing an "imposed solution" unfavorable to herself. President Nixon denied that the four-power talks sought to impose a solution, but pointed out they could make a definite contribution towards a settlement. Both moderate and radical Arab governments, led by Jordan and the UAR, have accepted the idea of four-power talks. However, other forces in the Arab world, especially the Palestinian guerrilla organizations, have condemned them. As settlement continued to be delayed, the power of these intransigent elements increased, making the survival of the governments of the Arab states increasingly difficult.

A. THE OUTBREAK OF WAR

69. The Palestinian Guerrillas Organize: Communique No. 1
From Headquarters of Asifa Forces
January 6, 1965

From among our steadfast people, waiting at the borders, our revolutionary vanguard has issued forth, in the belief that armed revolution is our only path to Palestine and freedom. Let the imperialists and Zionists know that the people of Palestine are still in the field of battle and shall never be swept away.

Our enemies have forgotten our strength and our history of revolutions. We are determined to resort to armed conflict whatever the obstacles, until all conspiracies are foiled. The Zionists have planned to stay long in our country by executing diversion and reconstruction projects aimed at increasing their potential for aggression and forcing the Arab world to accept the fait accompli.

Because of all these threats and since time is running out, our revolutionary vanguard had to move fast in order to paralyze the enemy's plans and projects. In this task, we rely upon our own strength and on the capabilities of the people of Palestine.

We hereby declare to the whole world that we are bound indissolubly to the soil of our homeland. Our moving force is our own faith that this is the only means which can reactivate our problem which has been dormant for so long. But we must also inform the world that we are bound, by our destiny and struggle, to the Arab nation which will help us, both materially and morally.

We appeal to the Arabs of Palestine, to our single Arab nation and to lovers of freedom everywhere to aid the fighting men of the Asifa in their heroic struggle. We pledge ourselves to fight until Palestine its liberated and resumes its place in the very heart of the Arab world. Long live the Arab nation. Long live our Arab Palestine.

70. Withdrawal of the UNEF from the United Arab Republic:
Report by Secretary General U Thant to Security Council
(excerpts) May 20, 1967

1. I have felt it to be an obligation to submit this report in order to convey to members of the Council my deep anxiety about recent developments in the Near East and what I consider to be an increasingly dangerous deterioration along the borders there.

2. The members of the Council will be aware of the Special Report on the United Nations Emergency Force which I made to the General Assembly on 18 May 1967.

3. I am very sorry to feel obliged to say that in my considered opinion the

prevailing state of affairs in the Near East as regards relations between the Arab States and Israel, and among the Arab States themselves, is extremely menacing.

*　　*　　*

6. A number of factors serve to aggravate the situation to an unusual degree, increasing tension and danger.

7. El Fatah activities, consisting of terrorism and sabotage, are a major factor in that they provoke strong reactions in Israel by the Government and population alike. Some recent incidents of this type have seemed to indicate a new level of organization and training of those who participate in these actions. It is clear that the functions and resources of UNTSO do not enable it to arrest these activities.

Although allegations are often made, to the best of my knowledge there is no verified information about the organization, central direction and originating source of these acts, which have occurred intermittently in the vicinity of Israel's lines with Jordan, Lebanon and Syria. All three of the latter Governments have officially disclaimed responsibility for these acts and those who perpetrate them. I am not in a position to say whether any or all of the Governments concerned have done everything they reasonably can to prevent such activities across their borders. The fact is that they do recur with disturbing regularity.

8. Intemperate and bellicose utterances by other officials and non-officials, eagerly reported by press and radio, are unfortunately more or less routine on both sides of the lines in the Near East. In recent weeks, however, reports emanating from Israel have attributed to some high officials in that State statements so threatening as to be particularly inflammatory in the sense that they could only heighten emotions and thereby increase tensions on the other side of the lines.

9. There have been in the past few days persistent reports about troop movements and concentrations, particularly on the Israel side of the Syrian border. These have caused anxiety and at times excitement. The Government of Israel very recently has assured me that there are no unusual Israel troop concentrations or movements along the Syrian line, that there will be none and that no military action will be initiated by the armed forces of Israel unless such action is first taken by the other side. Reports from UNTSO Observers have confirmed the absence of troop concentrations and significant troop movements on both sides of the line.

10. The decision of the Government of the United Arab Republic to terminate its consent for the continued presence of the United Nations Emergency Force on United Arab Republic territory in Sinai and on United Arab Republic controlled territory in Gaza came suddenly and was unexpected. The reasons for this decision have not been officially stated, but they were clearly regarded as overriding by the Government of the United Arab Republic. It is certain that they had nothing to do with the conduct of UNEF itself or the way in which it was carrying out the mandate entrusted to it by the General Assembly and accepted by the Government of the United Arab Republic when it gave its consent for the deployment of UNEF within its jurisdiction.

There can be no doubt, in fact, that UNEF has discharged its responsibilities with remarkable effectiveness and great distinction. No United Nations peace-keeping operation can be envisaged as permanent or semi-permanent. Each one must come to an end at some time or another.

UNEF has been active for ten and a half years and that is a very long time for any country to have foreign troops, even under an international banner, operating autonomously on its soil. On the other hand, it can be said that the timing of the withdrawal of UNEF leaves much to be desired because of the prevailing tensions and dangers throughout the area. It also adds one more frontier on which there is a direct confrontation between the military forces of Israel and those of her Arab neighbors.

11. It is well to bear in mind that United Nations peace-keeping operations such as UNEF, and this applies in fact to all peace-keeping operations thus far undertaken by the United Nations, depend for their presence and effectiveness not only on the consent of the authorities in the area of their deployment but on the co-operation and good will of those authorities. When, for example, the United Arab Republic decided to move its troops up to the line, which it had a perfect right to do, the buffer function which UNEF had been performing was eliminated. Its continued presence was thus rendered useless, its position untenable, and its withdrawal became virtually inevitable. This was the case even before the official request for the withdrawal had been received by me.

12. It is all too clear that there is widespread misunderstanding about the nature of United Nations peace-keeping operations in general and UNEF in particular. As I pointed out in my Special Report of 18 May 1967 to the General Assembly "The United Nations Emergency Force is, after all, a peace-keeping and not an enforcement operation." This means, of course, that the operation is based entirely on its acceptance by the governing authority of the territory on which it operates and that it is not in any sense related to Chapter VII of the Charter. It is a fact beyond dispute that neither UNEF nor any other United Nations peace-keeping operation thus far undertaken would have been permitted to enter the territory involved if there had been any suggestion that it had the right to remain there against the will of the governing authoriy.

13. The order for the withdrawal of UNEF has been given. The actual process of withdrawal will be orderly, deliberate, and dignified and not precipitate.

14. I do not believe that any of the Governments concerned are so careless of the welfare of their own people or of the risks of a spreading conflict as to deliberately embark on military offensives across their borders, unless they become convinced, rightly or wrongly, that they are threatened. Nevertheless, there is good reason to fear that the withdrawal of UNEF will give rise to increased danger along the Armistice Demarcation Line and the International Frontier between Israel and the United Arab Republic. The presence of UNEF has been a deterrent and restraining influence along both lines. There are some particularly sensitive areas involved, notably Sharm el-Sheikh and Gaza. The former concerns the Strait of Tiran. In the Gaza Strip there are 307,000 refugees and the substantial Palestine Liberation Army must also be taken into account.

15. It is true to a considerable extent that UNEF has allowed us for ten years to ignore some of the hard realities of the underlying conflict. The Governments concerned, and the United Nations, are now confronted with a brutally realistic and dangerous situation.

*　　*　　*

19. I do not wish to be alarmist but I cannot avoid the warning to the Council that in my view the current situation in the Near East is more disturbing, indeed, I may say more menacing, than at any time since the fall of 1956.

71. Closing of the Gulf of Aqaba: Speech to Armed Forces by President Nasser, May 22, 1967

The entire country looks up to you today. The entire Arab nation supports you.

It is clear that in these circumstances the entire people fully support you and consider the armed forces as their hope today. It is definite that the entire Arab nation also supports our armed forces in the present circumstances through which the entire Arab nation is passing.

What I wish to say is that we are now in 1967, and not in 1956, after the tripartite aggression. A great deal was said and all the secrets were ambiguous. Israel, its commanders and rulers, boasted a great deal after 1956. I have read every word written about the 1956 events, and I also know exactly what happened in 1956.

On the night of Oct. 29, 1956, the Israeli aggression against us began. Fighting began on Oct. 30. We received the Anglo-French ultimatum which asked us to withdraw several miles west of the Suez Canal.

On Oct. 31, the Anglo-French attack on us began. The air raids began at sunset on Oct. 31. At the same time, all our forces in Sinai were withdrawn completely to inside Egypt. Thus in 1956 we did not have an opportunity to fight Israel. We decided to withdraw before the actual fighting with Israel began.

Despite our decision to withdraw, Israel was unable to occupy any of our positions except after we left them. But Israel created a big uproar, boasted and said a great deal about the Sinai campaign and the Sinai battle.

Every one of you knows all the rubbish that was said. They probably believed it themselves.

Today, more than 10 years after Suez, all the secrets have been exposed. The most important secret concerns Ben-Gurion, when the imperialists brought him to France to employ him as a dog for imperialism to begin the operation.

Ben-Gurion refused to undertake anything unless he was given a written guarantee that they would protect him from the Egyptian bombers and the Egyptian Air Force. All this is no longer secret. The entire world knows.

It was on this basis that France sent fighter planes to Ben-Gurion, and it was also on this basis that Britain pledged to Ben-Gurion to bomb Egyptian airfields within 24 hours after the aggression began.

This goes to show how much they took into account the Egyptian forces. Ben-Gurion himself said he had to think about the Haifa-Jerusalem-Tel Aviv triangle, which contains one-third of Israel's population. He could not attack Egypt out of fear of the Egyptian Air Force and bombers.

At that time we had a few Ilyushin bombers. We had just acquired them to arm ourselves. Today we have many Ilyushins and others. There is a great difference between yesterday and today, between 1956 and 1967.

Why do I say all this? I say it because we are in a confrontation with Israel. Israel today is not backed by Britain and France as was the case in 1956. It has the United States, which supports it and supplies it with arms. But the world cannot again accept the plotting which took place in 1956.

Israel has been clamouring since 1956. It speaks of Israel's competence and high standard of living. It is backed in this by the West and the Western press. They capitalized on the Sinai campaign, where no fighting actually took place because we had withdrawn to confront Britain and France.

Today we have a chance to prove the fact. We have, indeed, a chance to make the world see matters in their true perspective. We are now face to face with Israel. In recent days Israel has been making threats of aggression and it has been boasting.

On May 12 a very impertinent statement was made. Anyone reading this statement must believe that these people are so boastful and deceitful that one simply cannot remain silent. The statement said that the Israeli commanders have announced they would carry out military operations against Syria in order to occupy Damascus and overthrow the Syrian Government.

On the same day, Israeli Premier Eshkol made a strongly threatening statement against Syria. At the same time, the commentaries said that Israel believed Egypt could not make a move because it was bogged down in Yemen.

Of course they say that we are bogged down in Yemen and have problems there. We are in Yemen. But they seem to believe the lies they have been saying all these years about our existence in Yemen. It is also possible that the Israelis believe such lies.

We are capable of bearing our duties in Yemen, and at the same time doing our national duty here in Egypt in defending our borders and in attacking if Israel attacks Arab country.

On May 13 we received accurate information that Israel was concentrating on the Syrian border huge armed forces of about 11 to 13 brigades. These forces were divided into two fronts, one south of Lake Tiberias and the other north of the lake.

The decision made by Israel at this time was to carry out an aggression against Syria as of May 17. On May 14 we took our measures, discussed the matter and contacted our Syrian brothers. The Syrians also had this information.

On this basis, Lieut. Gen. Mahmud Fawzi left for Syria to coordinate matters. We told them that we had decided that if Syria was attacked, Egypt would enter the battle from the first minute. This was the situation May 14. The forces began to move in the direction of Sinai to take up normal positions.

News agencies reported yesterday that these military movements must have been the result of a previously well-laid plan. And I say that the sequence of events determined the plan. We had no plan before May 13, because we believed that

Israel would not dare attack any Arab country and that Israel would not have dared to make such an impertinent statement.

On May 16 we requested the withdrawal of the United Nations Emergency Force (U.N.E.F.) in a letter from Lieut. Gen. Mahmud Fawzi. We then requested the complete withdrawal of U.N.E.F.

A big worldwide campaign, led by the United States, Britain and Canada, began opposing the withdrawal of U.N.E.F. from Egypt. Thus we felt that there were attempts to turn U.N.E.F. into a force serving neoimperialism.

It is obvious that U.N.E.F. entered Egypt with our approval and therefore cannot continue to stay in Egypt except with our approval. Until yesterday, a great deal was said about U.N.E.F.

A campaign is also being mounted against the United Nations Secretary General because he made a faithful and honest decision and could not surrender to the pressure brought to bear upon him by the United States, Britain and Canada to make U.N.E.F. an instrument for implementing imperialism's plans.

It is quite natural—and I say this quite frankly—that had U.N.E.F. ignored its basic mission and turned to achieving the aims of imperialism, we would have regarded it as a hostile force and forcibly disarmed it. We are definitely capable of doing such a job.

I say this now not to discredit the U.N.E.F. but to those who have neoimperalist ideas and who want the United Nations to achieve their aims. There is not a single nation which truly respects itself and enjoys full sovereignty which could accept these methods in any form.

At the same time I say that the U.N.E.F. has honorably and faithfully carried out its duties. And the U.N. Secretary General refused to succumb to pressure. Thus he issued immediate orders to withdraw. Consequently, we laud the U.N.E.F. which stayed 10 years in our country serving peace.

And when they left—at a time when we found that the neoimperialist forces wanted to divert them from their basic aim—we gave them a cheerful sendoff and saluted them.

Our forces are now in Sinai, and we are in a state of complete mobilization in Gaza and Sinai. We note that there is a great deal of talk about peace these days. Peace, peace, international peace, international security, U.N. intervention and so on and so forth, which appears daily in the press.

Why is it that no one spoke about peace, the United Nations and security when on May 12 the Israel Premier and the Israeli commanders made their statements that they would occupy Damascus, overthrow the Syrian region, strike vigorously at Syria and occupy a part of Syrian territory?

It was obvious that they approved of the statements made by the Israeli Premier and commanders.

There is talk about peace now. What is peace? If there is a true desire for peace, we say that we also work for peace.

But does peace mean that we should ignore the rights of the Palestinian people because of the lapse of time? Does peace mean that we should concede our rights because of the lapse of time? Nowadays they speak about a "U.N. presence in the

197

region for the sake of peace." Does "U.N. presence in the region for peace" mean that we should close our eyes to everything?

The United Nations adopted a number of resolutions in favor of the Palestinian people. Israel implemented none of these resolutions. This brought no reaction from the United States.

Today U.S. Senators, members of the House of Representatives, the press and the entire world speak in favor of Israel, of the Jews. But nothing is said in favor of the Arabs.

The U.N. resolutions which are in favor of the Arabs were not implemented. What does this mean? No one is speaking in the Arab's favor. How does the United Nations stand with regard to the Palestinian people? How does it stand with regard to the tragedy which has continued since 1958?

The peace talk is heard only when Israel is in danger. But when Arab rights and the rights of the Palestinian people are lost, no one speaks about peace, rights or anything.

Therefore it is clear that an alliance exists between the Western powers—chiefly represented by the United States and Britain—and Israel. There is a political alliance. This political alliance prompts the Western powers to give military equipment to Israel.

Yesterday and the day before yesterday, the entire world was speaking about Sharm el-Sheikh, navigation in the Gulf of Aqaba, the Elath port. This morning I heard the B.B.C. say that in 1956 Abdel Nasser pledged to open the Gulf of Aqaba.

Of course this is not true. It was copied from a British paper called The Daily Mail. No such thing happened. Abdel Nasser would never forfeit any U.A.R. right. As I said, we would never give away a grain of sand from our soil or our country.

The armed forces' responsibility is now yours. The armed forces yesterday occupied Sharm el-Sheikh. What is the meaning of the armed force's occupation of Sharm el-Sheikh? It is an affirmation of our rights and our sovereignty over the Aqaba Gulf. The Aqaba Gulf constitutes our Egyptian territorial waters. Under no circumstances will we allow the Israeli flag to pass through the Aqaba Gulf.

The Jews threatened war. We tell them: You are welcome, we are ready for war. Our armed forces and all our people are ready for war, but under no circumstances will we abandon any of our rights. This water is ours.

War might be an opportunity for the Jews—for Israel and Rabin [Maj. Gen. Itzhak Rabin, the Chief of Staff]—to test their forces against ours and to see that what they wrote about the 1956 battle and the occupation of Sinai was all a lot of nonsense.

Of course there is imperialism, Israel and reaction. Reaction casts doubt on everything, and so does the Islamic Alliance.

We all know that the Islamic Alliance is now represented by three states: the kingdom of Saudi Arabia, the kingdom of Jordan, and Iran. They are saying that the purpose of the Islamic Alliance is to unite the Moslems against Israel.

I would like the Islamic Alliance to serve the Palestinian question in only one way: by preventing the supply of oil to Israel. The oil which now reaches Israel through Elath comes from one of the Islamic Alliance states. It goes to Elath from Iran.

Who is supplying Israel with oil? The Islamic Alliance—Iran, an Islamic Alliance state.

Such is the Islamic Alliance. It is an imperialist alliance, and this means it sides with Zionism because Zionism is the main ally of imperialism.

The Arab world, which is now mobilized to the highest degree, knows all this. It knows how to deal with the imperialist agents, the allies of Zionism and the fifth column. They say they want to coordinate their plans with us. We cannot at all coordinate our plans with the Islamic Alliance members because it would mean giving our plans to the Jews and to Israel.

This is a serious battle. When we said we were ready for the battle, we meant that we would indeed fight if Syria or any other Arab state was subjected to aggression.

The armed forces are now everywhere. The army and all the forces are now mobilized, and so are the people. They are all behind you, praying for you day and night and feeling that you are the pride of their nation, of the Arab nation. This is the feeling of the Arab people in Egypt and outside Egypt. We are confident that you will honor the trust.

Every one of us is ready to die and not give away a grain of his country's sand. This, for us, is the greatest honor. It is the greatest honor for us to defend our country. We are not scared by imperialist, Zionism or reactionary campaigns.

We are independent, and we know the taste of freedom. We have built a strong national army and achieved our objectives. We are building our country.

There is currently a propaganda campaign, a psychological campaign and a campaign of doubt against us. We leave all this behind us and follow the course of duty and victory.

May God be with you!

72. United States Supports Independence and Integrity of All Nations in the Area: Statement by President Johnson, May 23, 1967

In recent days, tension has again arisen along the armistice lines between Israel and the Arab States. The situation there is a matter of very grave concern to the whole international community. We earnestly support all efforts, in and outside the United Nations and through the appropriate organs, including the Secretary General, to reduce tensions and to restore stability. The Secretary General has gone to the Near East on his mission of peace with the hopes and prayers of men of good will everywhere.

The Near East links three continents. The birthplace of civilization and of three of the world's great religions, it is the home of some 60 million people and it is the crossroads betweeen the East and the West.

The world community has a vital interest in peace and stability in the Near East, one that has been expressed primarily through continuing United Nations action and assistance over the past 20 years.

The United States, as a member of the United Nations and as a nation dedicated to a world order based on law and mutual respect, has actively supported efforts to maintain peace in the Near East.

The danger, and it is a very grave danger, lies in some miscalculation arising from a misunderstanding of the intentions and actions of others.

The Government of the United States is deeply concerned, in particular, with three potentially explosive aspects of the present confrontation.

First, we regret that the General Armistice Agreements have failed to prevent warlike acts from the territory of one against another government, or against civilians or territory, under control of another government.

Second, we are dismayed at the hurried withdrawal of the United Nations Emergency Force from Gaza and Sinai after more than 10 years of steadfast and effective service in keeping the peace, without action by either the General Assembly or the Security Council of the United Nations. We continue to regard the presence of the United Nations in the area as a matter of fundamental importance. We intend to support its continuance with all possible vigor.

Third, we deplore the recent buildup of military forces and believe it a matter of urgent importance to reduce troop concentrations. The status of sensitive areas, as the Secretary General emphasized in his report to the Security Council, such as the Gaza Strip and the Gulf of Aqaba, is a particularly important aspect of the situation.

In this connection, I want to add that the purported closing of the Gulf of Aqaba to Israeli shipping has brought a new and very grave dimension to the crisis. The United States considers the gulf to be an international waterway and feels that a blockade of Israel shipping is illegal and potentially disastrous to the cause of peace. The right of free, innocent passage of the international waterway is a vital interest of the entire international community.

The Government of the United States is seeking clarification on this point. We have already urged Secretary General Thant to recognize the sensitivity of the Aqaba question and we have asked him to give it the highest priority in his discussions in Cairo.

To the leaders of all the nations of the Near East, I wish to say what three American Presidents have said before me—that the United States is firmly committed to the support of the political independence and territorial integrity of all the nations of that area. The United States strongly opposes aggression by anyone in the area, in any form, overt or clandestine. This has been the policy of the United States led by four Presidents—President Truman, President Eisenhower, President John F. Kennedy, and myself—as well as the policy of both of our political parties. The record of the actions of the United States over the past 20 years, within and outside the United Nations, is abundantly clear on this point.

The United States has consistently sought to have good relations with all the states of the Near East. Regrettably this has not always been possible, but we are convinced that our difference with individual states of the area and their differences with each other must be worked out peacefully and in accordance with accepted international practice.

We have always opposed—and we oppose in other parts of the world at this very moment—the efforts of other nations to resolve their problems with their neighbors by the aggression route. We shall continue to do so. And tonight we appeal to all other peace-loving nations to do likewise.

I call upon all concerned to observe in a spirit of restraint their solemn responsibilities under the Charter of the United Nations and the General Armistice Agreements. These provide an honorable means of preventing hostilities until, through the efforts of the international community, a peace with justice and honor can be achieved.

I have been in close and very frequent contact—and will be in the hours and days ahead—with our able Ambassador, Mr. Goldberg, at the United Nations, where we are now pursuing the matter with great vigor, and we hope that the Security Council can and will act effectively.

B. THE GLASSBORO SUMMIT MEETING

73. President Johnson's Report to the Nation, June 25, 1967

On my return tonight to the White House after two days of talks at Hollybush, I want to make this brief report to the American people.

We continued our discussions today in the same spirit in which we began them on Friday—a spirit of direct face-to-face exchanges between leaders with very heavy responsibilities.

We wanted to meet again because the issues before us are so large and so difficult that one meeting together was not nearly enough. The two meetings have been better than one, and at least we learned—I know I did—from each hour of our talks.

You will not be surprised to know that these two meetings have not solved all of our problems. On some, we have made progress—great progress in reducing misunderstanding, I think, and in reaffirming our common commitment to seek agreement.

I think we made that kind of progress, for example, on the question of arms limitation. We have agreed this afternoon that Secretary of State Rusk and Mr. Gromyko will pursue this subject further in New York in the days ahead.

I must report that no agreement is readily in sight on the Middle Eastern crisis and that our well-known differences over Viet-Nam continue. Yet even on these issues, I was very glad to hear the Chairman's views face to face and to have a chance to tell him directly and in detail just what our purposes and our policies are—and are not—in these particular areas.

The Chairman, I believe, made a similar effort with me.

When nations have deeply different positions, as we do on these issues, they do not come to agreement merely by improving their understanding of each other's views. But such improvement helps. Sometimes in such discussions you can find elements—beginnings—hopeful fractions—of common ground, even within a general disagreement.

It was so in the Middle East two weeks ago when we agreed on the need for a prompt cease-fire. And it is so today in respect to such simple propositions as that every state has a right to live, that there should be an end to the war in the Middle East, and that in the right circumstances there should be withdrawal of troops. This is a long way from agreement, but it is a long way also from total differences.

*   *   *

As I warned on Friday—and as I just must warn again on this Sunday afternoon—meetings like these do not themselves make peace in the world. We must all remember that there have been many meetings before and they have not ended all of our troubles or all of our dangers.

But I can also report on this Sunday afternoon another thing that I said on last Friday: That it does help a lot to sit down and look at a man right in the eye and try to reason with him, particularly if he is trying to reason with you.

We may have differences and difficulties ahead, but I think they will be lessened, and not increased by our new knowledge of each other.

Chairman Kosygin and I have agreed that the leaders of our two countries will keep in touch in the future, through our able secretaries and ambassadors, and also keep in touch directly.

I said on Friday that the world is very small and very dangerous. Tonight I believe that it is fair to say that these days at Hollybush have made it a little smaller still—but also a little less dangerous.

74. Premier Kosygin's News Conference Statement, June 25, 1967

On June 25 a second meeting between the Chairman of the Council of Ministers of the U.S.S.R., Mr. Kosygin, and President Johnson of the United States, was held in the town of Glassboro, not far from New York. At the second meeting, as at the first, which took place on June 23, the exchange of views touched upon several international problems.

In connection with the situation in the Middle East, the two sides set forth their respective positions. It was stated on the Soviet side that the main thing now is to achieve the prompt withdrawal behind the armistice lines of the forces of Israel, which has committed aggression against the Arab states. This question is of signal importance for the restoration of peace in the Middle East, and it is in the center of the attention of the emergency special session of the General Assembly of the United Nations, and it must be positively resolved without delay. . . .

Both sides reaffirmed that they believe it important to promptly achieve understanding on the conclusion of an international treaty on the nonproliferation of nuclear weapons.

In the course of the talks, a general review was made of the state of bilateral Soviet and American relations. On the whole, the meetings offered the Governments of the Soviet Union and the United States an opportunity to compare their positions on the matters discussed, an opportunity both sides believe to have been useful.

C. THE STATUS OF JERUSALEM

75. United Nations Rejects Israel's Changing the Status of Jerusalem: General Assembly Resolution, July 4, 1967

Measures taken by Israel to change the status of the City of Jerusalem

The General Assembly,

Deeply concerned at the situation prevailing in Jerusalem as a result of the measures taken by Israel to change the status of the City,

1. *Considers* that these measures are invalid;

2. *Calls upon* Israel to rescind all measures already taken and to desist forthwith from taking any action which would alter the status of Jerusalem;

3. *Requests* the Secretary-General to report to the General Assembly and the Security Council on the situation and on the implementation of the present resolution not later than one week from its adoption.

76. United States Explains Its Abstention on the Jerusalem Resolution: Statement by the United States Mission to the United Nations, July 4, 1967

The United States abstained on the six-power resolution dealing with the city of Jerusalem contained in document A/L.527/Rev. 1.

Insofar as the six-power resolution expresses the sense of the General Assembly that no unilateral action should be taken that might prejudice the future of Jerusalem, the United States is in agreement. We were prepared to support a resolution to this effect. Some, if not all, of the sponsors were aware that the United States made a serious effort to get such a change incorporated in the resolution in the hope that we would be able to vote affirmatively. Regrettably, our suggested change was not accepted.

The views of the United States on the situation involving Jerusalem are contained in three recent statements. On June 28, in a statement issued by the White House on behalf of the President, the United States expressed the view that there "must be adequate recognition of the special interest of three great religions in the holy places of Jerusalem." On the same day the Department of State said the following: "The United States has never recognized . . . unilateral actions by any of the states in the area as governing the international status of Jerusalem." I reiterated in the General Assembly yesterday: that the "safeguarding of the holy places and freedom of access to them for all should be internationally guaranteed; and the status of Jerusalem in relation to them should be decided not unilaterally but in consultation with all concerned."

These statements reflect the considered views and serious concern of the United States Government about the situation in Jerusalem.

D. PLANS FOR PEACE

77. Five Principles for Peace in the Middle East: Speech by President Johnson (excerpts), June 19, 1967

Now, finally, let me turn to the Middle East—and to the tumultuous events of the past months. Those events have proved the wisdom of five great principles of peace in the region.

The first and greatest principle is that every nation in the area has a fundamental right to live and to have this right respected by its neighbors.

For the people of the Middle East the path to hope does not lie in threats to end the life of any nation. Such threats have become a burden to the peace, not only of that region but a burden to the peace of the entire world.

In the same way, no nation would be true to the United Nations Charter or to its own true interests if it should permit military success to blind it to the fact that its neighbors have rights and its neighbors have interests of their own. Each nation, therefore, must accept the right of others to live.

This last month, I think, shows us another basic requirement for settlement. It is a human requirement: justice for the refugees.

A new conflict has brought new homelessness. The nations of the Middle East must at last address themselves to the plight of those who have been displaced by wars. In the past, both sides have resisted the best efforts of outside mediators to restore the victims of conflict to their homes or to find them other proper places to live and work. There will be no peace for any party in the Middle East unless this problem is attacked with new energy by all and, certainly, primarily by those who are immediately concerned.

A third lesson from this last month is that maritime rights must be respected. Our nation has long been committed to free maritime passage through international waterways; and we, along with other nations, were taking the necessary steps to implement this principle when hostilities exploded. If a single act of folly was more responsible for this explosion than any other, I think it was the arbitrary and dangerous announced decision that the Strait of Tiran would be closed. The right of innocent maritime passage must be preserved for all nations.

Fourth, this last conflict has demonstrated the danger of the Middle Eastern arms race of the last 12 years. Here the responsibility must rest not only on those in the area but upon the larger states outside the area. We believe that the scarce resources could be used much better for technical and economic development. We have always opposed this arms race, and our own military shipments to the area have consequently been severely limited.

Now the waste and futility of the arms race must be apparent to all the peoples of the world. And now there is another moment of choice. The United States of America, for its part, will use every resource of diplomacy and every counsel of reason and prudence to try to find a better course.

As a beginning, I should like to propose that the United Nations immediately call upon all of its members to report all shipments of all military arms into this area and to keep those shipments on file for all the peoples of the world to observe.

Fifth, the crisis underlines the importance of respect for political independence and territorial integrity of all the states of the area. We reaffirmed that principle at the height of this crisis. We reaffirm it again today on behalf of all. This principle can be effective in the Middle East only on the basis of peace between the parties. The nations of the region have had only fragile and violated truce lines for 20 years. What they now need are recognized boundaries and other arrangements that will give them security against terror, destruction, and war. Further, there just must be adquate recognition of the special interest of three great religions in the holy places of Jerusalem.

These five principles are not new, but we do think they are fundamental. Taken together, they point the way from uncertain armistice to durable peace. We believe there must be progress toward all of them if there is to be progress toward any.

There are some who have urged, as a single, simple solution, an immediate return to the situation as it was on June 4. As our distinguished and able Ambassador, Mr. Arthur Goldberg, has already said, this is not a prescription for peace but for renewed hostilities.

Certainly, troops must be withdrawn; but there must also be recognized rights of national life, progress in solving the refugee problem, freedom of innocent maritime passage, limitation of the arms race, and respect for political independence and territorial integrity.

But who will make this peace where all others have failed for 20 years or more?

Clearly the parties to the conflict must be the parties to the peace. Sooner or later, it is they who must make a settlement in the area. It is hard to see how it is possible for nations to live together in peace if they cannot learn to reason together.

But we must still ask, Who can help them? Some say it should be the United Nations; some call for the use of other parties. We have been first in our support of effective peacekeeping in the United Nations, and we also recognize the great values to come from mediation.

We are ready this morning to see any methods tried, and we believe that none should be excluded altogether. Perhaps all of them will be useful and all will be needed.

I issue an appeal to all to adopt no rigid view on these matters. I offer assurance to all that this Government of ours, the Government of the United States, will do its part for peace in every forum, at every level, at every hour.

Yet there is no escape from this fact: The main responsibility for the peace of the region depends upon its own peoples and its own leaders of that region. What will be truly decisive in the Middle East will be what is said and what is done by those who live in the Middle East.

78. The United Nations Peace Plan: Security Council Resolution Passed Unanimously, November 22, 1967

The Security Council,

Expressing its continuing concern with the grave situation in the Middle East,

Emphasizing the inadmissibility of the acquisition of territory by war and the need to work for a just and lasting peace in which every State in the area can live in security,

Emphasizing further that all Member States in their acceptance of the Charter of the United Nations have undertaken a commitment to act in accordance with Article 2 of the Charter,

1. *Affirms* that the fulfillment of Charter principles requires the establishment of a just and lasting peace in the Middle East which should include the application of both the following principles:

(i) Withdrawal of Israeli armed forces from territories occupied in the recent conflict;

(ii) Termination of all claims or states of belligerency and respect for and acknowledgement of the sovereignty, territorial integrity and political independence of every State in the area and their right to live in peace within secure and recognized boundaries free from threats or acts of force;

2. *Affirms further* the necessity

(a) For guaranteeing freedom of navigation through international waterways in the area;

(b) For achieving a just settlement of the refugee problem;

(c) For guaranteeing the territorial inviolability and political independence of every State in the area, through measures including the establishment of demilitarized zones;

3. *Requests* the Secretary-General to designate a Special Representative to proceed to the Middle East to establish and maintain contacts with the States concerned in order to promote agreement and assist efforts to achieve a peaceful and accepted settlement in accordance with the provisions and principles in this resolution;

4. *Requests* the Secretary-General to report to the Security Council on the progress of the efforts of the Special Representative as soon as possible.

79. United States Gratification at Passage of November 22 Resolution: Statement by Ambassador Goldberg, November 22, 1967

The United States is gratified that the United Kingdom draft resolution has received the unanimous support of the Council. As I made clear in my brief intervention before the vote, we have voted for the resolution because we find it entirely consistent with the policy of the United States Government on the Middle East—the five principles enunciated by President Johnson in his statement of June 19 and my several statements in the Council since then.

*   *   *   *   *   *   *

We trust—and we believe this Council has the right to expect—that the parties concerned, without prejudice to their respective positions, will receive the United Nations representative and cooperate with him in the peacemaking process which this resolution sets in motion.

Success will depend, in the final analysis, upon the spirit in which the parties receive him and work with him to find solutions that will permit the Middle East to benefit from a permanent state of peace, security, justice, and tranquility. For this reason, we strongly urge all parties not only to participate in the peace-making process but to do so with the maximum spirit of accommodation, of respect for others' vital interests and legitimate grievances, of mutual accommodation and magnanimity.

Were it not for the fact that the United Kingdom resolution was so delicately balanced and our realization that the offering of any amendments, from any sources, could have upset that balance and jeopardized the chance of successful action by this Council, my delegation would have offered an amendment so that the Council could have endorsed the need to achieve a limitation on the wasteful and destructive arms race in the Middle East. This was one of President Johnson's five points. We have taken particular note of, and have been encouraged by, the fact that a provision to this effect was included in the draft resolution placed before the Council by the Soviet Union, as it was in our draft resolution.

We do not conceive that the mandate of the special representative to be designated by the Secretary-General excludes his exploring this important and urgent requirement of peace as he establishes and maintains contacts with the states concerned. His mandate encompasses the search for a just and lasting peace—and in pursuing this search, he should be encouraged by the fact that two great powers, the Soviet Union and the United States, have indicated a willingness to have the problem of a limitation on the arms race discussed and explored.

As for my own Government, we have stated before, and I renew that statement now, that the United States will use every resource of diplomacy including cooperating with the special representative to find a course which will put an end to the waste and the futility of the arms race in the Middle East. The beginning—but only a beginning—can be made if the United Nations, as we have proposed, would call upon all of its members to report all shipments of all military arms into the area and keep those shipments on file for all the peoples of the world to observe.

The special representative will need all the help and support he can get—both from the parties and from the international community. I have already given my Government's pledge on this score, and I wish to reiterate it again today: a pledge to this Council and to the parties concerned that the diplomatic and political influence of the United States Government will be exerted in support of the efforts of the United Nations representative to achieve a fair and equitable and dignified settlement so that all in the area can live in peace, security, and tranquility.

Similar pledges from other members of the Council and the United Nations, particularly those with great diplomatic and political influence, would be invaluable. For they would not only lend weight to the efforts of the special representative, but they would help to reassure all the peoples of the Middle East that they are not alone as they turn their attention to the search for the foundations of a just and durable peace.

In creating the framework of peace in the Middle East, the Security Council took the first step last June—by helping to bring about a cease-fire. It is vitally important that the cease-fire be maintained. Violations by any party cannot and must not be condoned.

Today we have taken a second step, the appointment of a special representative to go to the area in order to promote agreement and assist efforts to achieve a peaceful settlement. And for those who sometimes wonder about the value and effectiveness of the United Nations, perhaps in these two steps we have provided an answer to those worries and concerns.

80. "A Just and Dignified Peace . . . Is Possible": Speech by President Johnson (excerpts), September 10, 1968

Now let me turn to the Middle East. That is an area of deep national interest to the American people—to all of our people—for the safety and the future of small nations are not the concern of one group of citizens alone.

To you tonight, I assure you they concern all Americans.

Our society is illuminated by the spiritual insights of the Hebrew prophets. America and Israel have a common love of human freedom, and they have a common faith in a democratic way of life.

It is quite natural that American Jews should feel particularly involved with Israel's destiny. That small land in the eastern Mediterranean saw the birth of your faith and your people thousands and thousands of years ago. Down through the centuries, through dispersion and through very grievous trials, your forefathers clung to their Jewish identity and clung to their ties with the land of Israel.

As the prophet Isiah foretold: "And He shall set up an ensign for the nations, and He shall assemble the outcasts of Israel and gather together the dispersed of Judah from all the four corners of the earth." History knows no more moving example of persistence against the cruelest odds.

But conflict has surrounded the modern State of Israel since its very beginning. It is now more than a year that has passed since the 6-day war between Israel and its neighbors—a tragic and an unnecessary war which we tried in every way we could to prevent. That war was the third round of major hostilities in the Middle East since the United Nations established Israel just 21 years ago—the third round—and it just must be the last round.

From the day that war broke out, our policy—the policy of this Government—has been to work in every capital, to labor in the United Nations, to convert the armistice arrangements of 1949 into a stable and agreed regime of peace. The time has come for real peace in the area—a peace of justice and reconciliation, not a cease-fire, not a temporary truce, not a renewal of the fragile armistice. No day has passed since then without our taking active steps to try to achieve this end.

The atmosphere of fear and mutual suspicion has made communication between the two sides extremely difficult. In this setting the plans of reasonable men, both Arabs and Israelis, have been frustrated. Despite the patient and perceptive efforts of Ambassador [Gunnar] Jarring, little real progress toward peace has been made.

I am convinced that a just and a dignified peace—a peace fair to the rightful interests of both sides—is possible. Without it, the people of the Middle East cannot shape their own destinies, because outsiders are going to exploit their rivalries, and their energies and abilities will be diverted to warfare instead of welfare. That just should not happen.

No nation that has been part of the tragic drama of these past 20 years is totally without blame. Violence and counterviolence have absorbed the energy of all the parties. The process of peacemaking cannot be further delayed without danger and without peril. The United Nations Security Council resolution of last November laid down the principles of a just and lasting peace.

But I would remind the world tonight that that resolution is not self-executing. It created a framework within which men of good will ought to be able to arrive at a reasonable settlement.

For its part, the United States of America has fully supported the efforts of the United Nations representative, Ambassador Jarring, and we shall continue to do so. But it is the parties themselves who must make the major effort to begin seriously this much needed peacemaking process.

One fact is sure: The process of peacemaking will not begin until the leaders of the Middle East begin exchanging views on the hard issues through some agreed procedure which could permit active discussions to be pursued. Otherwise, no progress toward peace will be made.

In recent weeks some progress in this direction, I think, has been achieved. So tonight I appeal and I urge the leaders of the Middle East to try to maintain and to accelerate their dialogue. I urge them to put their views out on the table, to begin talking the substance of peace.

Many channels are open. How the talking is done at the outset is not very important tonight. But we just must not lose whatever momentum exists for peace. And, in the end, those who must live together must, in the words of Isaiah, learn to reason together.

The position of the United States rests on the principles of peace that I outlined on June 19, 1967. That statement remains the foundation of American policy.

First, it remains crucial that each nation's right to live be recognized. Arab governments must convince Israel and the world community that they have abandoned the idea of destroying Israel. But equally, Israel must persuade its Arab neighbors and the world community that Israel has no expanionist designs on their territory.

We are not here to judge whose fears are right or whose are wrong. Right or wrong, fear is the first obstacle to any peacemaking. Each side must do its share to overcome it. A major step in this direction would be for each party to issue promptly a clear, unqualified public assurance that it is now ready to commit itself to recognize the right of each of its neighbors to national life.

Second, the political independence and territorial integrity of all the states in the area must be assured.

We are not the ones to say where other nations should draw lines between them that will assure each the greatest security. It is clear, however, that a return to the situation of June 4, 1967, will not bring peace. There must be secure and there must be recognized borders.

Some such lines must be agreed to by the neighbors involved as part of the transition from armistice to peace.

At the same time, it should be equally clear that boundaries cannot and should not reflect the weight of conquest. Each change must have a reason which each side, in honest negotiation, can accept as a part of a just compromise.

Third, it is more certain than ever that Jerusalem is a critical issue of any peace settlement. No one wishes to see the Holy City divided by barbed wire and by machineguns. I therefore tonight urge and appeal to the parties to stretch their imaginations so that their interests, and all the world's interest in Jerusalem, can be taken fully into account in any final settlement.

Fourth, the number of refugees is still increasing. The June war added some 200,000 refugees to those already displaced by the 1948 war. They face a bleak prospect as the winter approaches. We share a very deep concern for these refugees. Their plight is a symbol in the minds of the Arab peoples. In their eyes, it is a symbol of a wrong that must be made right before 20 years of war can end. And that fact must be dealt with in reaching a condition of peace.

All nations who are able, including Israel and her Arab neighbors, should participate directly and wholeheartedly in a massive program to assure these people a better and a more stable future.

Fifth, maritime rights must be respected. Their violation led to war in 1967. Respect for those rights is not only a legal consequence of peace. It is a symbolic recognition that all nations in the Middle East enjoy equal treatment before the law.

And no enduring peace settlement is possible until the Suez Canal and the Straits of Tiran are open to the ships of all nations and their right of passage is effectively guaranteed.

Sixth, the arms race continues. We have exercised restraint, while recognizing the legitimate needs of friendly governments. But we have no intention of allowing the balance of forces in the area to ever become an incentive for war.

We continue to hope that our restraint will be matched by the restraint of others, though I must observe that has been lacking since the end of the June war.

We have proposed, and I reiterate again tonight, the urgent need now for an international understanding on arms limitation for this region of the world.

The American interest in the Middle East is definite, is clear. There just must be a just peace in that region and soon. Time is not on the side of peace.

Now, my friends, I know that these two areas of the world are of very great concern to you, as they are to me. Many of you have roots in Europe, from which you or your forebears came in order to enrich the quality of life here in America. Most, if not all of you, have very deep ties with the land and with the people of Israel, as I do; for my Christian faith sprang from yours.

The Bible stories are woven into my childhood memories as the gallant struggle of modern Jews to be free of persecution is also woven into our souls.

81. United States and Israel Support Spirit of November 22 Resolution and President Johnson's Five Principles of Peace: Joint Statement by President Johnson and Prime Minister Eshkol
January 8, 1968

President Johnson invited Prime Minister Eshkol to be his guest at the Texas

White House on January 7 and 8, during the Prime Minister's visit to the United States.

The President and the Prime Minister held several meetings during which they discussed recent developments in the Middle East as well as a number of questions of mutual interest in the bilateral relations between their two countries.

The President and the Prime Minister considered the implications of the pace of rearmament in the Middle East and the ways and means of coping with this situation. The President agreed to keep Israel's military defense capability under active and sympathetic examination and review in the light of all relevant factors, including the shipment of military equipment by others to the area.

The President and the Prime Minister restated their dedication to the establishment of a just and lasting peace in the Middle East in accordance with the spirit of the Security Council resolution of November 22, 1967. They also noted that the principles set forth by President Johnson on June 19 constituted an equitable basis for such a settlement.

The President and the Prime Minister noted that under that Security Council resolution the Secretary-General of the United Nations has designated Ambassador [Gunnar] Jarring as his Special Representative. They also noted with satisfaction that Ambassador Jarring is already engaged in discussions with the governments concerned and affirmed their full support of his mission.

The President and the Prime Minister reviewed with satisfaction developments in the relations between the United States and Israel since their last meeting in 1964 and expressed their firm intention to continue the traditionally close, friendly and cooperative ties which link the peoples of Israel and the United States.

Noting the mutual dedication of their governments and people to the value of peace, resistance to aggression wherever it occurs, individual freedom, human dignity and the advancement of man through the elimination of poverty, ignorance, and disease, the President and the Prime Minister declared their firm determination to make every effort to increase the broad area of understanding which already exists between Israel and the United States and agreed that the Prime Minister's visit advanced this objective.

82. An Arab Plan for Peace:
Speech by King Hussein of Jordan
(excerpt), April 10, 1969

My plea in all of this is to be even-handed in your support of the two sides, and to be even-minded in your thinking of the problems that confront us.

In conclusion, may I sum up for you just what it is that we are prepared to offer Israel? And [in] this I am speaking for President Nasser as well as myself.

On our part, we are prepared to offer the following as a basis for a just and lasting peace, in accordance with the Security Council resolution.

1. The end of all belligerency.

2. Respect for and acknowledgement of the sovereignty, territorial integrity and political independence of all states in the area.

211

3. Recognition of the rights of all to live in peace within secure and recognized boundaries free from threats or acts of war.

4. Guarantees for all [of] the freedom of navigation through the Gulf of Aqaba and the Suez Canal.

5. Guaranteeing the territorial inviolability of all states in the area through whatever measures necessary including the establishment of demilitarized zones.

6. Accepting a just settlement of the refugee problem.

In return for those considerations, our sole demand upon Israel is the withdrawal of its armed forces from all territories occupied in the June, 1967 war, and the implementation of all other provisions of the Security Council resolution.

The challenge that these principles present is that Israel may have either peace or territory—but she can never have both.

E. UNCERTAIN CEASE FIRE

83. The United States Condemns Violence on Both Sides: Statement Released by the Department of State, March 21, 1968

Further violence cannot bring a durable and stable peace to the Middle East. The Israeli military actions today against the territory of Jordan in response to terrorist attacks are damaging to hopes for a settlement of the real issues involved. Furthermore all of the parties know that peaceful channels are available.

We recognize the problems created by terrorism. We also recognize the disruptive effects of military action. Neither kind of action is in the true interests of the people of the area. Our main objective is to achieve a lasting peace. Israel and the Arab states should be adhering scrupulously to the cease-fire resolutions of the Security Council and working with the special representative of the United Nations Secretary-General in accordance with the Security Council's resolution of last November. Any action that delays his work is most regrettable.

We have made our position known repeatedly and as recently as 1 day ago; that is, that Arab-Israeli differences should be settled through the efforts of the United Nations and not through the use of force.

84. Condemnation of Israeli Attacks on Jordan: United Nations Security Council Resolution Passed Unanimously March 29, 1968

The Security Council,

Having heard the statements of the representatives of Jordan and Israel,

Having noted the contents of the letters of the Permanent Representatives of Jordan and Israel in documents S/8470, S/8475, S/8483, S/8484 and S/8486,

Having noted further the supplementary information provided by the Chief of Staff of UNTSO as contained in documents S/7930/Add. 64 and Add. 65,

Recalling resolution 236 (1967) by which the Security Council condemned any and all violations of the cease-fire,

Observing that the military action by the armed forces of Israel on the territory of Jordan was of a large-scale and carefully planned nature,

Considering that all violent incidents and other violations of the cease-fire should be prevented and not overlooking past incidents of this nature,

Recalling further resolution 237 (1967) which called upon the Government of Israel to ensure the safety, welfare and security of the inhabitants of the areas where military operations have taken place,

1. *Deplores* the loss of life and heavy damage to property;

2. *Condemns* the military action launched by Israel in flagrant violation of the United Nations Charter and the cease-fire resolutions;

3. *Deplores* all violent incidents in violation of the cease-fire and declares that such actions of military reprisal and other grave violations of the cease-fire cannot be tolerated and that the Security Council would have to consider further and more effective steps as envisaged in the Charter to ensure against repetition of such acts;

4. *Calls upon* Israel to desist from acts or activities in contravention of resolution 237 (1967);

5. *Requests* the Secretary-General to keep the situation under review and to report to the Security Council as appropriate.

85. 'A Talk with President Nasser': Interview with *Newsweek* Editor, February 10, 1969

In the ever-intensifying Middle East crisis no man plays a more central role than Gamal Abdel Nasser, the President of the United Arab Republic. Last week, in the first interview he has granted a Western journalist in more than a year, the Egyptian President gave Newsweek Senior Editor Arnaud de Borchgrave his views on the Arab-Israeli conflict and his thoughts about how it might be settled.

Q. *Mr. President, you have called for a more "even-handed" U.S. policy in the Middle East. What do you feel President Nixon should do?*

A. A fair policy means one that does not agree with the occupation of other countries' territories. Every day Israel says the occupation will continue and there is no reaction from the U.S. Does this mean the U.S. agrees? If you don't, all you have to do is say so. That would be a good start.

Q. *But the U.S. agreed to the U.N.'s Nov. 22, 1967, resolution.*

A. Agreeing to a resolution is one thing; condoning continued occupation is quite another. You say Israel should not withdraw before a settlement, but this then means a settlement unfavorable to the Arabs, because Israel now has the whip hand. If you give Israel Phantom fighter-bombers while they are occupying Arab lands, this can only mean you support this occupation. Otherwise, you would make delivery contingent on withdrawal.

Q. *What does the resumption of relations between the U.S. and the U.A.R. now depend on?*

A. On the point I just made. If the new Administration says it does not agree with this occupation, this will change the whole policy.

Q. *If, as you have often said, the Soviets do not control anything in the U.A.R., what leads you to believe that the U.S. could make Israel do something against its will?*

A. There is a difference between forcing Israel and stating your viewpoint. For instance, when there was a cease-fire proposal during the June war, it called for withdrawal, too. But the U.S. opposed this for the first time in the history of the United Nations. You were, in effect, encouraging Israel. You repeatedly supported the Israeli stand and were against any condemnation of the invasion. So this naturally gives us the idea that U.S. policy is to support their occupation. At first, the Israelis called them "conquered" territories, then changed the label to "occupied" and subsequently to "liberated," and the United States remained silent. It is not a question of American pressure against Israel. Just be fair and just. Instead, you gave them Skyhawk jet fighters and now Phantoms.

Q. *You apparently agree with King Hussein, who says the situation is deteriorating rapidly. In that case, what is the relevance of the Soviet peace plan?*

A. I was not optimistic about the U.N. resolution or the Soviet plan because I know Israeli strategy and views. I said to Gromyko when he came here just before Christmas: "The U.S. will not agree to your plan." Why? Because I know the U.S. supports Israel 100 per cent.

Q. *And if that were to change under President Nixon?*

A. We have to wait and see.

Q. *You have said that there will be no solution to the crisis until the Israelis believe that you are strong enough to push them out of occupied territories. When do you think Israel will become convinced of this?*

A. Well, of course, they have information about our military development. And from that standpoint, the situation is not deteriorating, as King Hussein suggests. He is in a very difficult position, because he was not able to make up the losses he suffered in the war. We are now in a much better position than last year.

Q. *Than before the war?*

A. [Laughing] You'd better not say that, or the Israelis will use it as another pretext to attack. No, better than last year. At first, I told my people we would have the strength to reconquer what belongs to us in six months. Then I raised it to twelve. We have now been patient for nineteen months. Every day we are getting stronger. But Israel is buying armaments everywhere it can and this, of course, affects the timing.

Q. *France has been Israel's biggest arms supplier, and French-made helicopters were used in the Beirut raid. Why, then, are you so grateful to France?*

A. I don't know about the helicopters. France kept very quiet about what it was doing. Its most important decision, however, was to embargo 50 Mirage fighter-bombers, and now they have frozen spare parts, too. For this we are indeed grateful.

Q. *If the Israelis had pulled back right after the June '67 war, how would the situation be different today?*

A. It was not all in our plans to attack Israel. I promise you, we had no plans for this. In fact, three of our best divisions were in Yemen at the time, and if we had been preparing for an attack, it would have been logical to bring them home first. What I did say, however, was that if they attacked Syria, we would retaliate by attacking them.

So I could not deceive myself and say that if they had pulled back right away we would have forgotten about their attack. But by not withdrawing, they have merely generated more hatred. There is a vast difference between occupation and nonoccupation, because occupation merely forces mobilization against the Israelis. I think if they had agreed to leave in accordance with the U.N. resolution this step could have been of tremendous effect in promoting a peaceful settlement. The resolution specifically mentioned a settlement. We agreed. We still agree.

Q. *And if they pulled back now, how would Israel's security be enhanced? What quid pro quo would the Arab states offer for evacuation?*

A. (1) A declaration of nonbelligerence; (2) the recognition of the right of each country to live in peace; (3) the territorial integrity of all countries in the Middle East, including Israel, in recognized and secure borders; (4) freedom of navigation on international waterways; (5) a just solution to the Palestinian refugee problem.

Q. *Do you insist on the choice of repatriation to what is now Israel or compensation for all refugees?*

A. The United Nations has said over and over again "the right to return or compensation."

Q. *Israel is convinced that neither you nor the Soviet Union wants permanent peace, but only a breathing spell in which to get ready for the fourth round. What can you say to convince Israel that both you and the Soviet Union want permanent peace?*

A. First of all, we were not preparing for the second or third round. We did not attack. In 1956 they attacked with the U.K. and France. Books by Western authors have made clear they had also been preparing for the third round, whose success was predicated on a pre-emptive first strike. Now they are preparing for a fourth round. So we must be prepared, too. You must believe me when I tell you the Soviet Union wants a peaceful settlement. I am convinced that their motives are sincere. As for us, we do not want to go on mobilizing everything for war. We crave peace. We desperately need peace for economic development. But we must defend ourselves. The Israelis have said many times their country stretches from the Nile to the Euphrates.

Q. *Do you really believe this is their objective?*

A. Of course. Remember what Defense Minister Dayan told the youth of the United Labor Party after the war. "Our fathers made the borders of '47. We made the borders of '49. You made the borders of '67. Another generation will take our frontiers to where they belong." Every day the Israeli Prime Minister, or Deputy Prime Minister, says they will not withdraw from everything they took, that big chunks will be permanently joined to Israel. They are settling Israelis in the Sinai, on the Golan Plateau in Syria and in Hebron in Jordan. So it is very hard to escape the conclusion that their *raison d'être* is expansion.

Q. *You have publicly supported the Palestinian commandos in their attacks on Israel. But you also support the U.N. Middle Eastern resolution of 1967 and the Soviet peace plan. How do you reconcile the two positions?*

A. Israel publicly refused the Soviet plan. And the U.S. answer to Moscow means the U.S. also refuses the Soviet plan. The Israelis, moreover, refuse to implement the Security Council resolution. We agreed to it. So really what choice do I have but to support courageous resistance fighters who want to liberate their lands?

Q. *Would you allow the Soviet Union, the United States, France and Britain to station troops in the Sinai as part of an agreement on Israeli withdrawal?*

A. No. We will not agree to the stationing of any soldier from the four major powers in our country.

Q. *But don't you already have Soviet military personnel in your country?*

A. No, they are advisers, not in uniform, and they take their orders from us.

Q. *Would you accept units from smaller countries under the U.N. flag?*

A. We would have no objection.

Q. *Would you agree to keep the Sinai demilitarized if Israel withdrew to its pre-June boundaries?*

A. No. We could only agree to the demilitarization of areas that are astride the boundaries.

Q. *If Israel were to pull back as the first phase of a settlement, would Egypt be prepared to sit down with the Israelis to discuss other issues?*

A. I could not give you an answer about that until they pull out. Obviously, you would not sit down with a foreign power occupying part of the U.S. until it withdrew. But I can tell you we sat down with the Israelis after the 1948 war under the armistice agreement until the 1956 war, and that we are prepared to do so again. We had joint committees with United Nations observers and it was Israel who refused to continue this procedure after 1956.

Q. *You have said that you recognize realities and that Israel is one of them. How does this differ from de facto recognition of Israel's prewar frontiers?*

A. This question has been complicated by the Israelis themselves. Under the 1949 armistice agreements, Arabs and Israelis were supposed to agree on the rehabilitation of Palestinian refugees. If this had been done, it would have been a mighty step toward lasting peace. But the Israelis refused to discuss rehabilitation. So the situation got progressively worse. Before, there were under 1 million refugees. Now, there are almost 1.5 million.

Q. *Could you spell out how you see a lasting solution?*

A. The only way is for Israel to become a country that is not based on religion, but on all religions—a nation of Jews, Moslems and Christians. They lived for centuries together with few problems, but as long as the Israelis insist on depriving the Palestinians of their rights, the crisis will be with us for 10, 20, 30, and 40 more years.

Q. *Do you see any chance for that kind of evolution?*

A. Perhaps the next generation in Israel. Some Israelis are beginning to say they should think another way. But present leaders are shortsighted.

Q. *Do you believe that Israel has a nuclear capability? If so, what do you plan to do about it?*

A. Our experts don't believe Israel will develop this capability soon. But, on the other hand, we know they are highly advanced in this field and are spending lots of money to speed things up. There is no doubt that this is one of their top priority objectives.

Since the latest U.S. news reports, we have re-examined our own position. I called a meeting of our top people. The conclusion was that we have the experts and the wherewithal, but not the money. It would be terribly costly.

Q. *How much?*

A. About $250 million. But we have no plans.

Q. *And if Israel did achieve nuclear capability?*

A. We signed the nonproliferation treaty. Israel refused. And under the treaty, the nuclear powers are obligated to guarantee us against nuclear blackmail.

Q. *If the events of June 1967 were repeated, what would happen this time? Would Russia intervene?*

A. We were not waiting for Russia last time, and we will not be waiting for her if there is a next time. We will defend ourselves. What helped the Israelis the last time was not so much their cleverness, but the conceit and complacency of our generals. They felt Israel would never dare to attack. They overestimated their own strength. And because of that, they failed to take elementary precautions. The situation is now completely different. It would be impossible for the Israelis to repeat June 5. They could strike first again, but they would certainly not destroy our air force.

Q. *Your detractors say that you have mortgaged your country to the Soviet Union. What is your answer?*

A. Well, we are not an independent country now, not because of the Russians, but because of the Israeli occupation. The Soviets have never asked me for anything. In Moscow last July, I told Brezhnev, Kosygin and Podgorny: "All I do is ask, ask and ask, but you never ask for anything. What can I do for *you* for a change?" They replied: "Nothing. We support your cause because it is a just one."

But if they asked me for something now, I would do it, if it helped me liberate my country from the Israelis. I need all the help I can get. [Chuckling] I would gratefully accept any help the United States could give us to achieve this objective.

The Soviets give us all the raw materials we cannot obtain in the West because of foreign-exchange shortage. They don't ask for money. They take anything we can give them—refrigerators, clothes, furniture.

Q. *Aren't you afraid of being absorbed into the Soviet-bloc economy?*

A. It is not as complex as you seem to think. When you are in debt to somebody, you are always in a strong position. [Laughing] Debtors are always stronger than creditors.

Q. *How do you assess Soviet strategy in the Arab world? Why the enormous military and economic aid?*

A. You are exaggerating what you seem to think is a grand design. They just don't want to be isolated. They are trying to win friends and counterbalance American influence. We are accused of giving the Soviets bases. They have no bases in Egypt.

Q. *Perhaps not, but they come and go as they please.*

A. Before the war, the U.S. Sixth Fleet was free to visit us, too. When your ambassador requested permission for a visit, we granted it. Warships from many countries came to see us.

Q. *Looking back on your seventeen years in power, what would you have done differently?*

A. There is little time for reflection in my job. It all looks like a machine. It must go forward. This is my destiny. I believe in God and destiny, and that one should not look back.

Q. *In 1948, as a young officer embittered by defeat, you resolved to overthrow the regime responsible. If you were a young officer today, wouldn't you be just as bitter and just as determined to overthrow the regime now in power?*

A. In 1948, we were a small army of ten battalions—no tanks, no planes. The reason for our revolt was a feudal regime, corrupt from top to bottom, that supported the British occupation of our country. That's how we were let down at the front. But after that, the army was able to get everything it needed. I see many young officers, of course, and they are bitter, but against Israel and U.S. support of Israel. They want to know how long they have to wait.

Q. *And what do you tell them?*

A. Be patient.

Q. *But how long can you go on telling them the same thing?*

A. Not indefinitely, of course. But as long as it takes.

86. 'Eshkol: A Reply to Nasser': Interview with *Newsweek* Editor, February 17, 1969

Two weeks ago, in an interview with Newsweek Senior Editor Arnaud de Borchgrave, President Nasser of Egypt gave his view of the Arab-Israeli conflict and indicated, in broad outline, the terms on which he felt it might be settled. Last week, in a two-hour conversation with de Borchgrave and Newsweek's Michael Elkins, Prime Minister Levi Eshkol of Israel explained his objections to Nasser's terms—and replied to some of the charges that the Egyptian leader had leveled against Israel.

Q. *How do you justify Israel's continued occupation of Arab lands?*

A. We have fought three wars in our brief lifetime of twenty years. If the Arab governments had accepted, as the whole world did, the establishment of the State of Israel, this would not have happened. In fact, there would have been no need to change our borders one jot. But after the six-day war, it is a miracle that we are still here. So why should we now crawl on our hands and knees to the Arabs and say: Please, do us a favor and take it all back . . . If we had lost the last war, our lot would have been the same as the nine Iraqi Jews hanged in public last week. Our occupation of the territory is the outcome of war. In 1948, Jordan conquered the west bank contrary to the resolution of the United Nations. In 1967 we conquered the west bank. You seem to forget the Arabs were the first to attack.

Q. *The Arabs attacked in 1967?*

A. They closed the Strait of Tiran, moved tanks and troops into Sinai, and were headed toward our borders. When they chased the U.N. troops out, we were faced with a blatant act of war; there was no way out for us. I tried to delay, hoping something would happen, something would intervene. It didn't . . . guarantees proved worthless. Ten years ago, President Eisenhower pledged that the Suez Canal would be open to us and that if President Nasser tried to stop it, the international community would have to deal with the situation with a firm hand. You know what happened.

Q. *President Nasser charges that your objective is a greater Israel, from the Nile to the Euphrates. What can you say that would convince him this is not so?*

A. It is difficult to say anything that would convince him. During the last two decades we have repeatedly said we are ready to discuss our problems with Nasser. I am still ready to fly to Cairo tomorrow. I don't want to talk to him as a conqueror. I want to rid his mind of the ridiculous notion of a greater Israel. He cannot base his policy on a phrase that has been uttered by individuals who represent nothing but themselves. Even the Bible doesn't use that phrase. The "river of Egypt" referred to in the Old Testament is not the Nile but the El-Arish River—a muddy stream a few miles inside Sinai. I can pledge my word to Nasser that greater Israel never has been and never will be our policy. I am ready to meet him anywhere, anytime, and I won't quarrel about procedure, agenda, or the shape of the table.

Q. *What about your plans for new Israeli settlements on the Golan Plateau in Syria, on the west bank of the Jordan River, and in Egyptian Sinai?*

A. You know what happened on the Golan Heights before the war—the Syrians shelled our settlements from there. Never again. Besides, these are not ordinary settlements but military agricultural outposts.

Q. *But why not an agreement to demilitarize Golan rather than settle Israelis in what is part of Syria?*

A. What is demilitarization? Who watches over the border? No one knows what demilitarization means.

We had a war. We won it. And as long as Golan remains a dangerous spot, we have to defend it. Besides we have no one to talk to on the Syrian side. They are not even willing to talk with Dr. Gunnar Jarring.

Q. *Are you prepared to give up these new settlements in occupied territories as part of a final peace settlement?*

A. It is not proper to answer iffy questions today. We are flexible on everything, but I don't want to get into specifics before negotiations.

Q. *Right after the six-day war, Israeli leaders said that they would make generous offers to settle the Palestinian refugee problem. What happened?*

A. We were perhaps a little overoptimistic on the chances for lasting settlement. Clearly the refugee problem can only be settled in cooperation with our neighbors. We must have a dialogue. The refugees are an international problem. We need land and water for them. we are a small nation with only 7,720 square miles of land and an annual water flow of 1.5 billion cubic meters. Jordan, Lebanon, Syria, Egypt and Iraq have between them 670,000 square miles of land and an annual water flow of more than 90 billion cubic meters.

Q. *I'm afraid I don't see your point.*

A. If these countries are interested in settling the refugee problem, there is much territory and much wasted water. We will pay compensation to the refugees or buy land for them to resettle in neighboring countries.

Q. *Arab leaders see no chance of peace because they are convinced you are determined to hold on to what you have conquered, come what may. Are they right?*

A. I am sure that Nasser knows that the opposite is the case.

Q. *How?*

A. Through channels I cannot disclose, Arab rulers have heard interesting things from us. They know we want peace.

Q. *But would you go back to your frontiers in return for peace?*

A. Let me say, clearly and unequivocally, there will be no return to the situation preceding the June war. The present cease-fire lines will not be changed except for secure and agreed lines within the framework of a final and durable peace. We must discuss new borders, new arrangements. The armistice agreements are dead and buried. We don't want any part of the settled area of the west bank—Nablus, Jenin and so on. What we say is that the Jordan River must become a security border for Israel with all that that implies. Our army shall be stationed only on the strip along that border.

Q. *You have repeatedly demanded direct negotiations with the Arab states, but if part of your country were occupied by Arab armies, could you afford to sit down with them face to face?*

A. Surely. No doubt. No doubt whatsoever. God forbid, but if we had been the losers and—miraculously—were still alive and they were to say "We are ready for peace negotiations," I cannot imagine that we would refuse.

Q. *You insist on a permanent peace with the Arab governments as the price of withdrawal. But do you think that is possible without a solution to the refugee problem?*

A. For our neighbors, the refugees are a convenient political football, not a life-and-death issue. If they want to begin with the refugee problem, we are ready. We are completely flexible on the agenda. It's all a package deal so it doesn't matter where you start.

Q. *The U.N. has said that the refugees should be given a choice between compensation and the right to their old homes. What is your stand on this?*

A. I would like to remind our friend Nasser that there was a time when we agreed to the return of 100,000 refugees—though I was against it as I didn't believe it would work out, because Arab leaders needed them as pawns. Today the situation has changed. Any returning refugees would be a time bomb for Israel. We cannot take them back, but we have agreed over the years to´return of 40,000 of the refugees on con passionate grounds. We are ready to pay compensation.

Q. *Would you withdraw from the occupied territories if the great powers would guarantee a settlement that gave you freedom of navigation, an Arab declaration of nonbelligerence, Arab recognition of the territorial integrity of Israel, and a demilitarized zone along your frontiers policed by the U.N.?*

A. No. We have learned a lesson. Remember the United Nations force in 1967? Nasser whistled and they packed their kit bags. And President Nasser speaks of freedom of navigation in "international waterways." What is "interna-

220

tional"? I am sure that he will say the Suez Canal is an Egyptian waterway. He has said it before.

Q. *What concessions do you insist upon in return for withdrawal from the Arab lands? Do you insist upon demilitarization of the Sinai Peninsula and a permanent military presence at Sharm el Sheikh?*

A. We don't insist on anything. Try us out and you'll be surprised on the degree of give and take we are prepared for. We have not made any demands for the demilitarization of Sinai. At Sharm el Sheikh, however, we must be in a position to protect the access to the Strait of Tiran—our backyard. We cannot rely on promises and outsiders to do it for us. We cannot live as a nation without a peace treaty. As for the Golan Heights, we will quite simply never give them up. The same goes for Jerusalem. Here there is no flexibility at all. I regret it. I would be very happy to say yes. But every time I look at the map I shake my head because there is no possible way to compromise on Jerusalem. It is the very heart of our state.

Q. *Some Israeli leaders are now suggesting that Nasser and King Hussein are too weak domestically to risk a peace settlement, and that eventually you will have to settle with the Palestinians directly. What do you think?*

A. If those two could work together—and if Nasser didn't stab the King in the back from time to time—I am quite sure they could sell a reasonable settlement to their peoples. I have met at least half a dozen times with Palestinian leaders on the west bank. They said they would go talk to Hussein and to Nasser. They did, but came back empty-handed.

Q. *Do you see the Palestinian commandos—Al-Fatah and the fedayeen—as a potentially important political factor in the Middle East?*

A. I don't want to brag, but the fedayeen have lost a lot of people. Many are leaving the movement dispirited. I do not believe the fedayeen will become as important as some people in Western countries seem to think. But if Al-Fatah wants to talk to us directly, we would not say no. If one day they overthrow established Arab governments, we would then have a new enemy and a new situation. But I don't believe this will happen because they feel better off as free lances, and are not at all anxious to take on the burdens of government.

Q. *You call the fedayeen terrorists. But how do they differ from other resistance movements through history?*

A. If people perpetrate terrorist acts they can, of course, call themselves a resistance movement. But what are they resisting? They cannot find shelter on the west bank; the Arabs there are not cooperating with the fedayeen. That hardly qualifies them as resistance fighters.

Q. *But in Gaza the local population is resisting your occupation. Doesn't that constitute a resistance movement?*

A. As a Jew, I will answer with another question. What difference does it make? Why should I glorify them with their own label? But, more seriously, I would point out that for twenty years Gaza was occupied by the Egyptians. The Egyptians' curfew there was much tougher than ours. The Palestinian refugees in Gaza resisted the Egyptians just as strongly as they resist us.

221

Q. *Do you think that Israelis and Palestinians might one day live together in a binational state, comparable to the Christian-Moslem arrangement in Lebanon?*

A. I would not like to be in the same position as Lebanon—that is, on a 50-50 basis. Lebanon could become 60-40 one day . . . and then what happens to the minority?

It's very important that you and your readers should understand that for 2,000 years we were persecuted minorities around the world. Never again. We must have our own place where we are a majority. Look at Cyprus. Twenty-three percent Turks, and look at what is going on. Is that what you want for us? Israel is and must remain a Jewish state.

Q. *In that case, how would you feel about a separate Palestinian Arab state?*

A. I am against it. Personally, I think Palestinian connections and ties should be with Jordan; they have the same customs, same religion, same language. But who knows? Jordan's behavior may force them to have a separate entity.

Q. *If the Jews are entitled to a homeland, aren't the Palestinians similarly entitled to their own country?*

A. What are Palestinians? When I came here there were 250,000 non-Jews —mainly Arabs and Bedouins. It was desert—more than underdeveloped. Nothing. It was only after we made the desert bloom and populated it that they became interested in taking it from us.

Q. *You expect Arab governments to disarm or control the fedayeen. But were Jewish leaders capable of controlling Jewish underground groups like the Stern gang at the time of your own struggle for independence?*

A. Yes, to a certain degree we were. But how can you compare? The Arabs have established governments with armies and police forces. We had nothing. We were just as illegal as the underground movements you just mentioned. And while trying to control them, we had at the same time to struggle against the British Army.

Q. *President Nasser told* NEWSWEEK *that Egyptian representatives are prepared to sit down with Israelis in joint committees with U.N. observers as they did under the 1949 armistice agreements. What are your objections to resuming such a dialogue—a dialogue, incidentally, which Nasser says your government ended?*

A. There was always a third party in these committees and this third party— the U.N.—was the decisive party. The U.N. observer nearly always said he never saw what happened. The arrangement had become a mockery, a travesty of justice. When Nasser launched the first fedayeen raids more than ten years ago, he acted as though he was free to do as he pleased while we were supposed to respect the armistice agreements. That's why the arrangement broke down. But if Nasser is ready to resume these joint committees and to sit with us there, why isn't he ready to sit with us under the U.N. Security Council resolution of Nov. 22, 1967?

Q. *Hasn't the time come for some new Israeli peace initiatives?*

A. We feel that every day is the time for this. The question is what and how. Let's sit down and discuss it. Let's reason together. We have said—and it certainly reached the ears of the Jordanian Government— that if Jordan needs a Mediterranean harbor we are prepared to give them free port facilities in Haifa or Ashdod. We can embark on all sorts of joint endeavors to develop their industry and export

222

business. Go talk to the Arab farmers on the west bank and they will tell you what we have done in a few months to increase their productivity—which had barely changed for centuries before. We dug wells for them where their own people had assured them there was no water. This is what we can offer. But there is a price. Either they maintain a state of war and nothing happens, or they want real peace and then the hopes for the future are unlimited.

Q. *If you were President Nixon and trying to counteract Russian penetration of the Arab world, wouldn't you find it necessary to inch a bit closer to the Arab view?*

A. It is always hard to put yourself in someone else's shoes, especially those of the President of the United States. But I am convinced that, although we fought alone, the six-day war enhanced the interests of the free world in the Middle East. There is much alarm about Soviet influence, but what do Egypt and Syria have to offer? And the states that do have a lot to offer—Saudi Arabia, Kuwait, Iran, Turkey, etc.—in those states Soviet influence is minimal. The value of Israel to the West in this part of the world will, I predict, be out of all proportion to its size. We will be a real bridge between three continents and the free world will be very thankful not only if we survive, but if we continue to thrive in secure and guaranteed borders.

F. NEW INITIATIVES OF THE UNITED STATES

87. 'A More Even-Handed Policy':
Governor Scranton's News Conference Statement
December 13, 1968

"America would do well to have a more evenhanded policy. . . . We are interested, very interested, in Israel and its security, and we should be. But it is important to point out in the Middle East and to people around the world that we are interested in other countries in the area and have friends among them."

88. 'We Are Not Going To Stand Back':
President Nixon's News Conference
February 5, 1969

Q. *Mr. President . . . on the Middle East, now that you have completed your review with the N.S.C., you spoke of the need for a new initiative. Can you tell us what your policy is going to be now and what initiatives you do expect to take?*

A. . . . my initiatives in the Mideast I think can well be summarized by that very word that you have used. What we see now is a new policy on the part of the United States in assuming the initiative. We are not going to stand back and, rather, wait for something else to happen.

Now, we're going to assume it on what I would suggest five fronts: We're going to continue to give our all-out support to the Jarring mission; we are going to have bilateral talks at the United Nations preparatory to the talks between the four powers; we shall have four-power talks at the United Nations; we shall also have talks with the countries in the area, with the Israeli and their neighbors; and in addition we want to go forward on some of the long range plans, the Eisenhower-Strauss plan for relieving some of the very grave economic problems in that area.

We believe that the initiative here is one that cannot be simply unilateral, it must be multilateral, and it must not be in one direction. We're going to pursue every possible avenue to peace in the Mideast that we can.

89. Progress Made Toward Middle East Talks: President Nixon's News Conference, March 4, 1969

Q. *Can you tell us whether or not, as a result of your talks with President de Gaulle and other government leaders in Europe, you are now encouraged about prospects for maintaining peaceful conditions in the Middle East?*

President Nixon: One of the tangible results that came out of this trip was substantial progress on the Middle East. Now, what that progress will be and whether it reaches an eventual settlement—that is too early to predict.

But I know that when I met with you ladies and gentlemen of the press at an earlier time, the question was raised as to the four-power talks, and there were some who thought that I—this administration was dragging its feet on going into four-power talks.

Frankly, I do not believe that the United States should go into any talks where the deck might be stacked against us. Now, as a result of the consultations that we had on this trip, the positions of our European friends—the British and the French—are now closer to ours than was the case before. We have a better understanding of their position; they have a better understanding of ours.

And also, we have had encouraging talks with the Soviet Ambassador. The Secretary of State and I have both talked with the Soviet Ambassador with regard to the Mideast. We will continue these bilateral consultations; and if they continue at their present rate of progress, it seems likely that there will be four-power discussions in the United Nations on the Mideast.

Now, I should indicate also the limitations of such discussions and what can come out of them. The four powers—the Soviet Union, the United States, Great Britain, and France—cannot dictate a settlement in the Middle East. The time has passed in which great nations can dictate to small nations their future where their vital interests are involved. This kind of settlement that we are talking about, and the contribution that can be made to it, is limited in this respect.

The four powers can indicate those areas where they believe the parties directly involved in the Mideast could have profitable discussions. At the present time they are having no discussions at all.

Second—and this is even the more important part of it—from the four-power conference can come an absolute essential to any kind of peaceful settlement in the Mideast, and that is a major-power guarantee of the settlement; because we cannot expect the nation of Israel or the other nations in the area who think their major interests might be involved—we cannot expect them to agree to a settlement unless they think there is a better chance that it will be guaranteed in the future than has been the case in the past.

On his score, then, we think we have made considerable progress during the past week. We are cautiously hopeful that we can make more progress and move to the four-power talks very soon.

Sources

Chapter I

1. U.S. Department of State. *The Suez Canal Problem, July 26-September 22, 1956* (Department of State Publication No. 6392). Washington, 1956. pp. 16-20.
2. Great Britain. House of Commons. *Correspondence Between Sir Henry McMahon, G.C.M.G., G.C.V.O., K.C.I.E., C.S.I., His Majesty's High Commissioner at Cairo, and the Sherif Hussein of Mecca* (with a map). Parliamentary Publications, 1938-39, Vol. XXVII (Accounts and Papers, vol. 12), Cmd. 5957. London: H.M.S.O., 1940, 16 pp.
3. *The Times* (London). November 9, 1917. p. 7.
4. *Congressional Record.* 65th Congress, 2d Session, vol. LVI, pt. 1 (December 8, 1917-January 18, 1918), p. 691.
5. U.S. Department of State. *Papers Relating to the Foreign Relations of the United States, The Paris Peace Conference, 1919, Vol. XII* (Department of State Publication No. 3009). Washington, 1947. pp. 787-99.
6. U.S. Department of State. *Papers Relating to the Foreign Relations of the United States, 1920,* Vol. II (Department of State Publication No. 814). Washington, 1936. pp. 651-55.
7. *Statutes at Large of the United States of America, Vol. XLII,* Pt. I (April, 1921, to March, 1923). Washington, 1923. p. 1012.
8. U.S. Department of State. *Papers Relating to the Foreign Relations of United States, 1923, Vol. II* (Department of State Publication No. 1262). Washington, 1938. pp. 717-18.
9. League of Nations. "Convention Regarding the Regime of the Straits, Signed at Montreaux, July 20th, 1936." *League of Nations Treaty Series, Vol. CLXVIII.* Geneva, 1936. pp. 214-41.
10. U.S. Department of State. *Nazi-Soviet Relations, 1939-41,* edited by R. J. Sontag and J. S. Beddie. (Department of State Publication No. 3023). Washington, 1948. pp. 255-59.

Chapter II

11. U.S. Congress. Senate. Committee on Foreign Relations. *A Select Chronology and Background Documents Relating to the Middle East.* 89th Congress, 2d Session. Washington, 1967. pp. 27-31.
12. *Ibid.,* pp. 31-34.
13. U.S. Congress. Senate and House. Committees on Foreign Relations and Foreign Affairs. *Legislation on Foreign Affairs* (Joint Committee Print), 89th Congress, 2d Session. Washington, 1966. pp. 524-27.
14. U.S. Department of State. *American Foreign Policy, 1950-1955, Basic Documents, Vol. II* (Department of State Publication No. 6446). Washington, 1957. p. 2187.
15. U.S. Department of State. *American Foreign Relations, 1950-1955, Vol. I* (Department of State Publication No. 6446). Washington, 1957. pp. 853-54.
16. U.S. Department of State. *American Foreign Relations, 1950-1955, Vol. II* (Department of State Publication No. 6446). Washington, 1957. pp. 2180-82.
17. *Ibid.,* pp. 2182-83.
18. *Ibid.,* pp. 2168-73.
19. U.S. Department of State. *American Foreign Relations, 1950-1955, Vol. I* (Department of State Publication No. 6446). Washington, 1957. pp. 1257-59.
20. U.S. Department of State. *United States Policy in the Middle East, Documents, September 1956-June 1957* .(Department of State Publication No. 6505). Washington, 1957. pp. 419-20.
21. U.S. Department of State. *American Foreign Policy, 1959* (Department of State Publication No. 7492). Washington, 1963. pp. 1020-22.
22. U.S. Department of State. *Department of State Bulletin,* Vol. LVIII, No. 1493 (May 13, 1968). p. 613.
23. U.S. Congress. Senate. Committee on Foreign Relations, *A Select Chronology and Background Documents Relating to the Middle East.* 89th Congress, 2d Session. Washington, 1967. pp. 15-23.
24. U.S. Congress. Senate and House. Committees on Foreign Relations and Foreign Affairs. *Legislation on Foreign Affairs* (Joint Committee Print). 89th Congress, 2d Session. Washington, 1966. pp. 544-45.
25. *New York Times.* April 25, 1957. p. 1.
26. U.S. Congress. Senate. Committee on Foreign Relations, *A Select Chronology, etc.* pp. 118-20.

Chapter III

27. U.S. Department of State. *American Foreign Policy, 1950-1955*, Vol. II (Department of State Publication No. 6446). p. 2230.
28. U.S. Department of State. *American Foreign Policy, 1956, Current Documents* (Department of State Publication No. 6811). Washington, 1959. pp. 603-04.
29. U.S. Department of State. *American Foreign Policy, 1963, Current Documents* (Department of State Publication No. 8111). Washington: 1966. pp. 612-13.
30. U.S. Department of State. *American Foreign Policy, 1964, Current Documents* (Department of State Publication No. 8253). Washington, 1967. pp. 721-22.
31. U.S. Department of State. *American Foreign Policy, 1965, Current Documents* (Department of State Publication No. 8372). Washington, 1968. p. 618.
32. U.S. Congress. Senate and House. Committees on Foreign Relations and Foreign Affairs. *Legislation on Foreign Affairs* (Joint Committee Print). 89th Congress, 2d Session. Washington, 1966. p. 266.
33. U.S. Department of State. *American Foreign Policy, 1965, Current Documents* (Department of State Publication No. 8372). Washington, 1968. p. 622.
34. U.S. Department of State. *American Foreign Policy, 1958, Current Documents* (Department of State Publication No. 7322). Washington, 1962. p. 1017.
35. *Ibid.,* p. 1072.
36. Murphy, Robert. *Diplomat Among Warriors.* Garden City, N.Y.: Doubleday and Co., 1964. pp. 412-13.
37. United Arab Republic. Department of Information. *For the Sake of Truth and for History, The Palestinian Problem* (Correspondence Exchanged Between President Gamal Abdel Nasser and President John F. Kennedy). Cairo, n.d. pp. 5-7.
38. U.S. Department of State. *American Foreign Policy, 1962, Current Documents* (Department of State Publication No. 8007). Washington, 1966. p. 784.
39. *Ibid.,* p. 783.
40. U.S. Department of State. *American Foreign Policy, 1965, Current Documents* (Department of State Publication No. 8372). Washington, 1968. p. 623.
41. *Ibid.,* p. 624.

Chapter IV

42. U.S. Congress and U.S. Department of State. Senate Committee on Foreign Relations. *A Decade of American Foreign Policy, Basic Documents, 1941-49* (Senate Document No. 123). 81st Congress, 1st Session. Washington, 1950. pp. 23-24.
43. *Ibid.,* pp. 808-10.
44. U.S. Department of State. *American Foreign Policy, 1950-1955, Vol. II* (Department of State Publication No. 6446). Washington, 1957. pp. 2271-72.
45. *Ibid.,* p. 2275.
46. U.S. Department of State. *American Foreign Policy, 1965, Current Documents* (Department of State Publication No. 8372). Washington, 1968. pp. 611-12.
47. U.S. Congress and U.S. Department of State. *A Decade of American Foreign Policy, Basic Documents, 1941-49* (Senate Document No. 123). 81st Congress, 1st Session. Washington, 1950. p. 906.
48. "President Johnson and Prime Minister Inonu." *Middle East Journal,* Vol. 20, No. 3 (Summer, 1966). pp. 386-93.
49. U.S. Department of State. *American Foreign Policy, 1964, Current Documents* (Department of State Publication No. 8253). Washington, 1967. pp. 686-87.

Chapter V

50. U.S. Congress and U.S. Department of State. *A Decade of American Foreign Policy, 1941-49* (Senate Document No. 123). Washington, 1950. pp. 23-24.
51. United Nations. General Assembly. *Resolution Adopted on the Report of the Ad Hoc Committee on the Palestinian Question.* A/RES/181 (II). Lake Success: 1947.
52. United Nations. General Assembly. *Resolution Establishing A Conciliation Commission for Palestine.* A/RES/194 (III). Lake Success: 1948.
53. U.S. Congress. Senate. Committee on Foreign Relations. *A Select Chronology and Background Documents Relating to the Middle East.* 90th Congress, 2d Session. Washington, 1967. p. 64.
54. United Nations. Security Council. *Resolution Adopted Concerning the Passage of Israeli Ships Through the Suez Canal.* Document S/2322. Lake Success: 1950.
55. U.S. Department of State. *American Foreign Policy, 1950-1955, Vol. II* (Department of State Publication No. 6446). Washington, 1957. pp. 2254-55.
56. *Ibid.,* p. 2255.
57. *Ibid.,* p. 2238.

58. U.S. Department of State. *U.S. Policy in the Near East, South Asia and Africa,* by Harry N. Howard (Department of State Publication No. 5801). Washington, 1955, p. 23.
59. U.S. Department of State. *American Foreign Policy, 1956, Current Documents* (Department of State Publication No. 6811). Washington, 1959. pp. 604-06.
60. U.S. Department of State. *United States Policy in the Middle East, September 1956-June 1957, Documents.* (Department of State Publication No. 6505, Near and Middle Eastern Series 25). Washington, 1957. pp. 148-51.
61. United Nations. General Assembly. *Resolution Establishing a United Nations Emergency Force.* A/RES/1000 (ES I). New York: 1956.
62. United Nations. General Assembly. *Presence and Functioning in Egypt of the United Nations Emergency Force: Report of the Secretary General.* Document A/3375. New York: 1956.
63. U.S. Department of State. *United States Policy in the Middle East, September 1956-June 1957, Documents.* pp. 199-204.
64. "Hammarskjold Memorandum on Mideast Peace Force." *New York Times.* June 19, 1967.
65. U.S. Department of State. *United States Policy in the Middle East, September ·1956-June 1957, Documents.* pp. 290-92.
66. United Nations. General Assembly. *Statement in the United Nations General Assembly by Israeli Foreign Minister Golda Meir, March 1, 1957.* U.N. Document A/PV.666. New York: March 1, 1957.
67. U.S. Department of State. *American Foreign Policy, 1963, Current Documents* (Department of State Publication No. 8111). Washington, 1966. p. 580.
68. *Ibid.,* p. 581.

Chapter VI

69. Khalid, Walid and Ibish, Yusuf, editors. *Arab Political Documents, 1965.* Beirut: American University of Beirut, n.d. pp. 4-5.
70. United Nations. Security Council. *Report by the Secretary General Concerning the Middle East Situation and Withdrawal of UNEF.* U.N. Document S/7906 New York; 1967.
71. U.S. Congress. Senate. Committee on Foreign Relations. *A Select Chronology and Background Documents Relating to the Middle East.* 90th Congress, 2d Session. Washington, 1967. pp. 131-35.
72. *Ibid.,* pp. 135-37.
73. U.S. Department of State. *Department of State Bulletin,* Vol. LVII, No. 1463 (July 10, 1967), pp. 37-38.
74. *Ibid.,* p. 38.
75. United Nations. General Assembly. *Resolution on Measures Taken by Israel to Change the Status of the City of Jerusalem.* A/RES/2253 (ES-V). New York: 1967.
76. U.S. Department of State. *Department of State Bulletin,* Vol. LVII, No. 1465 (July 24, 1967), p. 112.
77. U.S. Department of State. *Department of State Bulletin,* Vol. LVII, No. 1463 (July 10, 1967), pp. 33-34.
78. United Nations. Security Council. *Resolution on the Establishment of a Just and Lasting Peace in the Middle East.* S/RES/242. New York: 1967.
79. U.S. Department of State. *Department of State Bulletin,* Vol. LVIII, No. 1468 (December 18, 1967), pp. 842-43.
80. U.S. Department of State. *Department of State Bulletin,* Vol. LIX, No. 1528 (October 7, 1968), pp. 347-49.
81. U.S. Department of State. *Department of State Bulletin,* Vol. LVIII, No. 1493 (February 5, 1968), p. 174.
82. *New York Times.* April 11, 1969. p. 2.
83. U.S. Department of State. *Department of State Bulletin,* Vol. LVIII, No. 1503 (April 15, 1968), p. 509.
84. United Nations. Security Council. *Resolution Condemning Military Action Launched by Israel.* S/RES/248. New York; 1968.
85. "A Talk With President Nasser." *Newsweek* (February 10, 1969), pp. 33-36.
86. "Eshkol: A Reply to Nasser." *Newsweek* (February 17, 1969), pp. 49-54.
87. *New York Times.* December 14, 1968. p. 1.
88. U.S. Department of State. *Department of State Bulletin,* Vol. LX, No. 1548 (February 24, 1969), p. 159.
89. U.S. Department of State. *Department of State Bulletin,* Vol. LX, No. 1557 (March 24, 1969), pp. 240-41.

Legislative and Special Analyses Published to Date, 91st Congress, First Session:

LEGISLATIVE HISTORY, 90th CONGRESS, SECOND SESSION, AND INDEX OF AEI PUBLICATIONS

HIGHLIGHTS OF THE FEDERAL BUDGET FOR THE 1970 FISCAL YEAR

PROPOSALS TO DEAL WITH NATIONAL EMERGENCY STRIKES

THE NATIONAL DEBT CEILING PROPOSAL

PROPOSALS FOR REVISION OF THE ELECTORAL COLLEGE SYSTEM

THE BAIL REFORM ACT—An Analysis of Proposed Amendments and an Alternative

THE CONGLOMERATE MERGER TAX PROPOSAL (H.R. 7489—By Rep. Mills)

EXPENDITURE CONTROLS: EXPERIENCE AND PROSPECTS

THE SAFEGUARD ABM SYSTEM (Price—$3.00 per copy)

THE PROPOSAL TO REPEAL THE INTEREST RATE CEILING ON GOVERNMENT BONDS

THE INVESTMENT TAX CREDIT—SHOULD IT BE REPEALED?

UNEMPLOYMENT—PAST, PRESENT, AND FUTURE

MILITARY COMMITMENTS TO FOREIGN COUNTRIES—High School Debate Issue

Recent Long-Range Studies:

Goetz, Raymond. TAX TREATMENT OF PENSION PLANS—Preferential or Normal? April, 1969.

Haberler, Gottfried and Willett, Thomas D. U.S. BALANCE-OF-PAYMENTS POLICIES AND INTERNATIONAL MONETARY REFORM: A CRITICAL ANALYSIS. September, 1968.

Huston, Luther A.; Miller, Arthur Selwyn; Krislov, Samuel; and Dixon, Robert G., Jr. ROLES OF THE ATTORNEY GENERAL OF THE UNITED STATES. July, 1968.

Wright, Deil S. FEDERAL GRANTS-IN-AID. PERSPECTIVES AND ALTERNATIVES. July, 1968.

Van Cise, Jerrold G. THE FEDERAL ANTITRUST LAWS. Second Revised Edition. December, 1967.

Weidenbaum, Murray L. PROSPECTS FOR REALLOCATING PUBLIC RESOURCES, A Study in Federal-State Fiscal Relations. November, 1967.

Houthakker, Hendrik S. ECONOMIC POLICY FOR THE FARM SECTOR. November, 1967.

Schnitzer, Martin. THE SWEDISH INVESTMENT RESERVE—A Device for Stabilization? July, 1967.

Sebald, William J., and Spinks, C. Nelson. JAPAN: PROSPECTS, OPTIONS, AND OPPORTUNITIES. March, 1967 (Price—$1.00 per copy).

Buchanan, James M., and Wagner, Richard E. PUBLIC DEBT IN A DEMO-CRATIC SOCIETY. January, 1967 (Price—$1.00 per copy).

Antitrust Compendium

ANTITRUST CONSENT DECREES, 1906-1966—Compendium of Abstracts (Price—$30.00 per copy).

Analyses and Studies: $2.00 per copy except as indicated.
Discounts: 25 to 99 copies—20%; 100 to 299 copies—30%;
300 to 499 copies—40%; 500 and over—50%.

AMERICAN ENTERPRISE INSTITUTE
1200 - 17th Street, N.W., Washington, D.C. 20036